METAPHORS WE LEAD BY

We live in a leadership-obsessed society. The result is that we assume nearly any social or economic ill can be mended through better leadership. Sometimes, this commitment to leadership is followed by hero worshipping, wishful thinking and misplaced hope.

Seeking to understand the faith we place in leadership, the authors draw on a number of in-depth studies of managers trying to "do" leadership. It presents six metaphors for the leader: as gardener, buddy, saint, cyborg, commander and bully. Some of these offer unexpected insights into how leadership does and does not work. The book sheds light on a varied – often contradictory and sometimes darker – side of leadership.

Cutting through the management speak–drenched current literature on leadership, *Metaphors We Lead By* presents an enlightening and refreshing understanding of an important topic. It will be useful reading for students and researchers, as well as the thinking manager.

Mats Alvesson is Professor of Business Administration at Lund University, Sweden. He is also affiliated with University of Queensland Business School. Another of his recent books, *Changing Organizational Culture*, is also available from Routledge.

André Spicer is an Associate Professor of Organisation Studies at Warwick Business School, University of Warwick, UK. He is also a visiting research fellow at Lund University, Sweden. His recent publications (as co-author) include *Unmasking the Entrepreneur* and *Understanding Corporate Life*.

METAPHORS WE LEAD BY

Understanding leadership
in the real world

Edited by Mats Alvesson and André Spicer

Routledge
Taylor & Francis Group

LONDON AND NEW YORK

First published 2011
by Routledge
2 Park Square, Milton Park, Abingdon, Oxon, OX14 4RN

Simultaneously published in the USA and Canada
by Routledge
270 Madison Avenue, New York, NY 10016

Routledge is an imprint of the Taylor & Francis Group, an informa business

Typeset in Aldus and Gill Sans by
Florence Production Ltd, Stoodleigh, Devon
Printed and bound in Great Britain by
TJ International Ltd, Padstow, Cornwall

British Library Cataloguing in Publication Data
A catalogue record for this book is available from the British Library

Library of Congress Cataloging in Publication Data
Understanding leadership in the real world: metaphors we lead by/edited
by Mats Alvesson & André Spicer.
     p. cm.
   Includes bibliographical references and index.
  1. Leadership. 2. Metaphor. I. Alvesson, Mats, 1956–.
II. Spicer, André.
HM1261.U53 2011
303.3′4—dc22   2010018266

ISBN: 978-0-415-56844-9 (hbk)
ISBN: 978-0-415-56845-6 (pbk)
ISBN: 978-0-203-84012-2 (ebk)

CONTENTS

ACKNOWLEDGEMENTS

We are grateful to our colleagues Johan Alvehus, Magnus Larsson, Susanne Lundholm and Robert Wenglén for contributing with empirical work in the various research projects that this book draws upon. The research has been funded by Handelsbankens Research Foundation and Swedish Council for Working Life and Social Research (FAS).

MA & AS

CONTRIBUTORS

Mats Alvesson is Professor of Business Administration at Lund University, Sweden and affiliated with the University of Queensland, Australia.

Martin Blom is Assistant Professor in Strategic Management at Lund University, Sweden.

Gail Fairhurst is a Professor of Organizational Communications at the University of Cincinnati, USA.

Tony Huzzard is an Associate Professor of Business Administration at Lund University, Sweden.

Dan Kärreman is a Professor at Copenhagen Business School, Denmark and affilitated with Lund University, Sweden.

Sara Louise Muhr is an Assistant Professor of Business Administration at Lund University, Sweden.

André Spicer is an Associate Professor (Reader) at Warwick Business School, UK and Visiting Research Fellow at Lund University, Sweden.

Sverre Spoelstra is an Assistant Professor of Business Administration at Lund University, Sweden.

Stefan Sveningsson is an Associate Professor of Business Administration at Lund University, Sweden.

I

INTRODUCTION

Mats Alvesson and André Spicer

FOLLOWING THE EPIC FINANCIAL COLLAPSE of 2008, there has been much navel-gazing about what exactly the root causes were and how they might be addressed. Some have looked at problems to do with how the international financial system is organized. Others have blamed the way bankers were rewarded for increasingly risky behaviour. And still others have argued it was caused by mathematical specialists taking over the banking system. However, one of the most intriguing sources of blame has been leadership, or perhaps the lack of it. One Harvard Business School professor, Bill George, told *Business Week* that the collapse of many large financial institutions was due to 'failed leadership'. According to Professor George, many of the large financial institutions and banks were populated by people who were only in it for themselves and were not willing to exercise 'authentic leadership'. The great solution he offers are leaders who are willing to be authentic and build trust among their subordinates as well as contribute to the institution as a whole.

Bill George's claims about the importance of leadership are all too familiar. This is because we hear about the importance of true leadership in nearly every sphere of human endeavour. The leader has become one of the dominant heroes of our time. Of course we obtain information about leaders not only in business magazines and executive education programmes where many middle managers go to develop their 'leadership skills'. But the appetite has grown significantly in recent years. Now, we demand 'political leadership'. We think a captain of a sports team may have some serious insights on leadership. Schoolchildren are now having their lessons in more traditional fields of knowledge such as mathematics and grammar cut back in order to create space for instruction in the mystical arts of leadership. When faced with major crises, demands for better leadership inevitably appear. It seems that many politicians now believe that any serious public problem from a rising crime rate to a collapsed bridge can be confronted through more leadership. Whatever the problem, leadership has become the solution.

It seems that nearly everyone from politicians to priests wants to show their leadership abilities. Certainly many of the hordes of students graduating from business schools are eager to make a career as a leader. But how many have the ambition to become a good subordinate? It appears that few are satisfied with such a modest goal in life. Instead, the world is thus full of leader-wannabees eager to spend a lot of time in trying to lead other people.

The irony is that despite the increasing numbers of people who see themselves as leaders, organizations still need the great majority of people to be followers. Although some very junior people or individuals with a 'low self-concept' may be interested in following, other people may find such a position less attractive. But for leadership to be carried out, there needs to be followers and a willingness to be led. In fact people refusing to be led will often not last long in most organizations. This reminds us that the idea of leadership requires a considerable element of voluntary, even enthusiastic followers. Compliance alone is not good enough. People accept leadership not just because they are faced with serious penalties. Rather, they desire leadership because it offers them a sense of meaning, morale and a very often a sense of direction. In other words, leadership gives people a sense of purpose in the workplace.

In order to understand leadership, a thriving field of research has sprung up in the last five decades. Leadership researchers seek to offer attractive explanations about how leadership works. These researchers spend their days trying to sort out who are effective leaders and who are not. Part of this endeavour involves developing questionnaires and other tools that help us to identify what kind of leader we might be. But underlying this endeavour is an assumption that frequently goes unchallenged. This is that leadership is generally a positive thing: leaders do good things like improving schools, ensuring health care is delivered well or turning round a failing company. Leaders usually have a whole series of positive and very desirable characteristics attached to them – they are courageous, they have vision, they are excellent communicators, they have self-belief and so on. With such a glowing description, it is no surprise that most people whole-heartedly buy into the idea of leadership. Such a belief in the positive force of leadership is often easily converted into devoted and docile followers. In other words, because we believe in leadership we are willing to be led.

The widespread assumption that leadership is generally a good thing is simplistic and of course highly questionable. The often uncritical celebration of leadership reflects broader social beliefs in the power of the heroic individual to change the course of history (a belief particularly common in North America). But this assumption also reflects an unfortunate preference for avoiding what psychologists call 'cognitive dissonance' (Festinger 1957). This involves avoiding situations where positive things like leadership are linked with negative things like bullying. Instead we want to believe that good things go hand-in-hand and bad things do the same. If we assume that leadership is a good thing, then we also want to see the outcomes of leadership as good. For example, Hitler, Stalin and Mao are not seen as 'leaders' because they did evil things. This is despite the fact that if we applied many theories of leadership to these figures, we would quickly find that they were in fact exemplary leaders in many ways. The recent craze for 'authentic' transformational leadership is the other side of the coin. It assumes that a leader is an altogether good person who has noble ambitions and produces fine effects (Bass and Steidlmeier 1999). Others who might have a similar style but more opaque aims are regarded as 'inauthentic'. By keeping apart the good and the bad, many theories of leadership are able to offer us visions of a rather uncomplicated and generally positive world where people are led by good people to do good things. This may be reassuring for some, but we find it quite worrying that people make such crude categorizations which possibly encourage blind faith in leaders deemed to be authentic. It also pushes us to deny ambiguities, incoherencies and shifts in our great leaders. Such faith may actually be a key driver behind ethically questionable leadership behaviour, as history has shown us repeatedly.

Instead of seeking to avoid these dissonances, we want to tackle them head on in this book. We want to look at the contradictions of leadership. This involves giving up the comforting assumption that clear-cut examples of good leadership will deliver all sorts of good outcomes without costs. We find that leadership is a far more complex and contradictory phenomenon. Good leaders can do bad things; bad leaders can do good things, and frequently people claiming to be leaders do nothing. It might feel good to see oneself as a transformational leader, but subordinates are often not so easy to transform. Therefore for us, studying leadership is not about trying to identify positive examples of leaders and explain why they behave as they do. Rather, we seek to explore the many ambiguities, paradoxes and incoherencies associated with leadership.

OUR APPROACH TO LEADERSHIP

In this book we seek to grapple with the contradictions of leadership. The title of this book, *Metaphors We Lead By: Understanding Leadership in The Real World*, reflects our approach. The title includes four central ideas that orient how we look at leadership. These are understanding, leadership, the real world, and metaphors. Let us briefly explain what each of these ideas mean.

Our first point of orientation is *understanding*. For us leadership is not a physical object like a rock or flower that can be carefully measured using carefully calibrated instruments. Leadership is something that requires human understanding and interpretation. Indeed how we understand and interpret leadership is absolutely central to whether we actually respond to it. Leadership is all about meaning, understanding, performances, and communication. Take typical examples of style like task- or people-oriented. These are treated as if they were objective phenomena and that the leader, the subordinates and the researcher all agreed upon this. But is a certain set of leader behaviour intended to promote good social relationships necessary perceived as such by subordinates? Or is managerial behaviour that involves clearly defining what the follower should do understood as a concern only for production and result and not people? Some people, particularly young, inexperienced and uncertain individuals may see these as expression of consideration and people-orientation on the part of the leader. This suggests the same managerial behaviour may be viewed as being about distrust and control or as support and close contact. And how subordinates respond will vary with their interpretation. In order to capture how managers and subordinates understand leadership, we need to do much more than ask people to fill in questionnaires in a vain attempt to measure leadership (Alvesson 1996). Complex cultural phenomena cannot be measured using some kind of standardized scale. Instead they need to be interpreted. This requires an ambition to go deeper, to acknowledge uncertainty, work with imagination and be quite open about our insights. Understanding leadership involves acknowledging that any insights that we come up with will always be uncertain and preliminary. Eternal and robust truths are almost impossible to come by in a complex, situation-specific and dynamic area like leadership. All we can do is to expand the range of ways we can interpret leadership and hopefully provide some useful and engaging insights that we did not have before.

Our second point of orientation is the study of *leadership*. There are, as we will see in the next chapter, a range of views and definitions. It suffices for the moment to say that leadership is an influencing process involving some degree of voluntary compliance by those being influenced. It involves some work- or task-related purpose, and it is seen to benefit the group or the organization. For us, leadership needs to be considered not only in terms of behaviour and effects, but in terms of meanings, beliefs, identities and use of language. This involves considering how people try to make sense of the world and give labels to our various behaviours in the world. In order to explore this, we want to look at three major aspects of leadership. The first aspect involves understanding leadership as a practice. This involves looking at how leadership is actually done in normal everyday settings. The second aspect involves understanding leadership in terms of meaning (Ladkin 2010). This involves us considering how people doing leadership – both as leaders and followers – attribute meaning and significance to a whole variety of actions and activities in the workplace. It involves thinking about how some activities are labelled 'leadership' while others are not. The third aspect involves looking at leadership as a vocabulary for having conversations about what happens in the workplace. This involves attending to how leadership is used to talk about a whole range of concerns, hopes and distractions that accumulate in today's workplace. We should note that these three aspects may go together at some stages, but they can also diverge. We can try to observe what managers do, what they (and others) think they do and how people talk in terms of leadership. Sometimes people may ascribe different meanings to a specific behaviour or produce varied and incoherent talk. Careful studies often show that clear-cut intentions, styles or acts are not so common – leadership is difficult and people are often caught in ambiguities, confusions and incoherencies (Alvesson and Sveningsson 2003a, Carroll and Levy 2008).

Our third point of orientation is to focus on how leadership is done in *the real world*. Most people studying leadership believe that the real world should be taken seriously. However, doing this has some significant disadvantages. The real world is messy, ambiguous and often falls short of delivering the heroic examples of leadership or clear-cut styles that we like to read about in popular management books and business magazines. Research taking the real world seriously is difficult and time-consuming to carry out. Closer scrutiny of the reality of leadership efforts is thus less popular than polished, dramatized and sanitized examples delivering entertaining and encouraging examples which are often misleadingly taken for the real thing. We probably need these polished examples, but in the current book we have decided to take 'reality' quite seriously. In order to do this, we built on a number of in-depth cases that we collected over a number of years of people who claimed they did leadership. We were interested in seeing what such leadership looked like in reality. To do this we have not just asked people to respond to a questionnaire or participate in a single 60-minute interview. Rather we have combined repeat interviews with managers, observed them in action (and inaction) and interviewed subordinates. We also took time to learn about the organizational contexts where they sought to do leadership. By doing this, we were able to get into the often unglamorous and everyday world of leadership. We hope this will offer a corrective image to many of the airbrushed images of leaders which all too frequently stain our collective understandings. Moreover, we hope this will begin to disturb some of the heroic and damaging images of what a leader is and what they might do.

Our final point of orientation involves looking at *metaphors*. We are particularly interested in how different metaphors can and are indeed used to understand leadership. This involves leaders and the led seeing leadership though the prism of some other phenomenon. For instance they might understand leadership as creating growth, as moral goodness, or as bullying. During our studies of people exercising leadership as well as our reading of the infinite number of books and articles written on leadership, we noticed that metaphors were frequently used. It seemed to us that metaphors were an important way that people used to engage with leadership for a number of reasons. Because leadership as a day-to-day activity is so ambiguous and difficult to capture, people often compare the leader with more familiar figures like fathers or commanders. We are inspired by these metaphors used in organizations, but do, however, mainly use metaphors giving some perspective on the vocabularies, meanings and practices of the people studied. By using a set of metaphors, we are able to expand the range of ways we interpret leadership. While some metaphors may be well known and over-used, there are others that suggest new and potentially novel ways for understanding leadership. We think by exploring unusual metaphors of leadership, it is possible to begin to reveal interesting and perhaps useful aspects of leadership that are frequently missed. Our major purpose behind the selection of metaphors is to provide a range of viewpoints on leadership, considering both the lighter and darker aspects.

STRUCTURE OF THE BOOK

In this book, we seek to provide the reader with an understanding of leadership in the real world. To do this we will work through ten chapters. In this first introductory chapter we have tried to give the reader a sense of how we understand leadership and how we will look at it. In particular, we have sought to emphasize the need to examine leadership as a contradictory phenomenon. Doing this involves rejecting many of the common images of the leader as a good person who does good things. Instead, we have argued that leadership needs to be approached as a complex process to be understood through engaging with detailed analysis of real world processes and the creative use of metaphors.

In the next two chapters we look at two of the central concepts in the book – leadership and metaphors. The second chapter provides a brief introduction to existing thought about leadership. We begin by broadly defining leadership as attempts to give meaning to different activities using a vocabulary of leadership. We then go on to explore some of the more established theories of leadership, and look at the relationship between leaders and managers. After this we look at how leadership involves a close connection between context, leaders and followers. The chapter concludes with the call to understand leadership as an essentially ambiguous phenomenon. In the next chapter we look at metaphors. This chapter argues that because leadership is such an ambiguous and complex phenomenon, it is possible to use metaphors to understand it. We begin the chapter by outlining how metaphors are generally thought about and how they work. Next we go on to consider how metaphors have been used in the social sciences and the kind of insights that they have yielded. We then outline some of the benefits that come from metaphorical thinking as well as some of the critiques and questions associated with this approach. We conclude by briefly outlining how metaphors might be used to study leadership.

The following six chapters (four to nine) each look at one metaphor of leadership that emerged from our own studies of leadership. Chapter 4 looks at the leader as a saint. This explores how leaders are frequently understood as figures who encourage moral peak-performance and provide guidance to their followers through being very good people. The kind of leadership associated with this figure is one based on high levels of trust and authenticity. Chapter 5 looks at the leader as gardener. This is a figure who leads people through providing followers with opportunities for personal growth. This metaphor emphasizes how leaders seek to improve people by encouraging them to develop their self-esteem, and enhancement of competencies. Chapter 6 examines the leader as a buddy. This involves the leader seeing themselves as a friend in the workplace who makes people 'feel at home' by creating a 'cosy' environment. This often involves seeking to encourage the led to feel good about themselves and others around them. Chapter 7 examines the leader as a commander. This emphasizes leaders who try to set a strong direction by taking command, creating clear demands, using punishments and often embodying a powerful example of what should and should not be done in the workplace. Chapter 8 examines the leader as a cyborg. This involves emphasizing rationality and efficiency in the workplace. The cyborg leader is one who stands for machine-like efficiency and places great emphasis on delivering the results. Chapter 9 looks at the leader as a bully. This chapter examines how leaders often brutally sanction those who follow. This approach highlights how leadership involves underscoring norms and keeping up standards through bullying those not (perceived to be) contributing enough.

In the last two chapters we seek to draw the book together. In Chapter 10 we reconsider the idea of looking at leadership using metaphors. We seek to set this approach in the context of other ideas around leadership, in particular the idea of looking at leadership as a language game. We then consider some novel ways that the different metaphors that are included in the book can be combined and drawn together. We also suggest some unique and interesting combinations of metaphors that could be explored in future work. The final chapter recaps the central argument of the book, highlights how metaphors might be used in education and leadership more broadly, and calls for the exploration of new metaphors of leadership.

Chapter

2

THEORIES OF LEADERSHIP

Mats Alvesson and André Spicer

INTRODUCTION

W E ARE OFTEN TOLD THAT leadership is the vital ingredient in any
successful organization. It is what distinguishes thriving organizations from
languishing ones. The presumed importance of leadership fuels many
corporations' obsession with encouraging their employees to become leaders.
Many people think that perennial organizational problems such increasing
productivity, ensuring quality, driving innovation, building morale and
delivering strategies can all be dealt with through more and better leadership.
When things go wrong, one of the first things that a board of directors does
is look for new leadership. Even organizations that traditionally downplayed
leadership now ascribe more and more significance to it. Today schools,
hospitals and universities routinely try to encourage leadership in their ranks.

Given our confidence in leadership, we might assume it would have a clear
and distinct meaning. Sadly, this is not the case. A quick look at some of the
academic texts on leadership reminds us there is a very broad spectrum of
definitions. Yukl (1989: 253) points out that 'the numerous definitions of
leadership that have been proposed appear to have little else in common' than
involving an influence process. Yukl himself tried to bring a little order to this
complicated field by defining leadership as 'influencing task objectives and
strategies, influencing commitment and compliance in task behaviour to achieve
these objectives, influencing group maintenance and identification, and
influencing the culture of an organization' (p. 253). This definition makes sense
but it does not to say that much. Leadership is about influencing a range of
things. It seems that even the best definitions of leadership are often so broad
and ambiguous that they are of limited value and sometimes become fairly
meaningless. It is difficult to establish cognitive control over concepts like
leadership (and many other concepts as well, but leadership may still be one
of the trickiest). It works more through the associations it ignites.

The ambiguity of typical definitions of leadership can be seen if we ask ourselves the following question. Do leaders need to display all the characteristics listed by Yukl, or do they just have to do one or two of these things? If the former is the case then leadership is probably very rare. After all, it is very difficult for even the most super-human corporate warriors to exercise such a broad and far reaching influence. But if the latter is the case, then leadership is very common. Who does not then do it part of the time? We all influence each other at work. 'Leadership' easily becomes everything and nothing. And the use of the term easily oscillates between what everybody does and what only an exceptional group of 'real leaders' do. This means that it is not easy to sort out what leadership is and what it is not.

In this chapter we would like to argue that we must abandon the common assumption of many mainstream studies of leadership that it is possible to develop a universal theory of leadership. There have been many attempts to do such a thing. These universal concepts have come in different forms. Perhaps the most dominant way of thinking about leadership today emphasizes so-called 'transformational' approaches that see leadership as not just a matter of transactions for instrumental purposes, based on the manager rewarding/sanctioning subordinates. Rather, it involves attempts to appeal to followers' sense of a larger whole that they enthusiastically want to contribute to. Through being an inspirational example, having an appealing vision, showing consideration and being intellectually stimulating, the leader is capable of transforming subordinates into willing followers (Yukl 1999). But there has been a lot of criticism levelled at this heroic view of the leader recently. One result is that we have witnessed the rise of what could possibly be a new mainstream view of leadership. This involves advocating post-heroic leadership. According to this approach, leadership happens everywhere: You can lead your subordinates, your boss, your colleagues, even yourself! By drawing attention to the range of unusual and unsuspected ways that leadership occurs, this approach certainly represents an important advance in the study of leadership. However, post-heroic approaches are dangerous because they lead to the generalization of leadership: we begin to see almost anything and everything as 'leadership'.

While seeing leadership everywhere is interesting, we think it is ultimately unhelpful. After all, concepts benefit from some discipline and restriction. For us, studying leadership requires that we do not just see it everywhere, but rather that we recognize its limitations. The variation, incoherence and complexity of leadership need to be taken seriously. To capture this, we argue that we should develop an ambiguity-centred approach to leadership. This involves taking a much more sceptical stance towards ideas of leadership. Instead of seeing leadership as a fairly coherent process which can potentially happen anywhere, an ambiguity-centred approach sees leadership as a contradictory phenomenon that can be used in different ways by different people. This involves developing an approach to leadership that questions much of the common ideology about great leaders. This approach focuses on how leadership is actually done and interpreted/responded to in the messy real world. In particular, it involves a greater sensitivity to cultural contexts and recognizes the different meanings attributed to leadership. Despite what mainstream leadership authors and many managers claim, leadership is seldom self-evident and clear-cut. Examples of it are open to various interpretations and people often attribute different meanings to what the leader does and the consequences – if any – that may follow (Alvesson 2010a).

An ambiguity-centred approach involves listening to people in organizations and finding out when and why they talk about leadership, what they mean by it, their beliefs, values and feelings around leadership and different versions and expressions of it. One can, for example, probably identify leadership-oriented or 'leadership-free' organizational cultures of different kinds. It might also be possible to identify organizational cultures where there is less interest in heroic leaders or even leadership in other ways. The term may be seen as alien or of marginal relevance in some contexts. For instance, organizations with strong professional ideologies like universities or bureaucratic systems like retail banks could be examples here. We should remember that for some groups, leadership may actually be a fairly negative phenomenon. An emphasis on leadership could be equated with authoritarianism, elitism and non-professionalism. Does 'leadership' refer to different kinds of people and actions in different organizations? Perhaps for various groups it refers to the strong and decisive decision-maker, the superior technician or professional, the team-builder and coach, the educator and developer of people or the result-oriented number-cruncher carefully monitoring and putting pressure on people to perform. How people talk about leadership is indicative of wider cultural patterns in an organization or industry. And if there is such wide variation in what is thought to be good leadership, then it is very difficult to develop a definition of leadership which applies in all times and spaces. Instead sensitivity to people's meanings – held by groups, organizations, professions, industries and societies – become important to understand how people relate to leadership.

In order to capture this variation, we need a range of different ideas that will help us to understand leadership. We think that metaphors are helpful here. This book will develop such a range of metaphors that help us to understand the many aspects of leadership. These metaphors emphasize leadership as setting moral example, developing people, nurturing wellbeing, making firm decisions and providing direction, emphasizing efficiency and delivery, and kicking ass when needed. These are captured in Chapters 4 to 9 using the metaphors of the leader as saint, gardener, buddy, commander, cyborg and bully. We hope these metaphors provide a way of understanding leadership and all the ambiguity it entails. Or, to put this in the language of popular management: 'here is all you need to know to stop fearing ambiguity and start loving leadership (again)'.

To develop this ambiguity-centred approach to leadership, we proceed as follows. We begin by looking at one of the most basic ways people seek to define leaders – as being in some ways different from management. We note that it is often very difficult to make such a distinction. Next, we look at five dominant perspectives on leadership. We then focus on the possible short-comings of the currently dominant approach which emphasizes post-heroic leadership. We then begin to set out an ambiguity-centred approach to leadership. For us, this involves a focus on the ambiguity associated with how leadership is used, mobilized and done. We argue that to understand this ambiguity, we must be able to trace out the interactions between leaders, followers and contexts. By doing so, we become able to develop a far more nuanced and sceptical understanding of how leadership works. We hope such an approach allows us to begin to put leadership in its place.

MANAGERS VS. LEADERS

To repeat, leadership is a very difficult thing to define. One way researchers have tried to do this is by contrasting it with management. They often claim that managers rely on their formal position and work with bureaucratic processes such as planning, budgeting, organization and controlling. In contrast, leaders rely on their personal abilities, work with visions, agendas and coalition building and mainly use non-coercive means which affect people's feelings and thinking (e.g. Kotter 1988; Zaleznik 1977). Leaders influence by 'altering moods, evoking images and expectations, and in establishing specific desires and objectives . . . The net result of this influence is to change the way people think about what is desirable, possible and necessary' (Zaleznik 1977: 71). To put this another way, leaders are heavily involved in symbolic management while managers are more concerned with administrative processes.

This split between symbol-manipulating leaders and administrative managers seems appealing. It makes leadership sound like a glamorous, challenging, almost mystical pursuit. In contrast management appears as a kind of humdrum set of administrative tasks. These two caricatures seem to be heavily loaded with the ideology of what some have begun to call 'leaderism' (O'Reilly and Reed 2010). This involves a celebration of leadership as an essential component in creating continued and radical change. Leadership is viewed as inherently good and necessary for any dynamic organization. Every definition of management or leadership comes out to the leaders' advantage: it is much more dynamic, important and powerful. Given such an alluring image, people easily identify with leadership and regard themselves as 'leaders, not managers'.

However, this rigid distinction between leaders and managers is questionable. Most people who claim to or are believed to be doing leadership in organizations usually have a formal position, normally as a manager but it might also be as chair of a committee or a union representative. Such formal positions often tap into our deeply held belief that people can legitimately exercise influence over us when they are in formal positions of authority. Indeed, people usually gain access to these formal positions on the basis of what are taken to be 'informal' leadership capabilities. In most cases, people who are promoted to management positions are expected to have some qualities usually associated with 'leadership' like experience, education, intelligence and so on. They are also usually expected to 'look' like a leader, even if this just requires putting on a business suit and looking clean, tidy and reliable.

In practice, managers frequently rely on plans, they coordinate, control, and work with the bureaucracy. But they also try to create commitment or at least acceptance for plans, rules, goals and instructions. Managers working with these more formal mechanisms without any concern for what people think and feel usually accomplish very little. The mechanics of stimulus-response only works in simple and exceptional cases. There are few simple issues that can be communicated directly, resulting in behaviour that is easily monitored and adjusted. However, instructions call for understanding and acceptance. The hard work of helping people to understand the purpose of an instruction, and creating meaning around it, frequently transgresses any clear distinction between management and leadership. Therefore, it would seem to be more helpful to look at management and leadership as discreetly intertwined phenomena. By doing so, we are able to develop a more realistic account of how leadership is actually carried out.

We are not trying to say that all management is leadership, and vice-versa. Rather, we argue that leadership is frequently intertwined with management. However, there are many instances of managerial work that plainly do not involve leadership. Administration, for example, is not leadership. Everything that does not involve interaction or indirect communication with subordinates falls outside leadership, even if these activities could be seen as management. In addition, the strict monitoring of behaviour or output does not seem to be leadership. For us, leadership involves a strong ingredient of management of meaning (Ladkin 2010; Smircich and Morgan 1982), where the shaping of the ideas, values, perceptions and feelings is central, but this can involve also coercive elements (seen as legitimately enacted). To understand this process, it is important that we consider not just what the manager does, but how this is shaped by the entire context in which they seek to lead.

MAJOR PERSPECTIVES ON LEADERSHIP

The ongoing struggle to define what leadership is has produced a glut of perspectives, theories, models and typologies. Many people who are new to the field find the sheer amount and variety confusing, frustrating and perhaps even a little depressing. In order to make sense of this confusing mess, there have been varied attempts to carve up the field. One way of dividing up the field involves pointing to five broad approaches: traits of leader, leader behavioural style, contingency approach, transformational leadership, and post-heroic leadership (House and Aditya 1997; Parry and Bryman 2006).

The first approach involves an attempt to locate the personality *traits* that make someone into a leader (for a review, see House and Aditya 1997: 410–419). The central assumption here is that being a leader is caused by innate aspects of one's self. The major concern was to try to identify what the traits were that separate leaders from the led. Early research asked whether a series of personality characteristics like gender, height, physical energy, appearance and personality traits were linked with leadership. Despite deeply ingrained assumptions about these links (for instance men are more likely to be leaders), no defensible links were found. However, more recent work has tried to revive the trait approach by focusing on personality characteristics. Earlier research suggested that leaders would have higher levels of physical energy and higher intelligence than those they lead. Leaders would also seek to dominate others through showing what psychologists euphemistically call 'pro-social influence motivation'. This involves setting one's own goals and then contentiously and doggedly pursuing them. Another important trait for predicting leadership in some contexts is 'power motivation' which involves the desire to acquire positions of status and exercise that status over others for 'positive' (organizational, collective) purposes (e.g. McClelland and Burnham 1976). A third personality trait associated with leadership is high self-confidence. A final trait found in some studies of leadership is flexibility and social sensitivity. While trait based approaches have produced a significant body of findings, they have been roundly criticized by many studying leadership. In particular, many point out that personality traits rarely remain stable over time, the traits people display may change based on the situation they are faced with, and different traits might be valued in leaders in different kinds of organizations. By taking into account all these boundary conditions, many studies of leadership traits have become increasingly complex, confused in their goals, and often more confusing for poor readers.

To avoid the problems usually associated with trait approaches, some researchers turned their attention to examining the *style* of different leaders. The foundational research in this tradition argued that it was possible to distinguish between leaders who had a style which emphasized 'initiating structure' by designing and controlling the carrying out of work, and those who focused on issues of 'consideration' by being concerned about people issues (House and Aditya 1997: 419–421). This quickly congealed into what are seen as two dominant approaches to leadership – task-centred leadership which mainly focuses on getting things done, and people-centred leadership which involves significant concern for subordinates. While this approach certainly helped to divert attention from some presumed underlying list of personality traits that produced leaders, it continued to assume that there is a set of apparently universal behaviours that are associated with good leaders. This of course did not take into account the situational complexities usually associated with leadership. For instance, does one style of leadership work in knowledge intensive firms while another works in more routinized workplaces? Do people change the styles they use? Is there any cross-national variation? In short, behaviour style approaches did not address how context affects and shapes leadership.

To address many of the questions associated with the importance of differing situations on leadership effectiveness, researchers began to turn to contingency approaches to leadership. At the core of this work was the suspicion that different kinds of leaders would operate best in different kinds of contexts and organizational settings. Perhaps the best example of this was Fiedler's (1967) contingency model of leadership effectiveness. He argues that there are basically two types of leaders – task-oriented leaders concerned with getting things done and people-oriented leaders concerned with nurturing relationships. However, each of these different types of leaders will be more effective in particular situations. He argued that task-oriented leaders are suited to situations where there are high amounts of control and low amounts of control while relationship-oriented leaders are most suited to situations where there are moderate amounts of control. Fiedler's findings were highly influential, but they were called into question for a number of reasons. In particular, many of the results over time appeared to be inconsistent and it was difficult to measure some of the key variables. There was also a widespread feeling that how we actually thought about leadership had not significantly moved on from a myopic focus on task and person centred leadership.

More recently, there has been a very strong interest in a set of overlapping approaches called charismatic, transformational and symbolic leadership. We first address the former two which strongly overlap. We then move over to the latter, treating it separately. During the 1980s, the so-called *neo-charismatic* approach to leadership appeared. The central idea was that the leader's vision, commitment, strong ability to communicate and impressive personality create an irresistible enthusiasm and willingness to obey amongst followers. The leader is supposed to deeply influence the values and norms of followers and thus create or change organizational cultures. Leader-driven corporate cultures were the recipe for organizational effectiveness in the 1980s and early 1990s (e.g. Peters and Waterman 1982; Schein 1985). Apart from a strong over-emphasis on the leaders' significance and impact, this approach has been criticized for neglecting the negative side of charisma. This includes people becoming over-reliant on the leader and side-stepping critical and independent thinking. As the charisma ideal was downplayed, the partly overlapping but somewhat less heroic ideal of *transformational leadership* appeared. The focus here is how leaders manage meaning for followers. At the centre of this literature is the split between transformational leaders and transactional leaders (Burns 1978; Bass 1985). Transactional leaders have an instrumental relation with their followers and manage through formal means as well as rewards and sanctions. In contrast, transformative leaders create bonds with their subordinates, work with overall values and visions and try to make their subordinates feel committed to the overall purpose. Many popular writers argued that transformational leaders were particularly important for high performing companies because they helped to make employees feel highly committed to the organization and willing and ready to give nearly anything (e.g. Peters and Waterman 1982). The key was providing a vision to followers and communicating it (Bennis and Nanus 1985). Transformational leadership sounds appealing and is very popular, and researchers sending out questionnaires typically get positive correlations between measures of how transformative their leaders are and various good outcomes like reported satisfaction or performance. But in practice, it is often difficult to find pure examples as most managers would find it difficult to give up 'transactional leadership' behaviours such as handing out rewards and sanctions or pointing at bad performances. There are also a lot of contradictions and confusions regarding what precisely is transformational leadership. Often input (act) and output (response) are conflated, for instance being inspirational or intellectual stimulation (Yukl 1999). Transformational leadership also involves exaggerating the role of the great and powerful individual.

The leader is often thought to create high levels of morale, provide an inspiring example for the followers, and facilitate improvements in the organization. Symbolic forms of leadership are thought to involve far-reaching positive influence such as willingness

> to transcend self-interests for the sake of the collective (team or organization), to engage in self-sacrifice in the interest of the mission, to

identify with the vision articulated by the leader, to show strong emotional attachment to the leader, to internalize the leader's values and goals, and to demonstrate strong personal or moral (as opposed to calculative) commitment to those values and goals.

(Howell and Shamir 2005: 99)

Despite the rather alluring image associated with such neo-charismatic approaches, there have been many voices of dissent. One major issue is that it tends to focus our attention on a few exceptional cases of highly motivated top managers and ignore much of the fairly mundane day-to-day forms of leadership that occur in organizations. Another issue is that it can present a rather naïve understanding of leadership as creating corporate altruism, alignment, harmony, shared interest and dispelling self-interest, calculations and petty motives like money, status, power and career. Third, studies of transformational leaders often ignore what some have called 'the shadow of charisma' (Howell and Avilio 1992). This involves the narcissistic tendencies associated with transformational leaders that often makes it very difficult to see their own limitations and critically reflect on their actions (Kets de Vries 1994; 2003; Macoby 2000). It also involves the ability of charismatic leaders to induce blind faith and unflinching belief in their followers. Finally, the obsession with transformational leaders has often led companies to focus on appointing top executives who show charismatic traits and claim to have the capacity to radically transform their followers. While this may sound like a good thing, it can have some profoundly negative consequences such as overlooking other suitably qualified candidates and appointing people who engage in over-optimistic change programmes which destroy many of the central competencies of a company (Khurana 2002).

Transformational leadership certainly involves an important dimension of symbolic leadership. But symbolic leadership – or the management of meaning – can be approached in a less grandiose way than transforming subordinates. One such 'low-key' approach involves investigating symbolic leadership and how leaders try to influence frames, cognitions and meanings. This occurs when 'leadership is realized in the process whereby one or more individuals succeed in attempting to frame and define the reality of others' (Smircich and Morgan 1982: 258; see also Fairhurst 2005; Sandberg and Targama 2007). The focus of this more nuanced research has been on the leader and how she affects the meanings, ideas, values, commitments and emotions of the subordinates. Fairhurst (2001) refers to this as a monologic view; the alternative is a dialogic understanding where the interplay between leaders and subordinates is more important than how the leader manages the meaning for subordinates (Uhl-Bien 2006).

The growing awareness of the potentially darker side of charismatic and transformational leadership has pushed a range of leadership researchers to turn their attention to more participatory forms of leadership. This formed the foundations for what is known as 'shared' (Pearce and Conger 2003), 'distributed' (Gronn 2002) or 'post transformational' leadership (Storey 2004). We here refer to it as *post-heroic leadership*. Broadly, post-heroic leadership involves an attempt to move away from the study of heroic senior executives who propound grand visions and inspire followers. Instead, these studies of leadership engage with the more humble, everyday forms of leadership that happen in and around organizations. The focus is on how leadership is democratized and frequently shared within organizations, and is rarely the provision of a single great leader. This approach highlights how leadership is something distributed across the organization, collectively achieved through a range of people within the organization, and involves a process of mutual learning of how to work together in a productive way (Fletcher and Käufer 2003). For 'post-heroic' studies, leadership can function in nearly any direction. It involves focusing on shared leadership which 'is broadly distributed among a set of individuals instead of focused in the hands of a single individual who acts in the role of superior' (Pearce and Conger 2003: 1). This view recognizes that leadership does involve downwards influence (a boss leading an employee), but it is often not nearly as important as leadership studies have made it out to be. Indeed when downwards leadership is particularly influential, it often is based on a sense of authenticity on the part of the leader (George and Bennis 2008). Other equally important leadership processes include 'peer leadership' whereby members of a group will share the leadership activities depending on the context and the moment in the group process (Gronn 2002). Shared leadership approaches also emphasize how people can actually lead themselves, suggesting leadership from superiors is not necessary (Manz 1986; Manz and Sims 1991). Furthermore, this research also points towards instances of 'upwards leadership' where people actually lead their superiors in some cases (e.g. Useem 2001). The central theme in these studies is leadership does not necessarily need to come from top-level charismatic leaders. Rather leadership is something everyone can do in organizations. Following such post-heroic accounts, leadership appears to become something that is almost ubiquitous, evenly spread in organizations, and varying with the situation. Everyone becomes a leader. The result has been many activities in organizational life are considered as a kind of leadership.

Even though post-heroic notions such as shared or distributed leadership may sound attractive and open up for lines of thinking that do not over-emphasize the heroic central character, there are problems. One is that almost everything turns into leadership. For instance, Rost (cited in Uhl-Bien 2006) claims that for proponents of post-heroic approaches there are only leaders, not followers. This makes one wonder how coordination is possible and who is supposed to actually do the work.

CRITIQUES OF LEADERSHIP THEORY

Apart from the more specific difficulties with various perspectives on leadership there are some broader problems worth highlighting. The first issue is that despite an attempt to include many of the group dynamics associated with leadership, researchers continue to neglect those influenced by 'leadership' (Collinson 2005). Even though many post-heroic studies of leadership are attentive to followers' characteristics, they continue to assume that leadership will affect followers in a one-directional way. By just focusing on leadership (whether it be peer leadership, self-leadership or whatever), they (and many of us more broadly) tend to impose an understanding of leadership on complex and ambiguous organizational events, even when it is highly uncertain whether 'leadership' is the best way to understand it. As some advocates of attribution theory have suggested, there is strong inclination to attribute whatever outcome or effect to the leader being responsible for what is accomplished, irrespective of whether the leader had anything to do with it or not (Meindl 1985). This makes it very difficult, perhaps even impossible, to be aware of almost anything else going on. It can blind us to complex group dynamics, 'followers' taking initiative, and perhaps subtly changing the meaning of input (persuasive talk, instructions) from a seemingly salient key person, as well as more generally significant cultural, social and economic forces influencing organizational processes and outcomes. Assumptions of the significance of leaders mean that far too many organizational processes are attributed to leadership. The concept then becomes so widely used that it captures everything and nothing. The result is that we begin to neglect the ways that leadership may actually not work or play a minor role in some situations. Instead, we continue to celebrate leadership as the dominant way in which work is co-ordinated. This involves a continued disregard for the missing masses of leadership – that is those people who are actually led. Some versions of post-heroic approaches do away with these people by simply assuming that they are mini-leaders who lead themselves and almost anyone else around them. Everybody is a 'co-producer' of leadership. There are, of course, other concepts for grasping what goes on other than leadership, e.g. group work, shared decision making, organizing processes, mutual adjustment, professionalism, and autonomy. However, the colonializing use of leadership vocabulary has led to insensitivity to aspects that these concepts could draw attention to.

In addition to lacking an account of the interactional dynamics of leadership, many studies generally lack a deeper investigation of the practice of leadership and the meaning we attribute to it (Bryman 2004; Knights and Willmott 1992). This is because most of the literature has positivist aspirations. This means it promises a progressive accumulation of knowledge about leadership through the development and verification of hypotheses. However, this approach has not delivered the goods. Many practitioners feel the ideas that hypothesis-testing research has produced are abstract, remote and of limited relevance (House and Aditya 1997). It has resulted in a profusion of abstract categories and thin, context-insensitive understandings of leadership. As Meindl (1995) points out, 'much of the trouble with conventional leadership research is attributable to the conceptual difficulties encountered when theorists and research scientists attempt to impose outside, objective, third-party definitions of what is inherently subjective' (p. 339). The combination of a naïve belief in its objectivity and measurability with a profoundly subjective, local and vague subject makes leadership a difficult concept to handle. In order to counter these trends, some have turned to qualitative work (Bryman 2004). However, many of these studies only involve interviews with managers. This means they do not explore subordinates', colleagues' and superiors' constructions of leadership (Uhl-Bien 2006). Nor do they observe practices of leadership. This over-reliance on interviews with managers, and under-reliance on interviews with a broader set of those involved in leadership and a shortage of observations in the field is one important shortcoming in much leadership research (Conger 1998). Sometimes one may wonder what we actually know about leadership, in particular if and how people construct their relationships, means and objectives based on ideas around leadership.

Third, ideas that emphasize the importance of morality, involvement and authenticity in leadership are typically too romantic (see, for example, Meindl *et al.* 1985). They often speak more clearly to our ideological presuppositions than what leaders actually do. It is common to lump together many superior qualities in the all-embracing and ideological concept of transformational leadership (Yukl 1999). Close-up studies of leadership indicate that examples of this 'good' leadership are hard to find. This is because what most of those purporting to do leadership actually do is more instrumental and mundane (Alvesson and Sveningsson 2003a; 2003b; Bryman 2004). A profusion of superficial studies of senior managers, the persuasive effects of heroic (and now post-heroic) ideas about leadership, and a shortage of in-depth studies, means that much ideological writing ignores the less grandiose realities of managerial efforts to influence people (Bryman *et al.* 1996; Jackall 1988).

To pull together these points, there seems to be neglect or even denial of ambiguity of leadership. This is not surprising as a fear of ambiguity is something that characterizes much organizational and social research (Alvesson 2002; Martin and Meyerson 1988). Most research on 'post-heroic leadership' is based on a set of assumptions and methods that actually produces 'leadership': respondents are thought to be 'leaders' and asked to report about their leadership. Seldom are they asked to consider whether 'leadership' is a relevant term. Even less frequently are they asked to think critically about leadership. This obscures the fact that 'leadership' is a potentially problematic construction. It also overestimates and romanticizes leaders (Meindl *et al.* 1985; Pfeffer 1977). Perhaps, most importantly for us, it ignores the ambiguities and incoherence involved with leadership (Alvesson and Sveningsson 2003a; Bresnen 1995; Carroll and Levy 2008).

TOWARDS AN AMBIGUITY-CENTRED APPROACH TO LEADERSHIP

As we saw in a previous section, most studies assume that leadership 'exists' as a fairly coherent phenomenon. There are forms, types or styles of leadership. Keith Grint (2005) points out that the studies of leadership have typically tried to essentialize theories by claiming that leadership is located in a person (trait theories), in a situation (situational theories), and in person/situation combinations (contingency theories). While the expanding post-heroic views of leadership to some extent have challenged this, through seeing leadership as more distributed, much of this work still clings to the idea that it is possible to grasp some kind of 'essence-like' quality of what leaders do and what leadership is about. But dominant assumptions about the coherence and unity associated with these different types of leadership has been seriously called into question. More than 30 years ago, Pfeffer (1977) pointed at the ambiguity in definition and measurement of the concept itself. He questioned whether leadership has discernible effects on organizational outcomes. He also concluded that leadership is primarily 'phenomenological'. By this he meant that people construct or invent a version of leadership through drawing on their assumptions, expectations, selective perceptions, sense-making and imaginations of the subject matter. Others point out that leadership is a hopeless scientific concept, but it remains a particularly strong folk concept which people use everyday to negotiate their understandings of the organizational world (Calder 1977). When using this concept, they attribute leadership to some individuals and situations and not to others. According to this approach leadership '*exists* only as a perception . . . not a viable scientific construction' (p. 202, emphasis in original). More recently, a range of researchers have pointed out that leadership is a socially constructed phenomenon (Bresnen 1995; Fairhurst 2007; Fairhurst and Grant 2010). This means 'what counts as a "situation" and what counts as the "appropriate" way of leading in that situation are interpretive and contestable issues, not issues that can be decided on by objective criteria' (Grint 2000: 9). Attending to the ways in which different people understand and construct leadership opens up significant space for ambiguous interpretations, understandings and experiences of leadership. However, this ambiguity and incoherence are still neglected aspects in the study of leadership. There is a 'comparative lack of recognition given to the possibility that "leadership" can encapsulate a diverse range of meanings or multiple frames of reference' (Bresnen 1995: 496).

The book aims to investigate the ambiguity and fragmentation that seems to be at the centre of the processes of leadership. We hope to build on an emerging body of studies that recognizes such ambiguity. Early work on the topic recognized that many leaders in complex organizations spend a lot of time negotiating the ambiguity of the organization and their role. For instance, one study found that presidents in US colleges were charged with leading 'organized anarchies' (Cohen and March 1986). The goals of these organizations are unclear, the central technologies they rely on uncertain, and participation in the organization is very fluid. This makes it very uncertain what to do in many contexts, and indeed what their role as leader is. Similarly, a study of leadership in Canadian health care found that leadership in ambiguous conditions meant that what leaders could actually do was highly constrained and they needed to work through coalitions (Denis *et al.* 1996). This resulted in chaotic and non-linear change patterns. Still others have pointed out the ambiguity around the role of leaders in a schooling context means that many of the established theories do not work particularly well (Bess and Goldman 2002). Finally, Eric Eisenberg (2007) points out the ambiguity is often deployed in a highly strategic way by leaders to manage communication and change processes. Taken together, this work suggests that leaders need to cope with ambiguity, and often this ambiguity makes it unclear what their own role actually is.

More recent work on ambiguity and leadership has pointed out that it is not just that some leaders in particular organizations like health care and higher education operate under conditions of great ambiguity. Rather, they point out that leadership itself is something that is highly ambiguous. For instance, Tierney (1996) claims that

> the assumption about what constitutes good leadership is open for interpretation and redefinition ... (and we can assume that) multiple representations (of leadership) exist within one organization. The struggle becomes first how to develop those multiple interpretations, and then how to portray them.
>
> (p. 374)

This involves a suspicion that leadership itself is no more than a social attribution, a rationalization of perceived good or bad performance. This involves recognizing that at 'an individual level, people have very diverse views of what leadership represents and means to them' (Bresnen 1995: 498). It also involves attending to how 'how managers incoherently move between different positions of leadership' (Alvesson and Sveningsson 2003a: 961). By focusing on this we become aware of how 'the practical constraints and administrative demands . . . often overwhelm more "grandiose" leadership behaviors' (p. 982). It also draws our attention to how managers are very uncertain and indeed ambivalent about how they should relate to leadership (Carroll and Levy 2008). It reminds us that the meaning which we give to leadership, and what we understand as being leadership is essentially contested (Gallie 1955). That is, due to the ambiguities, uncertainties around the idea of leadership and the value which we attribute to it, it remains forever up for grabs. This makes it impossible to arrive at a final, agreed upon definition of what leadership is. It also condemns leadership to being a 'blurred concept' around and through which language games orient themselves and are played out in the practical accomplishment of other kinds of work (Kelly *et al.* 2006: 775).

Leadership is thus difficult to pin down and there are good reasons to see it as a construction that is an ambiguous and contradictory phenomenon. We are tempted to say that leadership does not have a meaning or a set of meanings. Rather it is more of a 'blurred concept' like 'goodness' that could mean almost anything and everything. It is used by different people to accomplish various rhetorical effects that they find desirable. Some examples include attributing responsibility to senior people for various outcomes, boosting identity for managers, selling courses to managers and other leader-wannabees, and creating faith that there is a solution to the miseries encountered in our work.

UNDERSTANDING AMBIGUITY IN LEADERSHIP

In order to understand the ambiguity around leadership, we need to consider the way ambiguity is created. To do this, it is necessary for us to move away from a view that focuses on the leader acting and a group of followers responding. Rather, leadership needs to be treated as a complex social construction where meanings and interpretations of what is said and done sit at centre stage (Fairhurst and Grant 2010). These attributed meanings are important sources of ambiguity. In what follows, we will argue these sources of ambiguous meaning are leaders themselves (who are often unsure about what it means to do leadership, and whether what they are doing is actually leadership), their followers (who tend to interpret different acts as leadership), and the context in which they operate (which tends to promote different understandings and ideas of what it means to lead). These three sources of ambiguity create tensions and strains between how leadership is thought of, practised and engaged with.

LEADERS

Leaders have always been the central focus in the literature on leadership. Much of the literature assumes that there are distinct, integrated 'types' of leaders who can be identified in a clear-cut way. There are transformational or transactional leaders (Bass 1985), level 1, 2, 3, 4 or 5 leaders (Collins 2001a), people-oriented or task-oriented leaders (Fiedler 1993) and so on. However, if we actually talk to leaders (which for us mainly means managers supposed to or claiming to exercise leadership), and observe them in action, we very rarely see such clear-cut instances of leadership. Often leaders move between different kinds of leadership processes. For instance, sometimes they will be task oriented, and at others times more people oriented. This fluidity about how one actually leads seems to be an important facet for many people who are considered to be successful leaders. Some leaders who become attached or even addicted to a particular approach seem to run into problems. For instance, one leader we followed became highly attached to the image of himself as a 'coach' (Wenglén and Alvesson 2008). Even when he was faced with situations that called for a far more hands-on approach, he was unwilling to relinquish his 'coaching' style. This resulted in things not getting done and a growing sense of disdain on the part of his 'followers'. In other words, because he became addicted to a certain image of himself as a leader, he denied the kind of ambiguity that seems to be necessary for a leader to negotiate their way through a tricky and complex organizational world. The knack of living with ambiguity seems to an important characteristic of many leaders.

In addition to not neatly falling into a single 'type', many leaders remain unsure about what kind of leadership they might in fact be engaged in. Our interviews with leaders suggest that they often have contradictory and conflicting understandings of when exactly they are engaging in leadership, what it takes to lead, and how they might go about doing this. During our research, we frequently asked people who identified themselves as being leaders when they had shown leadership. Usually this prompted a moment of head-scratching and a desperate search through their memory for a grand moment of leadership. The results were often quite ambiguous situations that showed little resemblance to the ideal. Many managers started to talk about working with strategic issues, the broader and long-term picture, visions, corporate culture and values. But then, when asked about what they do in practice, these 'leaders' mainly talked about taking part in a routine administrative task. The impression we were left with is that managers often swing between seeing leadership as something which involves heroic pronouncements and declarations and engaging in much more mundane and everyday behaviour such as small-talk, listening, and being friendly, in a rather disintegrated way. People often seem to be seduced by grandiose ideas about leadership, but cannot really integrate this into their daily tasks. There are exceptions, of course, but our experience is that many managers' interpretation of their own activities suggest it is far from clear when and how they are actually exercising leadership (Alvesson and Sveningsson 2003a, c; Sveningsson and Larsson 2006).

A final source of ambiguity within which people expected to exercise leadership themselves was their uncertainty about whether they were actually leaders at all. Usually, there is a widespread image of the leader as one who is very certain and adopts the mantle of leadership with ease. Indeed, some have argued that the problem may be that people become too sure of their capacity as leaders. Such certainty becomes a potent wellspring of self-delusion, narcissism and other highly destructive outcomes (Kets de Vries 1994). However, it is sometimes the case that people who we would assume see themselves as leaders in fact do not also see themselves in this way. Instead, they prefer to see themselves as professionals, as members of an occupation such as 'carpenter' or part of a social group. For some, identifying as a leader is not an attractive prospect: it appears pretentious, and diminishes the autonomy and value of other people who are supposed to follow them. It involves buying into a language that would actually destroy a lot of creditability among peers. This is particularly true in fairly egalitarian organizations which emphasize collaboration. Others have noticed that because the notion of leadership is so unclear and uncertain, many people feel very uncertain about the term and frequently retreat to a term which they understand a lot better – namely management (Carroll and Levy 2008).

In sum, leaders themselves can be an important source of ambiguity in the leadership process. This is largely because they rarely fit into the tight categories that are frequently used to describe leaders in most of the mainstream literature. Furthermore, leaders sometimes remain very uncertain about whether they have demonstrated leadership and exactly when this happened. In many ways they remain unclear about what exactly they do when they lead. In the end, some people who are designated as leaders (through their formal role as managers and constructed as leaders by the advocates of the leadership industry, like popular management authors, educators and consultants) remain very uncertain about whether they actually are able or want to be leaders. For a few, the concept of leadership is unattractive (French and Simpson 2006). This does not necessarily mean that they retreat from all sorts of behaviour that can be associated with leadership (in one sense or another of the term) but they rest with identities they feel more comfortable with than the perhaps rather pretentious one of being a 'leader'.

FOLLOWERS

In addition to leaders being an important source of ambiguity, their followers can create a sense of uncertainty around leadership. However, this important source of ambiguity has often been ignored in studies of leadership. This is because the strong focus on the leaders has reinforced the deeply held assumption that leaders act and followers follow. There are many theories that take into account follower characteristics: inexperienced and unqualified people cannot be led in the same way as experienced people who know their trade very well. But follower characteristics are still seen as something that the leader has to consider and adjust to, and then work on, rather than a source of active influence that shapes leadership. Leaders are still thought to be agents. They only need to consider how to exercise their influence in light of circumstances, including the characteristics of their subordinates.

Today, most people understand that leadership is a relationship and that followers are usually much more important and active than traditional ideas about leadership suggest (e.g. Kelley 1992). As Howell and Shamir (2005) argue, followers are actively engaged 'in constructing the leadership relationship, empowering the leader and influencing his or her behaviour, and ultimately determining the consequences of the leadership relationship' (p. 97). However, even those who criticize others for just paying lip service to the role of followers do not do much beyond stating that followers have different self-concepts that influence what the charismatic relationship with the leader will look like (e.g. Haslam and Platow 2001). So even if there is an expansion of the interest in the leadership relationship to include followers into the equation 'we know surprisingly little about how relationships form and develop in the workplace. Moreover, investigation into the relational dynamics of leadership as a process of organizing has been severely overlooked in leadership research' (Uhl-Bien 2006: 672), although there are studies on the conversational dynamics between managers and subordinates (Fairhurst 2007).

Attribution theorists have brought the followers to the centre of attention and downplayed the significance of the leader and his or her acts (Meindl 1995). It is the followers that 'attribute' leadership to something a leader might do. This leads attribution theorists to suggest that it is followers, not leaders, who are the 'active' ingredients in the leadership process. In the messy, uncertain and ambiguous world of work, followers are the key players in relating possible outcomes to people by labelling them 'leaders'. Expectations, reputations, sense-making and communication around what the leader is understood to do, mean or want are crucial in the process. Attribution theory is an important corrective to the excessive leader-focus of many accounts. But just focusing on the follower is not enough. It is vital that we seriously consider the interactions between leaders and followers (Collinson 2005). For us, meanings, intentions, interpretations are crucial elements in this dynamic. By thinking through this dynamic, we begin to recognize that there may be explicit clashes between the meaning attributed to a situation by leaders and followers. For example, in a change project in a large high-tech firm, top managers started the project and assumed that others should work on it. They appeared to see themselves as architects behind the change project that was to be carried out by junior managers taking local initiatives within the overall framework and vague and broad guiding values ('visible leadership', 'customer orientation'). However, junior managers expected top managers to be change agents driving change and saw themselves as following instructions. This clash of interpretations – where senior and junior people expected the others to do 'leadership' – meant that nothing really happened and the junior people in the firm saw the project as an indication that senior people were 'hypocrites'. Most participants felt that there was a lot of talk and promise, but no action or substance (Alvesson and Sveningsson 2008).

These kinds of clashes between how senior and junior people interpret a situation and role relations often create additional ambiguity. It can be produced by a clash between what leaders think it means to lead and what their followers think leadership looks like. For instance, in our own research we often found a mismatch between what managers and their subordinates thought of the relation in terms of leadership (Alvesson 2010a). This mismatch is a key aspect of the ambiguity of leadership. Is leadership what the leader thinks is happening in terms of influencing process, or how the follower may read and respond to it? Or may it be what the researcher 'objectively' determines, based on questionnaires or tests or observation protocols? But this may indicate another picture than the one experienced by the person exercising the leadership and those targeted by it. Ambiguity means that there is no alignment between various views. Indeed, there are frequently occasions when there is an outright clash between what followers think leadership is, and what leaders think leadership is. For instance, in a case we mentioned earlier, we found that one leader thought that adopting a 'coaching' style was the best way to lead. However, his subordinates did not regard this style as involving leadership at all – rather it was thought to denote indecisiveness, inability to act upwards and weakness (Wenglén and Alvesson 2008). Similarly, some groups seek to present themselves as being leaders, but are not thought of as leaders by their subordinates. Physicians for example seldom refer to senior hospital managers as 'leaders', but prefer to think of them as 'administrators' (Parker 2000).

Understandings around leadership do not then just diverge but often are contested. This of course means that it becomes very difficult to simply take a leader's word that leadership is actually happening. Instead, it is very likely that there is a whole range of different understandings in an organization about if, when and how leadership happens and what exactly it looks like. Followers may regard leadership or lack of it quite differently from the leader. Of course, also within the group of followers, there may be quite varied views that add to this ambiguity. It is very important to acknowledge this ambiguity and not – as in most leadership theory – simply deny or marginalize it through assuming that leadership normally leads to clarity and consensus.

CONTEXT

Alongside leaders and followers, the broad social context is an important source of ambiguity about leadership. This is because there is frequently tension between how leaders act, how they see themselves and the contexts in which they operate. This tension is often denied in much of the mainstream literature on leadership. This is largely due to the deeply held assumption that top leaders are able to shape the culture. Arguably, culture forms leadership rather than the other way around. Biggart and Hamilton (1987: 435) argue that 'all actors, but perhaps leaders especially, must embody the norms of their positions and persuade others in ways consistent with their normative obligations'. Societal and business culture set limits for the kind of leadership that might be accepted. For instance, in some countries (such as Sweden) a more relationship-oriented and participative leader is seen as acceptable and necessary. In other countries (such as the US), this approach would be seen as weak and a tougher results-oriented leader would be called for (Den Hertog and Dickson 2004). Even in countries often seen as culturally similar there may be more or less subtle differences in views on leadership and followers. Within Scandinavia, in Sweden, highly soft and participatory styles of leadership (if that is the right expression – in some other countries it may not count as leadership) can be contrasted with the more direct and authoritative leadership more common in Denmark. This can be understood partly due to institutional circumstances: in Sweden industrial legislation makes firing people very difficult; in Denmark it is easy and common – contributing to a different basis of authority and modes of superior–subordinate relations. Similarly, the culture of different industries can significantly shape the kinds of leaders who are thought to be appropriate. For instance, creative and hi-tech industries that celebrate freedom and autonomy will often encourage highly democratic leadership styles. In contrast, industries that are built on cultures of efficiency such as manufacturing or routine service work will often create more task-oriented, hands-on leaders.

Often people are trapped between different cultures that proscribe vastly different norms of good leadership. They might be caught between the values and norms held by senior managers and those promoted by their subordinates. The former may expect junior managers to implement strategies and policies from above and be sensitive to the wishes of their superiors, while the subordinates want their leaders to identify with the group and promote its interests. Frequently, subordinates are less interested in being led by their managers than by leaders being active in managing boundaries with other units, exercising influence upwards, protecting subordinates from what they see as stupid things harming their work (Alvesson and Blom 2009). Managers can also be caught in a conflict between the 'official' corporate culture and 'functional cultures' associated with production, R&D, personnel or marketing. This frames, influences and constrains also what kind of leadership is possible (or even if leadership is possible). Such conflicts or contradictions between cultures require leaders to negotiate very different kinds of normative frameworks and views on corporate reality. This can be illustrated by the case of a US coast guard who found his men – mainly college graduates whose expectations, interests and motives were at odds with the routines and lack of discretion of military life – bored and negative. Instead of trying to impose military discipline in a traditional way, he made a deal with his men about more discretion and certain liberties in exchange for more positive behaviour (Wilkins, referred to in Trice and Beyer 1993). The case illustrates how the values and orientations of a group of subordinates triggered a change in 'leadership' so that it resonated better with their values and meanings. It also reminds us how clashes between what is encoded into a context as good leadership, what a leader thinks is good leadership and what their subordinates think good leadership is can create significant tensions and uncertainties that need to be jointly negotiated.

COMBINING LEADERS, FOLLOWERS AND CONTEXT

Relating leaders, followers and context, is of course vital in any understanding of leadership. This is self-evident, but surprisingly rarely done. In the popular management literature as well as most academic studies, the leader's role is grossly overstated. They are treated as the key actor putting his own (or occasional) stamp on the followers as well as the context. Whatever the country, industry, organizational situation or group of employees a specific type of leadership is viewed as the best one. The follower-centric view sees the followers' constructions as the crucial element and reduces the leader's role to a projection of followers. Work emphasizing different fields or areas draws attention to the contexts (nations, organizations, professions) and sees cultural norms as the crucial element producing standards for leadership that people tend to follow. This marginalizes the actors as such and disregards their possibilities of acting in very different ways within one and the same cultural context. Clear patterns and little of ambiguity typically characterize these studies.

Our approach emphasizes that there are complexities and uncertainties in all the major 'ingredients' of leadership. We think that ambiguity – not clear-cut traits, styles, types, constructions or situations (professions, organizations) – should be taken seriously. What leaders do, if they do anything, is responded to and these different forms of ambiguity are negotiated. Leaders negotiate the ambiguities of different and incoherent meanings. If we combine the multiple ambiguities in different areas (leaders, followers and context), then we gain a richer and also 'more brutal' picture of the realities of leadership.

CONCLUSION

Leadership is a tricky concept. As we have argued in this chapter, it has multiple meanings and cannot easily be specified. Most academic definitions are vague and only modestly helpful. Indeed, two-thirds of all authors do not define the concept (Rost in Barker 1997). What is more, any simple distinction between social science and folk ideas about leadership is difficult to make. This is due to an overlap between the language used by researchers, educators, popular management writers and practitioners. Despite this uncertainty and lack of clarity about leadership, there still seems to be an increasing culture of 'leaderism' (O'Reilly and Reed 2010). This involves a widespread desire to see leaders as having a strong impact on organizational outcomes. This fits the self-image of many would-be leaders and reinforces their status and claims for high wages, prestige and authority. The result is a strong faith in efficacy of leadership, despite much evidence to the contrary. There are good reasons to suggest a more sceptical view, in which the uncertainties of any under-standing or assessment are taken seriously. This is a real deviation from the strong claims about patterns that dominate not only popular management but also the majority of leadership studies.

Leadership is ambiguous and complex, but we do not think that it is a hope-less concept. Rather, we want to recognize that leadership is an increasingly important language in many organizations. Organizations that traditionally have been seen as being professional and needing little 'leadership' like the church, schools and academic institutions have become targets for improvement through leadership. Increasingly managers seek to 'do' leadership, perhaps even when it is not required. This has made leadership an important empirical phenomenon. There is certainly an enormous amount of talk, writings, thinking, hopes, educational investments and more or less efforts to practise it.

Acknowledging the ambiguity associated with leadership does not make us totally liberal or agnostic in our approach to leadership. We don't think that an anything goes approach is helpful. For us leadership involves asymmetrical relationships, influencing processes and situations where people in some kind of formal and institutionalized dependency relationship are targeted.

Studying 'leadership' calls for a combination of a theoretical definition and a consideration of what a particular group means by 'leadership'. Some definition of leadership is needed. But there also needs to be an openness to local meanings. For different groups 'leadership' may have different meanings and values. For instance, in the police and in professional groups, 'leadership' has very different connotations (Bryman *et al.* 1996), but also within one and the same setting, there may be considerable variation. A certain act can be seen by some as leadership and others as just interaction or administration. Contexts can be defined in different ways and there is also the issue of how leadership is understood at different levels of the organization.

Studying leadership means facing up to a dilemma. On the one hand we would expect subjective, multiple, incoherent constructions of leadership in a setting. On the other hand, it does not make sense to talk about leadership without expecting some shared meanings about what a particular manager did (in terms of perceived leadership) and the outcome of this. Put differently, do multiple constructions of leadership in a particular setting converge or relate to each other? If not, what does that mean for the understanding of leadership as a theoretical construct? In the next chapters, we will argue that one way of addressing these questions is to use a set of rich and varied basic images or metaphors. We hope this will allow for a broader and more imaginative set of views of leadership than is common.

3

METAPHORS FOR LEADERSHIP

André Spicer and Mats Alvesson

IN THE PREVIOUS CHAPTER we argued that despite the fact that we talk about leadership every day as if it was a self-evident idea, it is a concept wracked by ambiguity and complexity. But just because leadership is difficult to get a handle on, it does not mean that we should necessarily dispose of the idea. Instead, we need to find a way that allows us to get hold of this complexity and try to capture the multiple possible meanings associated with the idea. In this chapter, we would like to suggest that one way we might be able to capture this ambiguity is through using metaphors to study leadership. Complex and multidimensional phenomena call for considering a variety of aspects, thereby acknowledging but also dealing with ambiguity.

Metaphors have been the subject of increasing attention in recent years, both in social science in general and organizational analysis in particular. The writings of Gareth Morgan (1980, 1986) have been groundbreaking in re-thinking how we use metaphors to understand the complexities and ambiguities of organizational life. Metaphors are seen as important organizing devices in thinking and talking about complex phenomena. They allow us a way of recognizing that we never relate to objective reality 'as such', but always do so through forming metaphors or images of the phenomenon we address. Organizations are, for example, seen as if they are machines, organisms, political arenas, brains, theatres, or psychic prisons. By using these metaphors, we are able to make sense of the confusions, complexities and difficulties that are often associated with organizational life.

Because metaphors help us to capture some of the difficulties of organiza-tional life, they have proved to be an increasingly popular tool for understanding a whole range of phenomena in organizational life including how we under-stand technology (Pablo and Hardy 2009), organizational change processes (Heracleous and Jacobs 2008), social capital (Andriessen and Gubbins 2009), organizational communication (Putnam and Boys 2006), identity (Alvesson 2010c) and research methodology to name just a few. Given the apparent usefulness of metaphors, we would like to use the idea to understand leadership in organizations. This will involve using metaphors as a way to capture the multiple and complex meanings at work. Indeed, some researchers have already begun to show that many of the difficulties and ambiguities around leadership can be explored by using metaphors (e.g. Hatch *et al.* 2006; Western 2008). These studies have identified a range of metaphors that might be used to think about leadership, including the leader as pedagogue, architect, commander, priest, and therapist.

These initial attempts to understand leadership by exploring a range of metaphors are interesting for a number of reasons. First, they have opened up communication about how both researchers and practitioners think about leadership. Instead of relying on what are often obtuse statistical tests, the exploration of metaphors has allowed researchers to begin to grapple with the meaning that people actually attribute to leadership. By looking at the metaphors that are used in leadership, it has also become possible to clarify some of the thinking around leadership. By capturing ideas of leadership in stark and striking images like the architect, it becomes possible to bring together many of the ideas and understandings which are usually hidden in the expert language of leadership researchers. This is particularly useful when it comes to trying to capture much of the 'folk knowledge' about leadership that most leaders (and the people they lead) use to understand and negotiate leadership. Finally, and perhaps most importantly, exploring leadership using a range of metaphors injects a note of creativity into what can often be a fairly staid and boring field of research. This opens up the notion of leadership to further exploration and creative insights that were often closed down through conventional modes of inquiry. Exploring novel and revealing metaphors associated with leadership helps us to think about the phenomenon in unexpected ways.

Existing accounts of leadership using metaphors have helped to communicate ideas about leadership, clarify how we think about it, and inspire creativity by broadening our sometimes heavily constrained palette of ways of talking and thinking about leadership. In this book, we hope to continue this endeavour by building on initial attempts to study metaphors of leadership. However, we aim to take these studies forward in three ways. First, we would like to go further by not just looking at what academic researchers think about leadership or what leaders claim in popular pronouncements such as letters to shareholders. Instead, we would like to explore a range of metaphors that can be aligned with or closely related to when people begin to 'do' leadership in the more mundane context of the workplace. We want to ask what the metaphors are that actually inform or inspire people negotiating leadership, either as the leaders or the led. Second, we would like to move beyond looking at metaphors that cast leadership in a positive or fairly neutral light. We will do this not only by focusing on the positive face of leadership, which is after all an all too commonly known side of leadership. We also want to look at the more questionable and disturbing face of leadership. Part of this will involve evoking some of the darker metaphors of leadership which rarely get talked about in the literature. Too often, less positive aspects are defined as 'not leadership' (but management, abuse of power or something else). It will also involve exploring how leaders frequently fail to live up to many of the great images that they espouse. By doing this, we hope to begin to develop a more realistic image of leaders and leadership than can usually be found in many books on the topic. Third, we aim for a broader and thus more helpful spectrum of metaphors for understanding leadership than offered by other writers, often emphasizing three metaphors (Hatch *et al.* 2006 talk about leaders as managers, priests and artists while Western 2008 views them as controllers, therapists and messiahs). We can do this by suggesting and elaborating on six metaphors, capturing moral, development, positive social support, commanding, machine like efficiency and sanctions as key themes around leadership. We use the metaphors of saint, gardener, buddy, commander, cyborg and bully to capture this broad range of leadership aspects.

In this book, we develop a distinct approach to metaphors of leadership. For us, this involves using metaphors in a creative and insightful way to understand the ambiguous phenomenon of leadership. This does not just involve using metaphors as a broad cognitive categorizing device that can be used to carve up the data in an interesting and engaging way. Rather it involves using metaphors as a creative device that allows us to develop new and interesting insight about how leadership can and might work. Moreover, we hope to explore some of the darker metaphors that are at play in leadership. By doing this, we hope to show how leaders often do not live up to the mythical proportions which are typically associated with them. Finally, in this book, we hope to adopt a more 'realistic' and less reductionist perspective on metaphors that are used to discuss and explore leadership. This involves recognizing how metaphors of leadership say something about ideas and meanings that are actually used in the difficult day-to-day work of executing leadership.

In the remainder of this chapter we explore the idea of metaphors in more depth. We begin by looking at what we mean by the concept of the metaphor, and provide some fairly elementary definitions. Following this, we examine the role that metaphors can play in the social sciences and the additional insights that they might bring. We then intensify this discussion by looking in more depth at the specific benefits that an analysis of metaphors can bring to the study of social life. Following this appreciation of the role of metaphors, we consider some of the possible shortcomings that might be associated with a strict analysis of metaphors. After assessing the possible benefits and problems with metaphor, we move on to outline a more in-depth understanding of how exactly metaphors work. We conclude the chapter with a brief account of existing studies of metaphors of leadership. This positions our own work in this broad tradition.

WHAT IS A METAPHOR?

At its most basic, a metaphor is created when a term (sometimes referred to as 'source') is transferred from one system or level of meaning to another (the 'target'), thereby illuminating central aspects of the latter and shadowing others. Put another way, metaphors 'involve the transfer of information from a relatively familiar domain (variously referred to as a *source* or *base* domain) to a new and relatively unknown domain (usually referred to as a *target* domain)' (Tsoukas 1991: 568, emphases in original). A metaphor allows an object to be perceived and understood from the viewpoint of another object. It thus creates a departure from literal meaning:

> a word receives a metaphorical meaning in specific contexts within which they are opposed to other words taken literally; this shift in meaning results mainly from a clash between literal meanings, which excludes literal use of the word in question.
>
> (Ricoeur 1978: 138)

A good metaphor depends on an appropriate mix of similarity and difference between the transferred word and the focal one. Where there is too much similarity, the point seems banal. Where there is too little similarity, the point may seem irrelevant.

A frequently used metaphor for understanding leadership is the teacher or pedagogue. In this metaphor, the leader is the target domain, and pedagogy is the source domain. Leadership is viewed as similar to teaching children in a classroom or tutoring students. By evoking pedagogy, we are reminded of all sorts of activity associated with teaching. These include the leader having more knowledge than his 'pupils', the leader seeking to improve the pupils through various kinds of teaching, and seeing the tasks as improving the student-like subordinates. The followers are re-envisaged as being students or pupils needing instruction.

This illustrates a key characteristic of metaphors. They call for some good will, imagination and knowledge of the subject matter. Indeed Brown (1976) points out that if a metaphor is taken literally, it usually appears absurd. A good metaphor 'makes us stop in our tracks and examine it. It offers us a new awareness' (p. 173). In this sense metaphors are 'category errors with a purpose, linguistic madness with a method' (p. 173). Metaphors must be approached and understood as if they were true at the same time that we are aware that they are fictitious – created and artificial.

A metaphor builds on the mixing of two elements. This means crossing or carrying over a concept or idea from one field to another (source and target domain, respectively). It is the interaction between the two elements that is of interest. In order for this interaction to work, the metaphor user (either as a producer/analyst or a consumer/reader) must emphasize the right elements in what is carried over as well as the focus of the object to be illuminated. Without that, the metaphor becomes pointless and frequently absurd. In the leader/pedagogue case, the metaphor presupposes a neglect of some of the more robust features of a teacher (like giving long lectures).

In a narrow, traditional sense, a metaphor is simply an *illustrative device*. In this sense, words that make language richer or more felicitous than formal models can both be regarded as metaphors (Brown 1976). If we think of metaphors as illustrative, they appear as helpful and nice, but not crucial and do not structure thinking. The researcher (or any other person) can in principle choose whether to use metaphors or not. But metaphors may also be seen as implying something more profound. In a very broad and basic sense, all knowledge is metaphorical in that it emerges from or is 'constructed' from some point of view. So, too, are our experiences. This means 'our ordinary conceptual system, in terms of which we both think and act, is fundamentally metaphorical in nature' (Lakoff and Johnson 1980: 3). Metaphor can thus be seen as *a crucial element in how people relate to reality*. Metaphors are, Morgan (1986) says, 'a way of seeing and a way of thinking' (p. 12).

If we address metaphor in this second, more profound sense, then they are viewed as 'a primal, generative process that is fundamental to the creation of human understanding and meaning in all aspects of life' (Morgan 1996: 228). This has implications for our understanding of science as well as our understanding of everyday life. Empirical evidence does not speak directly to the researcher. Rather, it is partially shaped by metaphors that researchers use to understand it. These metaphors draw attention to various aspects of the research object. In a similar way, managers or any other practitioners relate to and work within a universe that is filtered and constructed by the images of what management and business are all about.

DO METAPHORS HAVE A PLACE IN SOCIAL SCIENCE?

The idea of metaphors as a central element in social science (and perhaps in all science) has created a lot of debate. From a traditional scientific point of view, the problem with metaphors is that they cannot be translated into more precise, objective language and thus elude rigorous measurement and testing (Pinder and Bourgeious 1982). According to this approach, metaphors are useful and necessary in poetry and rhetoric, but they do not suit the precision of science that demands literal expression and well-defined words. The metaphorical usage of words involves fantasy and associations. This lends them generative power but limits their appropriateness for empirical investigation. The 'free' use of metaphors means that there is no strict theoretical definition of what is being studied.

Some argue that metaphors can be useful at the very beginning of developing knowledge about a novel or under-investigated phenomenon (Pinder and Bourgeious 1982). This is because metaphors allow the free play of ideas and experimentation with different concepts. Metaphors are seen as a kind of 'heuristic' or broad rule for simplifying reality that is a precursor to formal theory building. But once they have sparked off the process of exploration and discovery, metaphors can become a hindrance to a field. This is because it is important to state hypotheses in as clear and succinct language as possible. Metaphors make it difficult to be accurate. The slipperiness of metaphors also makes it difficult or impossible to prove a claim wrong through carrying out empirical tests. This argument is based on the assumption that 'objective reality' can be perceived and evaluated on its own terms. In other words, we do not need a gestalt or image standing between the reality out there to be understood and the researcher trying to make sense of what goes on. According to these critics, all we need is accurate definitions of what we are trying to examine and good measures that capture these definitions.

Many have disagreed with this scientific view of metaphors (e.g. Tsoukas 1991; Oswick *et al.* 2002). They argue that metaphors are a necessary element in the development of new approaches to research objects. However, they point out that metaphors are far more than just a precursor to the development of precise scientific theory. Metaphors are in fact far more fundamental to knowledge. According to this approach, metaphors play an important and perhaps inescapable role in science and organizational theory. It is impossible to let the 'objective data' speak for themselves (Brown 1976; Morgan 1983). Instead metaphors are vital in understanding any 'data' we get from the social world. Metaphors shape our thinking and language we use to talk about the social world.

If metaphors are so fundamental, it means all perception, including scientific studies, is guided by metaphors that provide a gestalt or a sense of the whole. The implication is that science should not be seen as the opposite of metaphor generation. Rather science may be seen as a creative process in which scientists view the world metaphorically, through the language and concepts which filter and structure their perceptions of their subject of study and through the specific metaphors which they implicitly or explicitly choose to develop their framework for analysis.

(Morgan 1980: 611)

Therefore it is impossible for knowledge generation to get away from metaphors. This means 'the choice for sociology is not between scientific rigour as against poetic insight. The choice is rather between more or less fruitful metaphors, and between using metaphors or being their victims' (Brown 1976: 178).

We agree that metaphors are useful for inspiring future scientific investigation. However, this does not mean we want to simply see scientific knowledge as the wild creation of new metaphors. Rather, working with metaphors involves seeking to be both imaginative as well as rigorous (Cornelissen *et al.* 2008). This involves balancing creativity and imagination with discipline in use of metaphors. Inns and Jones (1996) suggest that:

metaphor must be used as a rational tool for exploration and be somehow 'literalized' and be made less implicit. . . . The distinction is that metaphor is used primarily for gestalt understanding in poetry, and essentially for rational reductionist analysis in organization theory.

(p. 115)

They also suggest that while in poetry, metaphors and what they evoke may be the *end*, in social science they are mainly *means* for exploration, theory development and empirical analysis. Inns and Jones (1996) are, however, aware of the problems of emphasizing the dichotomy between poetry and science. To avoid these problems they seek to soften this strict distinction. The ability of metaphors to explore and express experiences for example indicates a shared ground between the poets and the researchers. We would add that careful interpretative work based on the conscious use of a metaphor requires an awareness of and tolerance for the ambiguities and tensions involved in the project – something that rigor and rational reductionist analysis tend to suppress. Furthermore, the development of a new metaphor may in itself be a major part of theoretical progress. Even though it needs to be explored and guided by theoretical and empirical work, it is certainly more than just a conceptual tool to be subordinated to conventional ideas of empirical inquiry.

WHAT DO METAPHORS DO?

If the disciplined use of metaphors is so fundamental to our knowledge about complex social phenomena like leadership, then we need to ask what metaphors do exactly. Perhaps the most obvious thing which a metaphor does when we are seeking to understand something like leadership is they add a certain aesthetic appeal or rhetorical flourish to how we understand a subject. By comparing the leader with an artist, a therapist or a coach, we can create attractive and rich mental images that can be easily grasped. In addition, many of these metaphors are highly appealing to would-be leaders. The use of attractive metaphors helps to make the text more engaging. It also lends a degree of imagination and freshness to what can sometimes become stale and fixed ideas. Yes, leadership is about influencing cognition, emotion, commitment, and claiming a leader has similar properties to a prophet, a military commander, a father or mother figure, a sports coach or an artist adds flavour to the idea.

But metaphors do more than just adding a little extra rhetorical spice. They also help to increase our communicative capacities. Metaphors can be used to communicate insight to others, for example as part of the production of scientific texts. People in organizations may also use metaphors to express their experiences. This means metaphors can help to facilitate our own understanding of other people's experiences. They help us to communicate ideas about complex and difficult to understand social phenomena such as leadership (Davidson 1978). This is because they help us to 'succinctly transmit a large amount of information simultaneously at a cognitive, behavioural, and emotional level' (Sackmann 1989: 482).

As well as facilitating communication, metaphors also allow us to develop new ideas and guide analysis in novel ways. Mastery of the metaphors involved in thinking and research may thus encourage creativity and provide insight (Grant and Oswick 1996; Morgan 1980; Schön 1979). This is because metaphors open up meaning and space of exploration around different phenomena. They allow a degree of 'interpretative variability' (Van Maanen 1995) and give the researcher space to explore the various meanings associated with a social phenomenon. This can open up what were often fairly closed and tightly guarded understandings of particular phenomena. This is, of course, not only relevant for academics. Many practitioners can also benefit. According to Palmer and Dunford (1996), managers are very positive about the idea of learning new metaphors and seeing things from different points of view.

This brings us to another function of metaphors – they can act as powerful cognitive tools. Metaphors are at the basis of our thought processes, and they help us to make sense of social reality. Metaphors aid us in delving into our unconscious thought processes and confronting how we frame reality (Lakoff and Johnson 1999). Considering metaphors also draws attention to the partiality of the understanding gained by an approach built on a particular root metaphor. This is because metaphors work as data-reducing devices (Inns and Jones 1996). They remind us that the intellectual operation such as making sense of something is shaped by the implicit images that we have of it. Being aware of the metaphors we use alerts us to the partiality and to some extent arbitrariness of how we see a phenomenon like leadership. It also hopefully facilitates a degree of openness and tolerance for alternative understandings of the phenomenon.

Combining the communicative and cognitive aspects could be to point at metaphors being useful to open up a semantic field, i.e. encourage the exploration and expansion of use of vocabularies and associated meanings. This enables people to make different yet related associations with a phenomenon that were not otherwise possible with literal language. In this sense metaphors act as a potential means for animating dialogue and assisting with interventions. When talking about leadership in a group introducing and then unpacking metaphors, new ideas and possibilities emerge. Yes, the leader as a teacher, but what types and meanings of teacher can be explored?

Yet another way that we can use metaphors is through encouraging critical scrutiny. A focus on metaphors could push us to examine the basic assumptions behind how we conceptualize something like leadership. It might draw out some of the more perverse but under-explored assumptions associated with a particular metaphor. For instance, if we look at the common metaphor of the leader as a commander, then we recognize some of the potential violence and aggression that can lurk behind leadership. Similarly, if we consider the metaphor of the leader as a saint, we are alerted to how leadership often evokes many religious images. In each of these instances, a metaphor helps us to grasp how the gestalt offered by a metaphor can be different from what the definitions and rhetoric suggest. Examining metaphors helps to move us beyond the relatively superficial level of much conceptual thinking about leadership.

A last point worth mentioning concerns irony. Metaphorical use involves a sense of irony as a good metaphor superficially appears like a category mistake. To see organizations as machines or pyramids is, in a sense, absurd. So is also the case with viewing the leader as an artist or therapist. Often irony is underused as a way to understand phenomena. In management and leadership positive-sounding expressions are too often used to impress audiences about how good leadership and leaders are. But metaphors also lend themselves to irony. For instance, when the transformational leader is described as Messiah then the tensions become readily apparent (Western 2008). In this book we will use metaphors in a way that seeks to inspire a slightly ironic understanding of the beliefs and practices of managers trying to do leadership.

THE PROBLEMS WITH METAPHORS

Despite the benefits that the use of metaphors appears to offer the study of leadership, it also presents some problems. These are to some extent the reverse side of what makes metaphors attractive. One of these is the risk of using 'bad' metaphors that actually cloud our understanding. An appealing metaphor may stand in the way of a less elegant but more accurate and elaborate description. For example, the garbage-can model (metaphor) for organizational decision-making (March and Olsen 1976) may have more rhetorical appeal than theoretical value (Pinder and Bourgeois 1982). According to the garbage-can model, decisions result from the random convergence of streams of problems, solutions, people, and situations. The degree of overlap between the type of decision-making process addressed and the garbage can is too small; the key features of the garbage can – its bad smell, its containing material packed together that is considered trash – seem of limited relevance (see Pinder and Bourgeois 1982). This problem basically concerns the level of expression and not so much the root metaphor (and other metaphors guiding thought) itself. As Tsoukas (1991: 32) remarks, the garbage-can metaphor is 'simply a figure of speech, a literary illustration to make sense of organizational decision-making and not a metaphor intended directly to reveal formal identities between garbage cans and organizations'. The metaphor does not necessarily have to be explicitly addressed, which would avoid the problem. March and Olsen could, for example, have conducted their analysis without referring to the garbage can and kept the metaphor (i.e. the signifier or expression) to themselves.

A related difficulty is the 'catchiness' problem that springs partly from the current popularity of metaphors in organization studies. This can easily lead to the excessive use of seductive metaphorical expressions, rather than the development of analytically helpful metaphors that really do shed new light on things. The very popularity of metaphors can make it 'too easy' to play with them, which in turn can lead to superficiality (Oswick *et al.* 1996). A popular metaphor can easily refer to everything and nothing, for example branding.

A third problem, once again related to the others, concerns the risk of a supermarket attitude to metaphors. It is possible that focusing on metaphors will draw attention away from the deeper or more basic levels of social research, such as the paradigmatic assumptions on which metaphors rely (on these various levels, see Morgan 1980). For example, Morgan's (1986) *Images of Organization*, despite its great value, may convey the impression that the more metaphors are employed the more comprehensive the understanding of organizational phenomena (Reed 1990). Instead, mastery of a particular perspective demands complete understanding of its paradigmatic roots and their existential and political aspects (on the relationship between metaphors and politics, see

Tinker 1986). Attempting to employ more than a few guiding metaphors often results in superficiality.

The final potential problem with metaphorical analysis is that it tends to draw out similarities rather than considering clashes and contractions (Oswick *et al.* 2002). By focusing on similarities, the study of metaphor can create a kind of over-simplifications that puts too much emphasis on a metaphor that is thought to guide and summarize a line of thinking. In these cases, it sometimes 'diverts attention away from ambiguity and alternative readings and (can) . . . actually undermine the formation of new perspectives' (Oswick *et al.* 2002). Because metaphors draw our attention to similarity, they can lead us to ignore the complexity of the phenomenon we deal with. For example, it is unlikely that any researcher sees leadership exclusively as pedagogical, exclusively as saint-like or even exclusively as a combination of the two. But when we use the metaphors it is easy to convey the impression that the expressions capture the 'essence' of the idea or thinking. The addition of further metaphors to 'capture' the framework may simply obscure and distort it; thinking and analysis are not the same as the aggregation of metaphorical bits. There is also the problem that language is restricted. The words that we have at our disposal do not always adequately signify just what we want to pin-point. To deal with this problem, Oswick and colleagues recommend that we should avoid consensual tropes like metaphors that emphasize similarity and instead focus on more dissensual tropes like anomaly, paradox and irony. They point out that what is essential in these kind of tropes is that they tend to focus on how something is *not* what it promises to be. The central task is to remind us of the gap between rhetoric and reality.

UNDERSTANDING METAPHORS

Despite the range of problems or cautions with using metaphors, they are clearly very useful for examining complex phenomena like leadership. Given the explosion of work using metaphors to understand organizational processes, the question 'is not whether metaphors exist and play a part in organizational theorizing – as this is now widely accepted – but to draw out how metaphors are actually used and are of conceptual value' (Cornelissen *et al.* 2005: 1545). Therefore, the most important question we need to ask ourselves is how exactly we look for a metaphor. What does a metaphor look like? How does it work? In order to begin answer these tricky questions, we need to look at some theories of metaphor in more depth.

Perhaps the most dominant approach to thinking about how metaphors work are correspondence theories of metaphor (e.g. Tsoukas 1991; Oswick *et al.* 2002;

Oswick and Jones 2006). This approach to metaphors involves an author picking a metaphor that elucidates the characteristics of the phenomenon that they seek to understand. Following this model, 'a metaphor is seen as a comparison in which the first term, A – that is, the target – is asserted to bear a partial resemblance (i.e. the ground) to the second term, B – that is, the source' (Cornelissen 2005: 754). This happens through drawing out similarities between a series of phenomena and a metaphor (Oswick *et al.* 2002). The central quest associated with finding a good metaphor is generating a good 'fit' between the stated metaphor and the phenomenon. This happens when there is not too much difference and not too much similarity. There are some metaphors that might fit too well and only produce fairly banal insights. For instance, using the metaphor 'the leader is a boss' tells us little that we already do not know about leadership. This would make it a fairly redundant metaphor. However, if we used a more outlandish metaphor like 'the leader is a bouquet of roses', then it would seem to have very little overlap with what we know about leadership and perhaps would seem absurd.

The comparison approach to metaphor continues to be the dominant way that people select metaphors to use in their analysis. However, it has recently been questioned by researchers who point out that metaphors do not just work through the creation of a fit between a source and a target. Rather, they involve a creative act where new meaning is generated through crafting an interesting link between the source and the target. This led Cornelissen (2005) to propose what he calls the 'domains-interaction' model of metaphor. According to this approach 'Metaphor involves the conjunction of whole semantic domains in which a correspondence between terms or concepts is *constructed*, rather than deciphered, and the resulting image and meaning is *creative*, with the features of importance being emergent' (p. 751). According to this model, metaphors are not simply found through identifying already existing characteristics within a target. Rather, meaning is creatively generated through the interaction of different domains. According to this model, meaning is generated out of the 'structural analogy' between two fields of knowledge. For instance, building a metaphor of 'the leader is a gardener' involves evoking all our knowledge about gardening and about leaders. Through evoking these two bodies of knowledge, a new kind of meaning tends to emerge. This leads to a kind of blending of concepts to create a new way of looking at or understanding a phenomenon. Talking about a leader being a gardener creates a new body of knowledge that one could not find either in leadership books or in a gardening manual. Building on this broad idea, Cornelissen (2005) argues that analysing a metaphor involves three generic steps: (1) developing a generic structure by identifying the various terms which are used in a metaphor, (2) developing and elaboration of the blend which comes from the interaction of two bodies of knowledge, and (3) then inputting the emergent broader meaning into broader theory. The crucial point here for us in this three-step process is that it indicates that working with metaphors does not just involve identifying previously existing metaphors, but actually involves a creative act.

The final approach to metaphor is conceptual metaphor theory (Lakoff and Johnson 1999; Andriessen and Gubbins 2009). Instead of seeing metaphors as involving a kind of intuitive fit between a target or source domain (as correspondence theories do), or entailing the creative interaction between two different domains of knowledge (as domain-interaction theories do), this approach seeks to reveal a set of deeper underlying metaphors. According to conceptual metaphor analysis, both correspondence theories and domain-interaction theories do not go far enough because they assume that 'the characteristics and the structure of the target domain exist independently of the metaphors used to describe them' (Andriessen and Gubbins 2009: 848). In order to avoid this problem, they argue that we should seek to identify what they call the 'primary metaphors' that appear in texts. These primary meta-phors are often based on very basic things such as our own bodies. Proponents of this approach claim that metaphors do not just occur randomly, but they tend to be conditioned or structured by deeper level metaphors. This approach argues that we should not seek to impose metaphors onto a phenomenon. Instead we should seek to discover or induct the primary metaphors that are already being used in the field. They suggest doing this involves six steps: (1) identify a concept under investigation, (2) sample a selection of texts around the topic, (3) highlight all target phrases, (4) identify the underlying metaphors, (5) group together all common phrases and identify the underlying concept, (6) count the various phrases which fit into each group. The authors argue that by going through these six steps it is possible to identify a small set of underlying metaphors. This would suggest that in the case of leadership, there is a series of underlying metaphors that are frequently used when discussions about leadership occur. These metaphors are in some ways deeply rooted in our cognitive makeup and are frequently shared in culture. The task of metaphorical analysis would then be to identify exactly what these are.

Each of these three models of how metaphors work provides some interesting and crucial ideas about how we might go about identifying metaphors associated with leadership. However, they each have significantly different recommenda-tions about just how we should do metaphor analysis. For correspondence theorists, metaphors are there to be found through an analyst looking for a good fit. For domain-interaction theorists, metaphors are constructed through the creative interplay between the source and target domain. For conceptual metaphor theorists, the central task is to deduce what the deep structure of a metaphor is. Each of these differs in two crucially different ways (Cornelissen *et al.* 2005). The first is the analytical focus of the different models. There are some, such as correspondence theorists, who tend to project metaphors onto a particular phenomenon using deductive reasoning. This involves the researcher imposing a metaphor that she thinks is a good fit with various phenomena in the social world. In contrast others follow a more deductive approach such as that used by conceptual metaphor theorists. This involves trying to elicit metaphors that are being used in a setting, a bottom-up approach whereby the research looks at the metaphors that are actually being used by people in a day-to-day way in organizations. Taking this approach would seek to identify the metaphors which people actually use in order to talk about leadership. The second major difference in how we can study metaphors is the analytical form. There are some, like conceptual metaphor theorists, who take a de-contextualized approach and tend to try to seek out the deeper structure that underlies particular metaphors that are used. They assume that there is a set of metaphors that holds good in nearly any context. There are others, which tend to take a far more contextually based view of metaphors, and are more interested in how these metaphors actually play out 'on the ground' in organizations. This involves attending to the ambiguities and complexities associated with how these metaphors are actually used.

METAPHORS IN LEADERSHIP

Much of the literature on leadership and metaphors notes that leaders make use of metaphors, i.e. when leaders try to influence they try to use persuasive language and here metaphors are an important part of the communication. These kinds of studies build on the insight that we encountered in the last chapter that leaders are symbolic 'managers of meaning' (Smircich and Morgan 1982). This involves attempts to provide meaning and give sense to the activities of the leader. Many leadership researchers have argued that an important way that leaders can seek to manage meaning is through crafting the 'culture' and the language that is used within the organization. Although many accounts over-estimate the ability of leaders to manipulate culture and language, we think this is an important insight. Leadership works through the use and manipulation of language and sign systems more broadly.

A range of researchers has sought to explore the vital importance of meaning in processes of leadership. One way they have sought to do this is through exploring the discourses of leadership (e.g. Fairhurst 2007). Another aspect is looking at how leaders actually use discourse in a day-to-day practical way to exercise leadership. This is what Alvesson and Kärreman (2000) call a small d approach to discourse. This involves looking at how leadership talk is achieved and the kinds of interactional dynamics that it gives rise to (e.g. Boden 1994; Fairhurst 2004; Cooren 2001). This research highlights attempts by leaders to convince their followers to do various things that they might otherwise not do and 'construct' a sense of reality for them. A second aspect of this is exploring how leadership is a broad socio-historical construct which constructs parameters around how we can speak and think about leadership. This is what we might call a big D approach to discourse, which emphasizes its muscularity and strength (Alvesson and Kärreman 2000). Leadership then is a framework, a line of reasoning built around categories and concepts that regulates thinking, expectations and norms of actors.

This research reminds us that leaders need to work with language in order to convince their followers that they are in fact 'leading'. In this sense, leadership is constructed in a certain way in the language that we use to talk about it. For instance, if we talk about leadership using a vocabulary of 'facilitation', 'care', and 'understanding', then we are likely to see particular acts as being leadership when they involve attempts to 'grow' people (see Chapter 5, on the leader as gardener). However, if a different vocabulary of leadership was used (for instance a language which emphasized direct orders and commands), then we would see very different acts as being leadership. The central lesson here is that the language that we use to describe leadership shapes what exactly we can understand as being leadership. Language here is both a matter of the overall framing and the specific use of vocabulary in specific settings.

One of the important features of the language of leadership are metaphors. Successful leaders are said to be adept manipulators of language, and one of the central tools in their linguistic tool kit is metaphors. The good leader is able to spin a good metaphor. This kind of argument can be found in a study by Mio and colleagues (2005) who argue that more charismatic leaders were those who made frequent use of metaphors. In their study of US presidents, they found that those who were rated as being charismatic leaders used about twice the number of metaphors in their speeches than those who were not rated as being charismatic leaders. Another study found that leaders put significant effort into trying to shape the way they were portrayed in popular media such as magazines (Chen and Meindl 2005). They found that the metaphors which leaders used changed over time as they tried to shape the way their performance was represented and they sought to make sense of their performance and subsequent failures in performance. What is common in these two studies is that metaphors are seen as functional for leaders. The message seems to be this: the more and better metaphors, the better the leadership. It is as if leaders are poets dwelling in the boardroom who are able to spin appealing metaphors.

METAPHORS OF LEADERSHIP

While studies that look at the functional use of metaphors by leaders are interesting, they do not address one of the deeper insights of most metaphorical analysis. They ignore how the metaphors of leadership are not just used by leaders, but can actually construct how we understand leadership and how it is done. In this sense metaphors are not just something which leaders make use of. Rather, leaders are constructed by the metaphors that frame and constrain what they do. This point has been picked up by a number of authors who use the concept of metaphors to identify some specific ways that we commonly think about and make sense of leadership. For instance, Western (2008) argues that three common metaphors found in the literature on leadership are the controller, the therapist and the messiah. Boleman and Deal (2003) identify the architect, the servant, the advocate and the prophet as four dominant metaphors in broad management thought. Drawing on a study of CEO interviews in *Harvard Business Review*, Hatch and colleagues (2006) identified three metaphors for the leader: the manager, the artist, and the priest.[1] What is interesting here is that each of these different studies has identified a fairly common set of metaphors which appear again and again when thinking about leadership.

While these are interesting studies that chart a range of metaphors that are more or less typically used, they have some shortcomings in our view. The first is that they tend to adopt a fairly decontextual view of metaphors of leadership, derived mainly from readings of theoretical and popular management texts. They assume that there is a set of fairly stable, and relatively universal metaphors that can be used to describe and understand leadership in most contexts. The other issue is that they tend to follow a more deductive approach to metaphors of leadership. This means they tend to identify metaphors of leadership from theory as it might be and then seek to apply these metaphors to a body of 'data' out there. This largely follows the 'correspondence' view of metaphors whereby the research seeks to identify the right fit between a source and a target. However, they rarely acknowledge the interplay between the source and target domain. Nor do they acknowledge the creative role that the researcher plays in crafting these links. Finally, when they go looking for metaphors of leadership, they tend to rely on existing theories of leadership or what leaders say about themselves. They do not explore the metaphors that are actually put into use in the day-to-day activities of doing leadership. This means that existing accounts of metaphors of leadership capture the metaphors in our espoused theories of leadership, but they perhaps do not really capture the metaphors that are frequently used in our practices of doing leadership.

OUR APPROACH TO METAPHORS

In this book, we seek to take existing accounts of metaphors of leadership somewhat further. We do this by analysing metaphors associated with leadership in a more inductive and contextualized way. By being inductive, we aim to look at which metaphors of leadership are useful in understanding how people frame and understand their doings of leadership. This involves looking at not just the metaphors that are frequently mobilized in heroic accounts of leadership that we find in the business press (as e.g. Hatch *et al.* 2006 have done), but also considering the metaphors that abound in the academic literature on leadership. Furthermore, we are not only interested in the discourse of leadership that appears in written texts. We are also interested in tracing out the metaphors that are in operation when people actually do leadership, in the sense of what people think they do when providing leadership. This does not just involve looking at what kind of metaphors leaders use to convince people or make their change efforts seem appealing or desirable. It also involves considering the kind of metaphors which leaders themselves use, as well as the metaphors those around them use to understand the ambiguous and paradoxical phenomenon of leadership.

Although we are committed to examining the metaphors that are actually in use in a field, we do not have a kind of naïve belief that metaphors can simply be 'found' in the data. An understanding of the leader as indicated by a metaphor like the leader as an overman or high priest only comes indirectly. To trace 'root' or background metaphors framing leadership calls for hermeneutic exercises, seeing what is visible as clues to an underlying image or metaphor. Following the domain-interaction model of metaphors (Cornelissen 2005), we recognize that identifying and engaging with metaphors is a creative act that requires some intervention on the part of the researcher. In order to identify the various metaphors of leadership, we engaged in interplay between the various theories of leadership as well as our own empirical work on leadership. By engaging in this long process of circling between theory and our data, we were able to identify some metaphors that were both novel enough to be interesting, but also close enough to the empirical material (data) to be well grounded. In addition to following a broadly inductive approach, we also sought to be context specific. This involved avoiding claims that the various metaphors that we have identified in this book are in some way universal 'primary metaphors' of leadership that can be found in any possible context. Rather, we have tried to identify how these metaphors were pressed into use in very specific contexts. We were interested in how they were actually being made use of by all the various groups including would-be leaders themselves, their followers, and all the people promoting ideas about leadership. To be context specific, we have tried to focus on how ideas about leadership were used in specific organizational settings. For instance, in the chapter on the leader as a cyborg, we look at how the machine-like approach to leadership played out in a large professional services firm. By being specific about context, we try to acknowledge that the ways we found metaphors of leadership playing out in this context could be quite different from how they played out in other quite different contexts. Indeed, each chapter acknowledges that these metaphors of leadership can be used in very different ways.

Finally, we try to avoid reproducing and reinforcing the highly respectful, indeed celebrating tone of a lot of leadership discourse, through reminding ourselves and the reader that leadership is seldom a matter of a great leader with a clear self-understanding who directs, supports and controls followers. Leadership is full of ambiguities, paradoxes, confusions, inconsistencies. The use of metaphors as an analytical tool might help to negotiate these.

CONCLUSION

In this chapter, we have looked at how metaphors might be used to understand leadership. Building on the ambiguity-centred approach to leadership we outlined in the previous chapter, we have argued that one way of making meaning of the contradictions and tensions which are at the heart of leadership is through metaphors. Metaphors are particularly valuable for this purpose because they allow us to develop creative insights in a clear way around a very indistinct phenomenon like leadership. Metaphors acknowledge the ambiguity of the phenomenon. They draw attention to the partiality and uncertainty of all understandings. We have argued that metaphors are more than just the precursors for scientific analysis. Rather, for us, the metaphors associated with leadership fundamentally shape and frame how we might understand what it means to lead and be led. Moreover, metaphors can help to communicate ideas about leadership, bring to the surface our deeply held cognitive assumptions about leadership, give rise to creative insights, and subject leadership to critical scrutiny. For us, these characteristics make metaphors an ideal tool for understanding how leadership works in the real world.

To put ideas of leadership to work, we have looked at some dominant approaches to studying metaphors in organizations. Putting aside comparison (e.g. Oswick *et al.* 2002) and conceptual metaphor theory (e.g. Andriessen and Gubbins 2009), we follow a domain-interaction approach to examining metaphors of leadership (Cornelissen 2005). This involves paying attention to the creative interplay between different domains of knowledge. This requires a kind of circling between the talk about and behaviours indicating leadership we encountered during a number of in-depth studies of leadership in organizations and theories about leadership. Engaging in this process of circling does not just involve identifying metaphors, but involves some degree of creative insight.

In the following chapters we look at six dominant metaphors of leadership we identified. These are the leader as saint, the gardener, the buddy, the commander, the cyborg and the bully. We thus point to six key themes of leadership, each summarized and framed by a specific metaphor for the leader:

- moral peak performance – the leader as a *saint* (-like figure) provides moral guidelines and relations high on trust;
- support with personal growth – the leader as a *gardener* helps people improve themselves, increasing competence and self-confidence;
- creating a cosy work climate – the leader as a *buddy* produces an attractive workplace where people feel good about themselves and others;
- setting direction – the leader being a *commander*, creates clarity and a powerful example for others to be inspired by and follow;
- underscoring rationality and efficiency – the leader as a *cyborg*, standing for machine-like efficiency bringing about the delivery of results;
- providing sanctions, including intimidating people – the leader underscoring norms and keeping up standards through *bully*ing those seen as not contributing enough or doing what the leader thinks is best.

Leaders and followers may adopt each of these metaphors more or less actively or skilfully. However, they all need to be considered – by practitioners when trying to exercise leadership (as leaders or followers) and by academics when developing knowledge about how leadership may work.

When identifying these metaphors, we wanted to identify metaphors that were well grounded in our research on how leadership was actually being exercised in real life. Each of these metaphors is based on how the leaders and the led thought about leadership. Furthermore, we were careful to ensure the metaphors we identified were not just limited to the cases that we looked at, but tended to have a broader importance. Indeed, elements indicated by the metaphors that we have identified have also been noted in other studies of metaphors of leadership. Finally, we sought to identify a range of metaphors that were potentially thought-provoking but also evoked the 'darker sides' of leadership. This involved looking at not just the typically celebratory metaphors we usually associate with leadership such as the great transformer. We also wanted to explore some of the darker metaphors usually associated with leadership such as the bully and the cyborg. By doing this, we hope to show that leadership is not just a positive phenomenon, but often has a far more sinister side.

NOTE

1   A different route to metaphors is offered by Armanic and colleagues (2006) through an analysis of letters to shareholders by Jack Welsh (the former CEO of General Electric). They identify five dominant metaphors of leadership at play in the letters: pedagogues, architects, commanders, saints, and physicians.

4

LEADERS AS SAINTS

Leadership through moral peak performance

Mats Alvesson

INTRODUCTION

IN CONTEMPORARY SOCIETY and business there is a booming interest in morality. There are debates on equal opportunities in relation to gender, ethnicity, disabilities, age, marketing methods and consumer issues, environmental responsibility, community involvement, business scandals, greed and overpayment for executives, whistleblowing, issues in the developing world like child labour and bad working conditions, and so on. Increased emphasis on individualism, consumerism and hedonism means that self-interest and egoism become more salient. Feelings of reduced community and increased secularization – combined with a renewed focus on religion – contribute to increased uncertainty around moral issues. Trends are seldom clear-cut, but these developments probably form a background to a contemporary interest in morality. This of course also infuses ideas around leadership. There is an interest in how leaders can address these moral problems involving the interface between leadership and 'explicitly' moral phenomena. But the link between leadership and ethics is not constrained to address 'hot' issues such as corporate social responsibility and the moral shortcomings of contemporary working life. Most people interested in leadership are concerned more generally with questions such as what a good leader is and what constitutes good leadership. It is surely not a matter of just being tough, intelligent, having a strong will, being persuasive, result-oriented and other possible effectiveness-inducing qualities. It is also very much about being of the right moral stuff, of being good and caring to the subordinates.

The moral worries of our time form a background to many of the contemporary popular ideas in the leadership literature and self-understanding of practising managers. It is common in reasoning about leadership to emphasize the leader's high moral standing. This is hardly new, but such a framing and focus has become much more salient during the recent decades.

Integrity and high ethical standards are often viewed as characteristics of a good leader. Sometimes authors claim that when the leader is not of the right moral calibre, it is not a case of leadership, but something less noble. For instance, some researchers claim that transformational leaders 'must incorporate moral values as a central core' (Bass and Steidlmeier 1999) if they want to be assessed as authentic. Put in the crudest form, many assume that a real leader is good. If he or she is bad then he or she is not a leader. This seems to indicate that people are eager to preserve some purist and idealized notion of the leader, possibly blocking this category from critical reflection.

The problem is, of course, that the enthusiasm of devoted followers may have little to do with Bass and Steidlmeier's idea of what is authentic and not. As Grint (2010) claims, there is

> preciously little evidence that admiring followers of Mao, Stalin, Hitler or Osama bin Laden followed their leaders because they were psychopaths ... and much more evidence that they followed them because these followers assumed they were ethical.
>
> (p. 97)

It is very common to describe leadership in positive ways. Moral issues are not here necessarily clearly espoused, nor are they the dominating feature. However, the undertone is one of positive features scoring high on morality. There is often an interest in for example 'the collaborative subtext of life, the numerous acts of enabling, supporting, facilitating, and creating conditions' (Fletcher and Käufer 2003: 23). Such acts dominate in settings characterized by 'shared leadership'. This is about 'a dynamic, interactive influence process among individuals in groups for which the objective is to lead one another to the achievement of group or organizational goals or both' (Pearce and Conger 2003: 1). In shared leadership the 'influencing process involves more than just downward influence on subordinates by an appointed or elected leader' (p. 1). This 'more' is indicated to not just be a matter of quantity but of qualitative moral superiority. In a similar tone, Chemers (2003) claims that 'effective leaders provide subordinates with direction and support (i.e. coaching) that helps them to accomplish their goals' (p. 11). The effective leader 'provides' and 'helps', thus occupying a morally positive role. That leaders may build on downward influence is not made explicit, so any moral doubt in this respect is avoided. It is, however, clearly morally superior to advocate a form of leadership that is 'more than just downward influence'.

Efforts to boost moral qualities of leadership are common. One example of this is 'SuperLeadership'. This involves encouraging followers to lead themselves through empowerment and the development of self-leadership skills.

The SuperLeader exhibits orientations that match the gardener metaphor (next chapter), but the moral qualities are also worth highlighting – the altruism and care attributed to the SuperLeader being a supermoral person. The SuperLeader is a fine person who 'focuses primarily on the empowering roles of helping, encouraging and supporting followers in the development of personal responsibility, individual initiative, self-confidence, self-goal setting, self-problem solving, opportunity thinking, self-leadership, and psychological ownership over their tasks and duties' (Houghton *et al.* 2003: 133). The SuperLeader does this through a range of orientations and behaviour, all of which echo positive moral ideals such as encouraging learning from mistakes, avoiding punishment, listening more, talking less, creating independence and interdependence, avoiding dependence, and so on.

The assumption that (good, real) leadership involves moral peak perform-ance points towards one of the most important metaphors that lurk in discussions about leadership, regarding the leader as a saint. Of course, as with all metaphors this means an exaggeration of certain characteristics. We know that few managers perform moral miracles or are referred to as ethically strongly outperforming other people. And few would speak of most business people as saints. Nonetheless, there remains a strong assumption that effective leaders have a high level of integrity, honesty, and ethics – they are almost saint-like in their qualities of being authentic, putting their followers first and so on.

The saint metaphor invites us to consider themes such as sacredness, worship and miracle. These are certainly themes in a lot of the thinking about leadership, although more pronounced about political and religious leaders and a few mass media business heroes than in most cases of managerial leadership (Grint 2010). But for some management authors, it is a mistake to emphasize the profane nature of business. Hatch *et al.* (2006), having studied a number of articles in *Harvard Business Review*, claim that 'stories about the founders of business, the glory of its leaders, or its employees' extraordinary efforts reference the sacred within the business settings that are misconstrued as strictly profane' (p. 60). In the more extreme writings, the authentic leader is pure and sacred. Many of the most enthusiastic and naïve leadership writers (and perhaps part of the public as well) seem to worship the very idea of the fantastic leader. They are portrayed to perform something not too far from a miracle – the transformation of bored office workers into emotionally, socially, intellectually and spiritually better beings has such a particular ring about it.

Of course, an interest in more realistic aspects of leadership in fairly typical business and public contexts means that we find little of these qualities. We are not primarily interested in the mythology of the Catholic Church.

And we are not interested in those few public figures that always appear when 'evidence' of morally peak performing leadership is to be delivered (Mahatma Ghandi, Martin Luther King, Mother Teresa and Nelson Mandela). As our interest is primarily in the 95 per cent or so of those managers in organizations that are not top managers in large organizations, it needs to be emphasized that we use the metaphor mainly in order to highlight claims to moral peak performance and not literal canonization processes. Also here there is frequently an undertone of sacredness, purity, miracles, when followers look up to the leader. But it is often a modest element and as we are mainly interested in the nuanced understanding of leadership through the help of a metaphor, rather than imposing the latter and stretching it to or beyond its limit, the reader's expectations of exceptional leadership should not be too high.

We will explore various ideas of the good leader being a moral peak performer in its varied forms in this chapter. We shall start with empirical illustrations from our own research, then 'unpack' the saint metaphor and point to some versions of it, discuss the mechanisms and processes making saint-like leadership likely to work, assess the broader relevance of the metaphor and then, before concluding, critically discuss contemporary ideas of leadership as moral peak performance.

ILLUSTRATIONS

This image of the good leader as saint-like is not only popular in the leadership literature but also characterizes the self-perceptions of many of our 'real-life' examples. This usually involves managers presenting themselves as very good people, although they do not always explicitly stress moral virtues or claim ethical peak performances. However, in several cases, managers talked extensively of their moral qualities and seem to think that these are core aspects of how they exercise good and influential leadership. The saint metaphor helps us illuminate these examples. In empirical studies, we found many examples of managers claiming that moral qualities are a key dimension in leadership. One example of this is George Steinbrenner, engineer and manager of a small group of engineers engaged in a diverse set of complex and specialized technical work. This and to some extent the fact that George is relatively new in the firm means that he knows very little of what his co-workers do:

> I build my leadership on showing respect for those really sitting there with the tasks. And I don't have this inclination to point and control but rely heavily on trust and respect, am very open so to speak.
>
> (George)

Apart from being 'very open' and in close dialogue with the co-workers, George claims that one must

> engage in the co-workers, not just what they are to produce but also to a certain level their lives, that is self-evident. And openness is then very much a matter of they should feel that I am on their side. I work for them, i.e. I bring their interests further and inform about constraints, e.g. we can't allocate all the time in the world on tool development and so on.

In his self-narrative, George comes through as a very good man. Respect, confidence, openness, being on the side of the co-workers, working for them, advocating their interests are key issues, emphasized again and again in presentations. George's saint-like self-image as a leader can be related to his difficulties in contributing that much to technical discussions and other substantive issues. He says that:

> Earlier I had worked a lot from that I have a very good insight in the technical tasks people are working with. I have realized that is incredibly tough here.

There is a new product segment in which people are doing 'very complex' and specialized work, which George finds 'extremely difficult to understand':

> I feel that this is a handicap for me. I have to rely heavily on people in my group – and I do. What they say, it very much determines time frames, etc., their recommendations, etc. But I try to show a genuine interest in what they are doing, even though I will not be able to reach that level that I really will be able to coach in technical issues. And then I am much in favour of being available, visible and take your responsibility as a leader, not hiding from issues and problems. We have one who has been on sick leave for depression, I have no problems what so ever in handling, if you say so. And to take those possible conflicts that exist.
>
> I am sure that, or believe that, if you think what you think that I am open and offer very much of myself. I am, sort of, talk about my private situation and I say what I am capable of and not. Many at my previous workplace said that I am very good at being accessible and listen. The response from my co-workers was very clear that I was good here.

It is common in high-tech settings that managers have limited knowledge of what most scientists and engineers actually do and can neither participate in discussions nor assess performances and progress (Alvesson 2004; Rennstam 2007). George's leadership then is a matter of making a virtue out of necessity.

In our field work, we found that many others emphasize moral qualities as part of a broader set of positive traits. Warner, another R&D manager at the same company where George works, talks of integrity and emphasizes:

> I am steady in terms of principles so I think that treating people equally is important, that people get the same space for they have such different needs. There is nothing that irritates me so much as when someone comes in and says that now I should have that because now he has got it. Then I become really mad . . . I think it is an ineffective way to steer like that everybody should be the same, but all should be treated equally considering their needs.

Despite Warner's desire to be a morally good leader, he also recognizes that there is of course a lot of complexity involved:

> I do think that other managers see me as obnoxious because I don't give in, I did think that my manager thinks it is a bit cumbersome because he can't tell me what to do but must negotiate with me, so I think I have a high level of integrity. I have a very strong impact in the organization due to this. It is difficult to say no to me, so it is perhaps easier just to do it. I never give orders to people but ask kindly, but I do not give up before I get what I want.

Warner also claims to have a 'high accessibility, people can always come in and talk with me'. In this and many similar cases, the saint metaphor has only moderate interpretive power, although it still throws some light on how managers understand their leadership.

A third example of leaders who present themselves as being on a high moral level is Hale. He has a background as a manager and consultant. He subsequently accepted the job as a headmaster in a newly founded private school. During the initial year, he had six teachers working with him. He described himself as 'less of a manager and decision maker' and more of a 'coach'. He said his 'goal is that the teams make decisions themselves', and his 'own role is largely giving (his) knowledge about group processes and getting round personal obstacles', that he was 'very much personnel-oriented', and if the co-workers felt at home and 'feel that they get enough of a challenge, then it will go well'. Basically Hale suggests that his work is more about facilitating the subordinates in their work than about deciding; more about setting the work potential free than about discipline; more about empowerment than holding on to authority and responsibility; and more about constructive dialogues in complex work situations than giving expert advice. These ideas about coaching sound seductive, and the idealization of what appears as morally and cognitively superior easily leads to strong identification (Wenglen and Alvesson 2008). Hale was convinced he could not be a more 'authoritarian' manager:

> No, I don't want that. My work builds on commitment ... My leadership builds on the belief that it's about having fun and then that doesn't work. Then it's like Sara says. 'If you tell me what to do then you might as well do it yourself.' Forget that, then I'm not needed.
>
> Just because I'm a headmaster I don't solve problems for others, or decide which projects we should have. We have a dialogue around this so that everybody will have to take responsibility. That is probably not the traditional view of what a headmaster does, I think.

Hale believed that coaching was an efficient and morally superior leadership style. At the start this was appreciated by the teachers, but it did not last. During the year, the teachers were dissatisfied with a lot of things, including some of the basic ideas and arrangements of the school. These sources of dissatisfaction included what were seen as rigid policies, lack of sufficient resources and also Hale's leadership – or perhaps rather the lack of it.

> The coaching style didn't work at all. Completely miserable ... He wasn't the right man at all for the business. He didn't dare to make any decisions, partly because he was strictly controlled by top management. He said he would sleep on it and get back to you even when it came to small details such as buying material, books or something like that. He was spineless and incapable of taking decisions.
>
> (Mary, teacher)

One source of critique was Hale's shortcomings in key respects, partly relating to weak moral qualities.

> During our endless discussions with Hale he always emphasized our participation in the decisions that were being made. And then, during Easter when Hale was 'burned out' we found out from Aretha that we had no part in the decisions or goals concerning the number of pupils for the second year. And then you really feel deceived.
>
> (Mary)

Hale in his turn criticized the teachers' inability – or lack of willingness – to understand the concept of the firm:

Either you are with us because you agree with the underlying concept or you choose not to be a part of the system. You can't do both. I have a hard time accepting people staying in the system with the aim of changing it. If we're a concept business, that's what we are.

Hale here echoes a commander view of management (see Chapter 7). A sense of loyalty and discipline justified by the great cause of the organization is invoked here, blending the saint and commander images of leadership. He also felt that his subordinates were the wrong persons to appreciate coaching, being more used to working in isolation and preferring a manager who gives them instructions, something that Hale refused to do. In short, they were beyond help:

I feel I've done what I can and from what I've seen I would never have been able to change these people.

In the case of Hale, problems and conflicts can to some extent be seen as the clash of different moralities. For Hale, high morality is to provide coaching (and to not be authoritarian) and for all employees to accept the basic idea and conditions of the firm and be loyal to it. For employees, coaching means avoiding responsibility, lacking the courage to make decisions and unwillingness to support employees when they call for changes. For Hale it was morally problematic not to accept the overall idea of the firm, for the teachers to uncritically accept was the opposite. For Hale this was disloyalty, while the teachers saw it as professional responsibility. Different frames and identification then informed moral positioning: for Hale being part of and loyal to the firm provided the moral base, while the teachers defined themselves as professionals knowing what is best for the pupils. The case illustrates that morality appears in very different ways depending on your point of view. Trying to take what oneself believes is a high moral stance is not necessarily something that is seen by others as good. It is not necessarily regarded as socially acceptable and effective leadership. According to Hale's followers, the morally laudable ideal of not being authoritarian meant that pragmatic and forceful behaviour was avoided and important issues neglected.

COMMENTS

The three cases illustrate different ways in which the moral aspects of leadership are salient. It is typically about being good to people (thus to some extent overlapping the buddy metaphor, Chapter 6), rather than adhering to higher moral principles, like putting God and the country first.

In the case of George, his moral positioning seems more unproblematic, as his co-workers did not seem to care that much about what he was doing. They worked independently and did not regard themselves as very much part of a coherent group or particularly dependent on interference or support from the manager. Warner faces, as he sees it, a varied and messy environment, which seems to make any coherent or rigid stance difficult. Complexities of organizational life sometimes lead him to become angry and impatient with people. In the case of Hale, his leadership style, and the moral positioning it embraces, accelerated rather than prevented a clash with the subordinates.

The saint-like self-positioning can be seen as compensating for being ignorant about what one's followers do. Perhaps George would not emphasize moral virtues so strongly if he was more knowledgeable about substantive matters and could contribute more actively to the work. This can be seen as a rather weak compensation for an almost total lack of effective task leadership. But advocates of this view do not see it like this. Through his high moral standing and good example, George thinks he can address certain problems of a more social nature, but also make people loyal and committed to the unit and himself. He hopes this may reduce opportunism and other problems. However, both his and Hale's self-presentations as providing morally high-level leadership may be understood as an identity and self-esteem saving project which compensates for a lack of status and respect in substantive matters. So even if Hale was heavily damaged by the conflict with his subordinates, he – in his own eyes – came out as the morally intact, refusing or incapable of changing to a more 'authoritarian' leadership.

UNPACKING THE SAINTS I: SAINT LIGHT AND SAINT HEAVY

As mentioned in the introduction and illustrated by our examples, most views on leadership typically attribute a moderate moral value to leadership. There are also more extreme instances of saint-like moral peak performances in the leadership literature and research. The former, 'saint light version', is common in both academic and popular management texts on leadership as well as leaders who talk about their own views of themselves. For instance a headteacher that we studied, Eva, told us that 'I am here for the pupils. I am where I am most needed', 'I can and am not afraid of making decisions, but I want them (the co-workers) with me', and 'I want them to feel that they have a leader prepared to listen to their views' (Wenglén 2005). The kinds of views expressed by this headteacher involve an altruistic quality which is quite distant from the opportunistic self-interested 'human nature as we know it', assumed by people drawing upon economic theory emphasizing self-interest (e.g. Williamson

1985). In a quite different league of leaders from our headmaster, is former General Electric CEO Jack Welch, perhaps the most admired business leader in recent times according to various polls. Jack may be different in terms of power, prestige and pay than the middle managers who form the major concentration of leaders (or at least those claiming to exercise leadership), but nevertheless presents himself as an equally morally high standing person in his letters to shareholders. He claimed to lead a firm of 'saintly feats' (Amernic *et al.* 2007: 1853). According to Welch in his letters, General Electric is a firm of the highest standards, creating 'the spirit and soul of a small company', 'of never putting one foot 'outside the line of absolute integrity' (cited in ibid.). Of course, Welch focuses here on what is moral within a specific (economic, shareholder-friendly) context, and does not relate to religious, social welfare, environmental or other moral frameworks. He does, also, express in his communications qualities and characteristics other than moral ones, meaning that saint-like features are only a moderate part of his profile. We will come back to Welch later in the discussion of commander metaphors. This probably does more justice to his practices, but in this chapter we concern ourselves also with the ideas and claims of what people do when they lead.

Although these ideas on 'saint light' are those most frequently expressed, it is, however, not uncommon to go beyond such an average moral template in constructions of leadership, both in academia, in popular management writings and, although less frequent, in the expressions of managers and other people in organizations claiming practical knowledge and experience of the subject matter of leadership. There is a wealth of literature and general popular reasoning emphasizing that a high moral standard is essential to good leadership. Here the saint metaphor does not seem too far stretched to do injustice to the ideas it throws some light on. In a popular and expanding literature on 'servant leadership' moral virtues are stressed to such an extent that the good leader has virtues quite different from the great majority of people. Much of this literature is explicitly (and uncritically) religious, with references to Bible stories and the great leadership feats of Jesus Christ. Hatch *et al.* (2006) see the priest as being one of the faces of the leader, together with the manager and the artist. The priest-leader then is empathetic, ethical, inspiring, comforting, focusing on faith, soul, transcendence and purity, and embraces the saviour as the heroic ideal. Most leadership literature and a lot of thought and discussion originating from the US bear strong imprints of North American ideologies. We find ideas like 'servant leadership requires that leaders lead followers for the followers' own ultimate good' (Sendjaya *et al.* 2008: 403) and that 'the sine qua non of servant leadership is followers' holistic moral and ethical . . . development' (p. 403). Servant leaders are said to put 'followers first, organizations second, their own needs last' (p. 403). Servant leaders are authentic, altruistic, humble, and create 'an intensely personal bond marked by shared values, open-ended commitment, mutual trust, and concern for the welfare of the other party' (p. 407). Those served by the servant leaders 'are positively transformed in multiple dimensions (e.g. emotionally, intellectually, socially, and spiritually' (p. 408). The good leader then is a saintly figure capable of producing moral peak performance and avoiding all the vulnerabilities that characterize the large majority of the population. These are not necessary sinners, but it is assumed that the good leader stands out as different from the morally imperfect masses. But there is salvation, as the servant leader may sanctify the followers by turning them into leaders as well (Greenleaf 1977).

Bass and Steidlmeier (1999) also make a case for there being truly good leaders. There are some concerns that charisma may not be so good all the time, leading to questions of whether transformational leadership is necessarily a blessing. These authors confidently claim that authentic transformational leadership is always on the side of the good, it 'must rest on a moral foundation of legitimate values' (p. 184). The opposite is inauthentic or pseudo-transformational leadership, where leaders act in bad faith. All sorts of good things characterize this authentic leader. For instance, some claim that authentic leaders 'call for (a) universal brotherhood' and focus 'on the best in people' whereas inauthentic leaders 'highlight fictitious "we-they" differences' and 'tend to focus on the worst in people' (pp. 187, 188). The authentic transformational leader may experience a need for power, but 'channel the need in socially constructive ways into the service of others' (p. 189). As it seems very difficult, most of the time, to assess this, and Bass and Steidlmeier mention that behaviours as well as the self-view of people may be misleading, one wonders where all this knowledge about the characteristics of the authentic and the pseudo leader comes from or who is supposed to determine the truth. It seems to call for a God-like ability to see through appearances and find the hidden truth. There is a prophet-like quality in the writings of authors like Bass, Greenleaf and others and a self-confident set of insights coming from having seen the Light.

UNPACKING THE SAINT 2: VARIOUS VERSIONS

As mentioned, there is great variation in the level and centrality of morality in the various representations of leadership. There are also variations in terms of what the key qualities of this high morality leadership might be. A review of the literature and our empirical impressions point at a number of different 'types' of moral heroes who exercise the kind of leadership that makes it possible for employees, shareholders and others to sleep well at night, stop worrying and learn to trust and love the leader. Among the types we find are the person with great inner moral strength, the martyr, the one driven by a great cause (personifying the Protestant work ethic) and Mr or Ms Nice Guy. Of course, most of these types can be and are often combined.

INNER MORAL SUPER(WO)MAN

One kind of saint is the character who has an extraordinary inner strength. According to one popular Harvard Business School book on the topic, leaders:

> are able to dig below the busy surface of their daily lives and refocus on their core values and principles. Once uncovered those principles renew their sense of purpose at work and act as a springboard for shrewd, pragmatic politically astute action. By repeating this process again and again throughout their work lives these executives are able to craft an authentic and strong identity based on their own rather than someone else's sense of what is right. And in this way they begin to make the transition from being a manager to becoming a leader.
>
> (Badaracco 1998)

One could fear that limited interest in other people's sense of what is right may risk a moral detour, but the author seems to believe that real leaders have their own – and superior – sense of what is right. Another author emphasizes the importance of controlling one's inner world (or 'invironment') in order to lead people:

> the ability to remain calm amidst all this stress and strain is an important trait of effective leaders. [. . .] By paying attention and learning to control their **in**vironment they are able to be effective amidst a changing **en**vironment. [. . .] These leaders are happy with who they are and what they do. They've found the resources within themselves to be at peace. As a consequence they're not dependent on external conditions – money, recognition, power, and so on.
>
> (Blanchard and Waghorn 1997: 202)

A more sceptical view would be that these internally focused leaders could possibly also be asocial, self-assured, socially unresponsive and rigid in their attitude. But as they are portrayed as morally superior to more average mortals, these shortcomings are not indicated to be part of the picture. Instead they are, according to popular leadership mythology, clearly different from ordinary people – who hardly develop a sense of what is right totally disconnected from the views and assessments of more humble people and who are hardly totally independent of money, recognition and power, and who probably find that a dynamic, complex, turbulent and often ambiguous reality invites doubt, uncertainty and openness rather than self-sufficiency.

THE MARTYR

Another version of the saintly leader is the one who is willing to sacrifice themselves. Sacrifice by the leader means that he or she is willing to engage in risky behaviour to serve the goals and the mission of the group or organization. They are also willing to be scapegoated if everything goes wrong. Some researchers and popular management authors argue that the perception of sacrifice leads to experiences of trust that is good for cooperation:

> communicating concerns for the group and its members by means of self-sacrifice and exhibited commitment on behalf of the group (in addition to respect and exhibited fairness) are indeed effective to establish effective relational leadership.
>
> (De Cremer 2003: 119)

The martyrdom business in most workplaces is one of fairly diminutive proportions. The religious or political leader who shoulders profound suffering for a greater good is totally different from the CEO of a shoe sales firm or a head librarian. But some authors also claim that the ability to draw out some positive insights from hardship and frustrating experiences is vital for all leaders. For example, Bennis and Thomas (2002a), in an article with the title 'Crucibles of leadership', are of the opinion that 'one of the most reliable indicators and predictors of true leadership is an individual's ability to find meaning in negative events and to learn from even the most trying circumstances' (p. 39). Suffering then would be good for (future) leaders, one may assume, although only those of the right stuff may benefit from this, those with 'adaptive capacity' composed of 'ability to grasp context' and 'hardiness': 'this is the stuff of true leadership' the authors assure us (p. 45). The idea that leadership involves sacrifice is then part of the picture, feeding the religious mythology that many leadership researchers are fond of (Grint 2010). Unfortunately, Bennis and Thomas do not provide any definite clues about exactly who will benefit from a prison trip, participation in a war or working for a Sony camcorder factory in rural Japan ('the hardest thing I've ever done', according to a person benefiting from this event) – to use some of their examples – in their leadership career. Presumably, there are many ex-prisoners, war veterans and camcorder factory workers that do not make it to the top executive jobs where those addressed by Bennis and Thomas ended up. Given the value of suffering, one wonders if an implication of their ideas would be to cultivate a harsh leadership style, for example, including bullying, to produce the beneficial experiences fostering 'adaptive capacity'.

CHAMPIONS OF THE GREAT CAUSE

Another kind of moral leader is the one who undertakes the great cause without being driven by selfish motives. The leader's attachment to a higher, almost sacred purpose produces the moral peak performance. Here it is not inner qualities like peace or a stable identity that are the focus and it is not martyrdom. Instead, it is the overall cause, in business typically building an organization with extraordinary good results. The best for the company is the overall guideline. Personal interest and ambition for their own part are insignificant for those committed to these larger-than-life missions of producing excellence. Strong will overlaps with inner qualities and also the great transformational mission of the saint-leader. But it is the overall purpose that stands in the centre, even though this is fuelled by the saint's engagement. Many radical change projects are believed to be driven by leaders who have a great faith in their morally superior ideas. Transformational leaders seek to change attitudes, values and behaviours by projecting 'extremely high levels of self-confidence, dominance, and a strong conviction in the moral righteousness of his/her beliefs' (House, cited by Amernic *et al.* 2007: 1842). This is, for example, the self-view promoted by General Electric CEO Welch in his letters to shareholders, mentioned above. Whether this moral righteousness is shared by followers is another matter. However, most researchers assume that if there is a transformational leader then those targeting transformation buy into the righteousness. Whether an external observer looking at this in more depth would agree with either the moral manager or the possible devoted followers is another matter.

Of course, many people have worked at creating great companies and impressive transformations, but the saint does so without any narcissistic motives. Self-interest should not interfere with the great cause, we are told. Rather than the self-focused charismatic leader who may inspire and seduce people at the cost of creating strong dependencies, the post-heroic leader has different and superior moral qualities. Sometimes the post-hero is not remarkable; he or she is just a good and well-intentioned person lacking obvious bad traits. But sometimes the post-hero figure is, according to the clear-sighted researcher, really heroic, behind an appropriate modest surface. Collins's (2001a) idea of the level 5 leader could exemplify this. People on this level are superior as leaders to everybody else, i.e. leaders on levels 1–4, Collins argues. The trick of level 5 leaders is humility plus strong will and professionalism. There are elements of the Protestant work ethic here that one should work very hard and ambitiously as a value in itself. In this account there are some exceptional people, admired and worshipped by the author (and judged by the sales of Collin's book, many readers), who created very good companies but hold a low profile and even deny their own contributions. These were modest about themselves. Instead they credited their co-workers with the great work. This is sometimes counted as an example of a post-heroic leader (Western 2008), but their heroism is really only reinforced by their reluctance to boast or put themselves centre stage. A true hero does not seek the spotlight, is the (moral) undertext to this. She or, normally, he performs miracles but is very humble about it, reinforcing the greatness of the exceptional achievement.

THE GOOD GUY

A much less spectacular but probably much more common version of the leader as saint(-like) is Mr or Ms Good Guy. This is the one we met in the beginning of this chapter and, according to our studies, a very common position. Here the leader is open, honest, considerate, non-pretentious and in general a very good person, producing various positive experiences and motivation-raising effects on co-workers. For the most persons eager to emphasize their high morality, this is the easiest and most accessible version of saint-like leadership. This is a character well regarded by other people. Claiming exceptional inner moral strength, unresponsive to the morality of others sounds impressive, but may not be appreciated by people around, including followers. And although many people like to complain, credible martyrdom is rare. In most firms, performance is not much better than average and the contribution to mankind is perhaps not so exciting so the commitment to the great cause may not be entirely credible. But being the good guy, as expressed by most of the middle managers we studied, seems to be a leader position that can be taken in most settings and by most managers. Being both accessible and harmless it is quite popular in many organizations. So at least according to the managers themselves (particularly in Sweden) and to some extent also the leadership industry, a recipe for good leadership – which they fit into – is a fine moral profile, creating satisfaction, trust, cooperation among co-workers and thereby, presumably, good results in the workplace. The Good Guy moral peak performer overlaps with the leader as a Buddy, something addressed in Chapter 6.

MECHANISMS AND PROCESSES IN MORALLY EXEMPLARY LEADERSHIP: POSSIBLE LEADERSHIP ADVANTAGES OF THE SAINT MANAGER

Why should the moral superiority of the leader and his or her example lead to productive effects on subordinates? This is not obvious. The high morality of a manager could be met with suspicion and seen as misplaced in a highly political context. Perhaps subordinates are more interested in their boss being a good power-player able to outsmart competitors for resources. A morally minded manager may seem to be naïve and subordinates, superiors, clients and colleagues may want to exploit the saint-like figure. A person preaching and practising openness and honesty is possibly easier to manipulate and outflank than someone hiding their cards and acting in ways less easy to predict by people with conflicting interests, competing for resources and status for themselves and their units, or moral qualities could be seen as simply irrelevant or of marginal importance in a context where issues of efficiency and performance are supposedly what matters. I will come back to this in a critical discussion of the view of leaders as saint-like. One can, however, argue that a high moral standing could be performance-facilitating in at least three different ways. First, moral leadership may influence patterns of reciprocity. If a manager is viewed as having a lot of moral qualities, arguably he or she may be at the same time perceived as doing positive things for their followers. Being open, honest, and considerate are all actions that, at least when read and framed in these positive terms (other and less positive labels are also possible), call for a positive response from those presumably benefiting from these positive behaviours. People who receive goodness feel a need to do good in return and may be more inclined to make an effort to deliver. This is the norm of reciprocity, a universal norm according to Gouldner (1960). You do the same things to the manager as he or she does to you and then the relationship becomes smoother and functions better. Leadership gets easier to carry out as people are more receptive and positive to the leader's suggestions and requests.

Another way moral qualities may work is through faith and trust. The less trust there is, the greater the risk of cheating, and the higher the cost of monitoring and controlling people to constrain their opportunistic tendencies. In the managerialist literature, it is usually only subordinates who are opportunistic and optimize their self-interest at their employer's expense. But this is of course a two-way issue. Both managers and subordinates may have more or less well motivated feelings of distrust, leading to the careful monitoring of the other party and a preference for formal agreements. High morality means trust, good will and that promises are relied upon. People assume that their good performances will be rewarded fairly in the long run and that in a fair relationship one gets what one deserves. This is perhaps most relevant in contexts where transaction costs are high because it is difficult to monitor the relationship between contributions and rewards. If subordinates have trust in the manager the former may give the latter the benefit of the doubt in ambiguous situations. This may lead to the avoidance of conflicts and reduction of bad feelings and opportunism.

A third way in which saintly leadership works is through creating identification. The more transformational leaders relate their vision to underlying generalities associated with positive human and/or spiritual values, the more it seems that 'querying any aspect of the vision becomes an illegitimate act, incompatible with continued participation in the organization's activities' (Amernic *et al.* 2007: 1854). High morality breeds trust and the overall cause attracts an extra sense of identification and solidarity. This dampens the acceptance of deviating views. Saintly metaphors thus promote conformity and compliance, which may (or may not) be good for business, but it is probably frequently seen as good for senior managers, if they prefer a loyal and docile work force.

BROADER ASSESSMENT OF THE USE OF METAPHOR

The saint metaphor seems to be fairly common in the literature and managers' talk about leadership. As mentioned above, in most cases reasoning around leadership by academics, popular management authors and practitioners falls short of claiming such a centrality and moral superiority as the saint metaphor implies. A real manager rarely lives up to the hagiographies we find in leadership texts. The majority of interviewed managers and also a very large part of the leadership literature strongly emphasize moral virtues without seeing these as the most significant feature. It is still, however, implied to be an important quality in leadership – a good leader is indeed a morally good person.

When addressing high morality it is important to consider the standards people rely on in an assessment of what is good. For some, the things considered to be good are related to a world where a communicative and empowerment ethos dominates. Other ethical schemas relate to the environmentally sustainable, or being incorruptible or following due process (bureaucratic ethos). At the same time, most authors talk about morality without being very specific. This is particularly the case in the literature, where being selfless, authentic, using power for the good of society, or integrity are used in excessively vague ways. The middle managers that we have studied are somewhat more specific and typically relate to being good to their co-workers, sometimes to the organization and/or the customers (clients, students).

Many authors emphasize the payoff of this, arguing that high integrity and honesty can create efficiencies (Salam 2000). But the surprisingly large and expanding literature on authentic leadership and servant leadership preaches extreme moral virtues. This is sometimes viewed as the way to counteract all sorts of bad things in business and society (Sendjaya *et al.* 2008). Here the saint metaphor works very well to understand this (naïve) thinking. In a bad business world we need the saviour, in the form of the saint-like leader. The underlying assumption here is that financial and environmental scandals could be avoided if only we had the (morally) right leaders at the top. Anything systemic such as institutions, capitalism, political (de-)regulations, and consumer culture encouraging maximization of self-interest and greed are all downplayed. Instead, the focus remains trained squarely on the great leader.

Ideas about morally high-standing leadership seem to be the norm in at least parts of the Western world, at least in terms of what is espoused. The more extreme versions of this seem to be mainly popular in the US and among (other) people strongly influenced by religious ideas. In some (secular) countries moral example and influence is more low key, but still persistent. For instance, in Sweden the idea of leadership as coaching is often given a moral meaning, through the implication that you should not be authoritarian or bureaucratic, nor should you constrain or punish. Instead, to be a good leader you should be helpful and supportive. The gardener and to a degree the buddy metaphors also point at these qualities.

The impression from having interviewed many managers is that almost all of them are deeply concerned with scoring high on moral positioning. Other managers are regarded as not sharing the same saintly virtues. One manager compares other managers' inauthentic appearance with his own lack of pretence:

> I've seen leaders who come in and pretend everything. I haven't done that. These guys (his subordinates) have all the experience, they've got the knowledge.

As the following quotation indicates, Warner's superiors show little respect when they mess around with details, something he himself does not do:

> I am a person with integrity which means that I become irritated when my superiors start to mess around with details. I try not to do so with my co-workers.

Not only the superiors but also the subordinates do not score so high all the time in terms of the virtues held by the interviewed managers. For instance Warner told us that:

I become angry with people not being honest and apparently argue for not doing something they don't feel for doing. Unfortunately there are quite a lot of people that find all sorts of reasons for not doing things.

Laurent (1978) found that while the interviewed managers all informed their co-workers about planned changes – thus showing a considerate attitude to them – the interviewees' own superiors generally did not. We can thus conclude that the people studied had a much higher moral standing than people not directly interviewed or asked to fill in questionnaires. Most managers' self-understanding includes a view of having high morality and this being a moderately to significantly important leadership quality. Managers are hardly alone in having a self-serving bias about their virtues, but the normative pressure of 'good leadership' may reinforce such a tendency. The great majority of the leadership literature seems to promote the opinion that good leadership includes a fair to large dose of high morality, but this probably reflects contemporary ideologies of moral goodness more than actual managerial practices or the qualities of managers.

SCEPTICAL DISCUSSION

Assumptions and reasoning that can be illuminated through seeing the leader as a saint are popular, but have some deep problems. According to Greenleaf (1977), the major author of servant leadership,

> the real enemy [of all bad things] is fuzzy thinking on part of the good, intelligent, vital people, and their failure to lead, and to follow servants as leaders. Too many settle for being critics and experts, there is too much intellectual wheel spinning . . . [There is] too little disposition to see 'the problem' as residing in here and not out there. In short the enemy is the strong natural servants who have the potential to lead but do not lead, or who choose to follow a non-servant.
>
> (p. 133, emphasis in original)

One might assume that very few academics would be tolerant about someone having little patience with critique, suspicion of intellectual activity and seeing expertise as 'the real enemy'. Surprisingly, there are a lot of academic authors seduced by Greenleaf's ideas, claiming expertise through the use of psychological scales for (supposedly) measuring authenticity (e.g. Sendjaya et al. 2008). It is of course very easy to claim a high moral standing in self-reports, managerial development programmes and other situations where idealized self-images can be expressed. In 'real life' settings key virtues may less frequently be salient.

MORALITY AS WINDOW-DRESSING

It is of course very easy to express a high moral standing (saintliness) when a researcher asks about your management style, when you attend managerial development programmes or you are interviewed by a journalist about your recipe for leadership. However, in 'real life' settings many virtues may less frequently be evident. One could of course claim that people's true morality is difficult to comment on. Normally what matters are the impressions conveyed. This reminds us that role requirements and mass media manipulations are crucial for leading actors' moral performances. Of course, political leaders are particularly exposed to the glare of the media, but also senior managers have a public face that needs to be preserved. Within organizations there is a need to engage in impression management and to appear to have the right moral posture. Sometimes 'right' here means holding ethics high, sometimes not involving ethics, but adapting to the requirements of the customers, hard competition, minimizing costs, and so on. What is 'right' is to make the customer happy.

According to Brunsson (2003) organizations display hypocrisy in the sense that talk, action and decision are often separated and various ingredients are used in order to meet different demands and expectations. This may sound morally questionable, but Brunsson suggests that this is necessary in order to create flexibility. It allows morally sound appearance to solve issues of legitimacy and have limited destructive bearing on productive activity. The important thing for managers is not so much to have a firm (and thus rigid) moral position, but sometimes act and exhibit high morality and sometimes be flexible and adaptable to situations not easily assessed in terms of morality. This gives a manager the leeway they might not have if they were constrained by a strong sense of personal morality and strong expectations of others on appearance. Perhaps contemporary complex society and business, with a variety of expectations and demands from diverse groups, undermine the chance of senior people in organizations developing and maintaining a strong sense of ethics.

THE IMMORALITY OF BUSINESS MORALITY

The fundamental problem of peak moral performance in business is of course that firms are not designed or rewarded primarily for the maximization of possessing high moral qualities. If leaders insisted on these high moral standards, they would create a lot of problems for themselves and their firms and would not last long. For instance a sales manager, himself being committed to ecological ideals, refrains from trying to influence his customers as it would be wrong to impose his own values on them (Fineman 1998: 243):

> But it is not for me to bring personal prejudice of my own opinion into the marketplace. What's important from my point of view is to reflect my customers' requirements. So whatever I happen to think is irrelevant. I must give customers what they require.

Here we find a 'market morality': the customers are (morally) right and other moral considerations are subordinated to what the customer wants. Ethics is re-framed as personal opinion. This may be one way out: the labelling 'high integrity' is fine and used when it is fairly easy to adapt to the situation, but framing one's view as 'personal opinion' allows us to refrain from insisting on acting in line with one's own convictions.

Integrity certainly sounds fine – it involves loyalty to one's rational convictions in action and it may foster trust and all sorts of positive co-worker responses (Salam 2000). However, this quality may be very difficult to adhere to in a business world with strong demands on flexibility and adaptation. Of course, a manager's conviction may be 'customer orientation' or profit maximization, but we see little point in labelling this as 'integrity'. According to Jackall (1988), people in firms who insist on high morality are generally met with suspicion. They are seen to be inflexible characters importing ideas relevant for the Sunday school into the wrong context. Integrity may then lead to distrust. An important moral rule is to avoid moral pretence and not to try play 'holier than thou'. This rule does not seem to apply to managers interviewed by leadership researchers about their values and practices. Here an undertone of 'holier than the rest' (the followers, other managers) is common. When people emphasize that they are honest, open, considerate, etc., they imply they are so much more than other people. But these virtues mainly refer to being nice to people. Morality in relationship to what organizations do, including producing and marketing products and services that include harmful elements (cruelty to animals, negative effects on health, pollution, waste of natural resources, encouraging gender stereotypes, manipulating customers, etc.), is a completely different matter and here claiming morality may mean entering an ethical minefield.

One way of trying to cope with the tricky issue of morality vs. profits is to twist morality so that it becomes adapted to business logic. General Electric CEO Welch, in a communication to shareholders, insisted on the moral virtue of making some people redundant, arguing that good management is to routinely 'remove' the bottom performing 10 per cent of staff; to not do so is likened to 'management failure', 'false kindness' and a form of 'cruelty'

(Amernic *et al.* 2007: 1855). Collins (2001b) also expresses the opinion that firing people that are not 'the best' is not a matter of ruthlessness but of high principles about creating excellent results. We have here a specific take on morality, which includes a fair dose of what many people may see as the opposite. We will return to this example in Chapter 7, where it will be addressed from the point of view of the commander metaphor for the leader.

THE SITUATIONAL QUALITIES OF MORAL RIGHTEOUSNESS

A basic problem with a lot of ideas on management and leadership is the inclination to emphasize fixed properties. The servant, super, transformational, post-heroic, level 5 and so on leader is like this or that. Few would deny that there is a degree of flexibility amongst the most saint-like leaders. However, moral positioning is probably much more contingent and varied. This is not just in the pragmatic sense of that leaders need to switch back and forth between moral and not-so-moral positioning for the sake of legitimacy and efficiency. It is also the case that very different employment situations will produce – or give space to – different sets of morality and what it takes to be good. In a safe situation as a superior it is easier than if the business is shaky or you receive intense pressure from powerful actors. For instance, one executive, House (who we will meet in Chapter 6) claimed to be highly moral (honest, trustworthy) in his previous job. This was the position of branch manager for a bank in a very stable and secure setting. However, in his new position as a CEO of a real estate firm, where rough owners interfered in sometimes intimidating ways, being open and honest were hardly ideals easy to live up to. Subordinates saw shortcomings in his performances in these respects. As mentioned above, most business settings provide little space and tolerance for managers with very high moral ideals. Nonetheless, in some contexts it is easier to be moral and sometimes there may even be a payoff. Customers and people you are collaborating with may see this and appreciate this. Interestingly enough, high morality among people that we have studied is typically expressed in the context of the wellbeing, trust and satisfaction of co-workers and/or customers. It is a form of popularity or profit-enhancing morality that is emphasized. Animal rights, environmental issues, help for the poor, etc., are seldom included in how middle and senior managers typically present themselves as good leaders with a strong moral standing. Seldom, if ever, does the intensive bombardment of consumer propaganda increasingly colonizing public life and leading to self-doubt, lowered self-esteem, reinforcement of gender stereotypes and life goals oriented towards consumption bring much happiness (see Kasser 2002; Klein 2000) if marketing is targeted for ethical reflection. Of course, many firms have some ingredient of corporate social responsibility, but this is typically a policy issue rather than part of the leadership exercised by middle-level managers. There are few examples of senior executives willing to refrain from enjoying salaries fifty times higher than their workers, even though during crises they may claim they will refrain from such greed.

In many cases executives exhibit a lot of variation and incoherence in their moral positioning and performance. Jack Welch emphasized high integrity and other virtues, but was also known at General Electric as 'Neutron Jack' because of his ability to eliminate people while leaving buildings intact (Amernic *et al.* 2007: 1841). This of course nicely exemplifies the commander metaphor (see Chapter 7).

MORAL LEADERSHIP AS THE INFANTILIZATION OF FOLLOWERS

The idea that moral leaders should exercise a strong influence over the weaker souls without integrity, moral righteousness, and commitment to a noble cause expresses a specific form of elitism. It suggests that leaders are like wise parents, while followers are like savage children with a lower level of morality. Western (2008: 116) echoes this point when he claims that:

> The suggestion that a leader brings intelligent, adult employees to a new moral maturity is reminiscent of the Victorian paternalistic ideology which attempted to bring a new morality to the working class.

Strongly emphasizing an asymmetry between moral leaders and their followers who are in need of moral guidance places high expectations and a heavy burden on managers. It means that in addition to all their other duties and tasks, they should also work as parent-like moral activists who should model what is right for their children. That managers have a formal responsibility that their subordinates act according to laws and broadly accepted moral standards is one thing. That they should have a responsibility for the moral transformation of subordinates (as suggested by some advocates of servant leadership and 'authentic' transformational leadership) is quite another. Of course we might doubt that managers are generally of higher moral quality than their co-workers. Some may say that good qualities lead to promotion, that in the job there is an encouragement to take a broader responsibility or that the pay-off of moral trust will cultivate the right leadership orientations and behaviours. This is possible, but it may also be the case that careerism, a focus on quick results, manipulation of performance indicators, politically astute behaviour, and the treatment of subordinates in a purely instrumental way might help people rising through the ranks who are far from models of morality. Indeed, the long climb up the corporate greasy pole may be an exercise which beats almost any sense of high morality out of even the best people (Jackall 1988). Perhaps there is sometimes reason to hope that subordinates are able to raise the moral standards of their superiors as much as the other way around. A one-sided focus on managers or leaders as being superior moral educators may hardly raise ethical standards in business and working life.

SUMMARY AND CONCLUSION

As I mentioned at the beginning of this chapter, there are signs that we live in a time of moral degradation, or at least in a time where people worry about moral standards. There are environmental and financial scandals. Enormous resources are invested in images and branding. The increasing focus on marketing involves a lot of manipulation and half-truths and creates a wide-spread sense of scepticism. There are many negative mass media reports indicating how bad large parts of contemporary corporations are. Executives are for example regularly portrayed as overpaid and greedy. This seems to fuel the popularity of business ethics, CSR and a hope for saint-like leaders. Portrayals of good leaders as saint-like figures may be comforting, but business contexts typically constrain moral excesses and most organizations socialize and reward people that are flexible and do not let strong personal convictions get in the way of corporate results (Jackall 1988). Expecting the Messiah to arrive in the open plan office is not realistic. All the prophets claiming that Messiah-like leaders are already here are probably deluded.

Of course managers, like all people, consider moral issues in work and life. Given contemporary worries about morality and the (over)emphasis on leadership for solving all problems, managers may feel that they were chosen as champions of ethics. Despite some scepticism about the claims and self-images of managers as moral peak performers, I do not doubt that ethics for a manager is potentially a good thing. In many ways it is promising that many interviewed managers and most contemporary leadership literatures emphasize moral qualities. Encouragement to think through ethical stances of social and business relations, and specific themes like environmental issues, animal rights, social inequalities and injustices, and misuses of power, is important.

There are, however, strong reasons to be critical of much contemporary thinking around these issues. The leadership literature and many of the managers studied indicated naïve and highly individualistic approaches to morals. It is common to claim a moral level in one's leadership due to one's own internal moral standards. And often this involved indulging in a celebration of one's own moral prowess. One may even question the tendency to celebrate one's own fine values and moral elevation above inferiors. And the literature embracing authentic leadership suggests rigid distinctions between good and bad people that are perhaps not entirely 'authentic'. So more critical thinking is surely needed here.

It is important here not to just emphasize the personal qualities of managers. Leadership is not done in splendid social isolation. Corporate and societal context is crucial. So also are interactions with followers, whose characteristics and influence (for better or worse) on the leadership produced may be more significant than the impact emerging from the manager and his/her efforts. One key point of this chapter is that moral peak positioning can be seen as a compensation for other inadequacies of managers in relationship to subordinates. In organizational contexts where managers cannot contribute expert knowledge to subordinates more knowledgeable about their work, nor run by numbers or rely on rules and standards, the good moral example is one of the few remaining options. Others include trying to make people happy (see Chapter 6). In some contexts, saint-like leadership constructions may be appealing. Morality then becomes a position and resource for the manager. In order for this to work, just being an ordinary good person is insufficient. Appearing to be much better than the norm (authentic, open, spiritual, having integrity, altruistic, adhering to fine values) is necessary.

Perhaps it is hardly surprising that while almost all the people studied told us they were very moral (using words like honest, open, considerate, non-authoritarian, disliking micro-management), other people referred to by them came out as sometimes inferior to those studied. This would indicate that many people have an exaggerated and naïve view of their own moral qualities. A leader's saintly ambitions often say more about wishful thinking and fantasies than 'objective reality'. A challenge is to save ethical reflections and stances from moral storytelling, feel-good exercises and the aggrandizement of fictitious Moses-like figures doing authentic transformational leadership. Critical analysis and reflection are needed in order to rescue the idea of the leader as a moral example in a corporate world where the morally good and the profitable do not always stand in a one-to-one relation, from being wishful-thinking, identity boosting and ideological. Integrity, honesty and other moral virtues are perhaps better viewed as a struggle than a position to choose or a fixed set of qualities to search for in the selection of people for managerial jobs. If our moral struggles lead to partial success and compromise it is probably a comparatively good result. In a corporate and organizational world where market adaptation, careerism, fashionability and flexibility are routinely rewarded, the values of integrity, authenticity and honesty can sometimes be a serious hindrance for a leader on the make.

Chapter

5

LEADERS AS GARDENERS

Leadership through facilitating growth

Tony Huzzard and Sverre Spoelstra

INTRODUCTION

IN THIS CHAPTER WE EXPLORE the metaphor of the leader as gardener: as someone who helps develop employees into people who reach their potential in a way that benefits the organization they work for. The image of leadership as facilitating growth is very popular in leadership theories such as coaching, self-leadership, SuperLeadership, spiritual leadership, and authentic leadership, to name but a few of the more influential alternatives on offer. In this literature, leadership appears as a beautiful thing: it fosters creativity, morality, authenticity, spiritual growth, and so forth. However, this chapter argues that such an ideal picture is hardly an adequate description of the new forms of leadership that are emerging in the organizations that we have studied. Leaders often like to see themselves as people-improvers, but their practices are often more ambivalent. The leader is seen as someone who finds a balance between the laws of nature on the one hand and care for their employees on the other. Our aim is to show how the growth metaphor in leadership discourse tends to underplay the importance of the laws of nature in favour of a happy image of care, tenderness, and authenticity. Organizations are not simply at the mercy of things beyond their control – the laws of nature – rather, leadership interventions can make a difference.

The chapter is structured as follows. In the first section we discuss the discourse of growth that we currently see in the leadership literature. Next, we illustrate how leadership as the facilitation of growth has also emerged in managerial practice, paying special attention to an office manager, Janet, in the Swedish Public Employment Service. In the section that follows we explore different possible meanings of 'growth', but also note that authors and managers are rarely specific about the term. Whilst carrying superficial connotations that are apparently positive and productive, on deeper reflection what is suggested is not clear-cut. This leads us to a more critical discussion of the leader as growth-facilitator as well as to broader connotations of the gardening metaphor in the context of leadership in working life and beyond.

THE GROWTH METAPHOR IN LEADERSHIP DISCOURSES

The idea that leaders and employees must 'grow' has become part and parcel of the managerial language of our times. To grow as a person within the sphere of work is today's utopia for many knowledge workers or people working in the creative industries. The goal is no longer just to have a successful career or to do meaningful work. The ultimate goal for contemporary work is described rather in terms of 'personal fulfilment' or 'reaching one's potential' and the way towards this blissful state of affairs is growth. The neuro-linguistic programming guru Anthony Robbins captures this ideal rather well in one of his videos:

> success without fulfilment is failure. . . . You can only be fulfilled by the final two needs. . . . These are the needs of the spirit. No. 5 is YOU MUST GROW. In fact if you don't grow, you what? You know the answer, you what? You die.

Growth for Robbins is clearly not optional. Just like a plant dies when it stops growing, people symbolically die when they fail to live up to their 'potential'. But personal growth is of course not just good for the person who grows. The crux of the matter is that personal growth is deemed necessary for *organizational growth*. Within a knowledge economy, the growth of the company is increasingly associated with the growth of its people. The knowledge-intensive firm needs the 'full person' on the job, not just a labouring body or a pair of hands. Within this story, the leader appears not only as someone who is great at growing him- or herself, but especially as the person who facilitates growth in others. Indeed, in the words of Harvey Firestone, founder of Firestone Tyres, 'the growth and development of people is the highest calling of leadership'.[1] This, then, is what the metaphor of the leader as gardener today exemplifies: someone who enables his or her employees or followers to grow.

The metaphor of growth within an organizational context has been around for quite a while. It goes back at least back as far as Myles L. Mace's *The Growth and Development of Executives*, first published in 1950. This book would not raise many eyebrows today. Much of what Mace argues is now considered managerial common sense: for a company to be thriving one must carefully examine and monitor the skills and attitudes of employees by means of, for example, appraisal interviews and psychological tests. The key success factor for developing people is to guide nature in the right direction:

> The farmer does not grow wheat. The wheat grows, but the success or failure of the crop depends in large part upon what the farmer does or does not do about helping it grow.
> [...] The father does not develop a family. The children grow and develop themselves, but the nature and the extent of growth depend not alone on inherited qualities but in large part on the environment within which they live, an environment where the father is a major figure.
>
> (Mace 1950: 113)

The Growth and Development of Executives was ahead of its time: it would take another 40 years before the growth and development perspective truly took off, with its peak probably yet to come.

Much of the current popularity of the idea of personal growth in business is informed by the (predominantly) North-American self-help tradition that has preached personal growth for many decades (see McGee 2005). In this tradition people are called to focus on their personal development first as the basis for a successful social and professional life. Self-improvement guru Stephen Covey (1992) calls this the 'Inside-Out' approach, in which the exploration of one's inner motives, assumptions and character provide the basis for dealing with the 'outside' world. If successful, the world will magically agree with your inner being resulting in personal and professional success.

Today the majority of the leadership literature is, explicitly or implicitly, drawing upon such an inside-out perspective: the leader can only enable growth of employees and the organization by growing him- or herself first. In other words, s/he must adopt an inside-out approach in order to effectively facilitate an inside-out approach on the part of subordinates. The benefits of such an approach to leadership are endless: it leads to motivation, creativity, happiness, profits and even higher moral standards (which is a convenient bonus in times of moral and ecological crisis). John C. Maxwell's multimillion bestseller *The 21 Irrefutable Laws of Leadership* (1998) takes this idea to the extreme. His law no. 20 tells us that leaders must grow 'leaders of leaders of leaders', which consequently results in 'explosive growth' for the company.

Of course, this 'discourse of growth', is not limited to leadership texts. Talk about growth and the development of people has become common parlance in many organizations and is equally popular in fields like Human Resource Management or Knowledge Management, and frequently occurs in texts on consulting, mentoring and empowerment. However, in this chapter we shall limit ourselves to the literature that explicitly refers to leadership. Of particular relevance are leadership theories and fashions that are sometimes called 'post-heroic' (see Chapter 2). We shall briefly mention some of the most influential ones.

The first to mention is the coaching literature. The term 'coach' is often used to refer to external consultants, like executive coaches or life coaches, but it has also become a popular way of describing a style of leadership. The leader as coach does not try to document progress through social or cultural learning. He or she must get rid of social and cultural ballast to free up the natural potential of individuals. Accordingly, leaders who see themselves as a coach often present themselves in humble ways, as someone who merely cleans the path for natural growth. The coach is indeed like a gardener in that he or she waters and creates a fertile soil for each individual plant (co-workers, individuals) to grow. For example, much like Mace, who was also a pioneer on coaching as a leadership style, David B. Peterson and Mary Dee Hicks advise the following:

> Approach your coaching like a gardener who does not try to motivate the plants to grow, but who seeks the right combination of sunlight, nourishment, and water to release the plant's natural growth. A gardener provides an environment conducive to growth, much as a coach creates the conditions in which personal motivation to develop will flourish.
>
> (Peterson and Hicks 1996: 35)

Second, the growth metaphor also figures prominently in the (interconnected) ideas around self-leadership and SuperLeadership (see also Chapter 4). Self-leadership has been defined in various ways but it usually comes down to Covey's inside-out idea: one should 'lead' or 'manage' one's inner life as the basis for leading others. The ultimate aim of self-leadership is to inspire self-leadership in others. This leads to SuperLeadership: leadership that stimulates self-leadership in one's followers, which feeds back into the strength of the (Super-) leader (Manz and Sims 1990). In the end, everyone grows and flourishes, especially the company:

> The SuperLeader's strength is greatly enhanced since it is drawn from the strength of many people who have been encouraged to grow, flourish, and become important contributors. The SuperLeader becomes 'Super' through the talents and capabilities of others.
>
> (Manz and Sims 1990: 34)

Compared to the leader as coach, the idea of SuperLeadership puts more emphasis on the greatness of the individual leader. Unlike heroic leadership theories, however, the SuperLeader is not born as a superman/woman but turned into one by his or her 'growing' employees. A central aspect of their job becomes seeking to nurture employees and using all their skills to ensure that they too grow into leaders.

Third, we also encounter the growth metaphor in texts on spiritual and authentic leadership, which often refer to notions such as 'moral growth' or 'spiritual growth'. One of the guiding ideas here is that the best and most successful leaders are true to their authentic self. For this reason 'Authentic Leadership Development' programmes are designed to bring leaders into this delightful state of being (Avolio and Gardner 2005). Like coaching and self-leadership, the best employees in a knowledge-intensive environment are thought to be true to their inner selves (rather than the values of the organization). By expressing their authentic being – mostly by having 'fun' and being 'playful' (see Fleming and Sturdy 2009) – employees would be more creative, passionate, ethical and ultimately more valuable to the company.

Lastly, we should note that some of the 'heroic' theories also incorporate development and growth elements in their picture of the ideal leader. Transformational leadership authors in particular speak of the ideal of leading followers into self-leadership by means of 'intellectual stimulation', which has been identified as one of the four dimensions of transformational leadership (see Chapter 2). Transformational leadership has also been linked to authenticity by distinguishing between 'authentic transformational leadership' and 'pseudo-transformational leadership' (Bass and Steidlmeier 1999).

We could have mentioned more leadership concepts, like 'shared' or 'value-driven' leadership, that also draw frequently upon ideas around the growth of leaders and/or employees. For now it suffices to say that the leader as gardener metaphor, in its most basic form, signifies that leaders should provide the conditions for employees to reach personal fulfilment for the benefit of themselves and the organization. We could also have chosen other metaphors to capture this main idea. Indeed, metaphors like farmer, father, mother, therapist are occasionally used for the same effect. However, we chose to focus on the metaphor of gardening for two reasons. First, we noticed that many of the leaders who we talked to spoke extensively about growth and nurturing. Second, the metaphor of the gardener also points towards some darker connotations like cutting and pruning which are not captured by similar metaphors.

ILLUSTRATIONS

We have seen that developing people is something that the leader does indirectly, or to put it another way, that he or she establishes the right conditions for people to grow. Managers who we have interviewed expressed many of the themes found in the leadership literature. This includes the creation of the conditions for growth and the importance of self-knowledge (or 'self-leadership'). Many of the managers we have interviewed also think of themselves as offering growth opportunities for their subordinates.

A common theme among those who see themselves as growth-facilitators was avoiding authoritarian leadership styles:

> I don't want to have an authoritarian leadership style . . . a positive and developmental climate builds on everyone feeling that they are involved. That's my belief.
>
> (Eve, head of a private school)

> They should be able to grow while I'm in the back [. . .] I've had two very special managers. My last manager in particular had a leadership style that I didn't like; I've seen too many negative effects. I saw how my colleagues were treated, controlled, and which consequences it had on them [. . .] I don't think you need to use a big sledgehammer. I think one can get people to grow in other ways.
>
> (Monica, social insurance office)

Here we can recognize the idealistic picture of authentic growth that one also finds in strands of the leadership literature. However, not all managers see leading growth as the solution to all problems. As a headmaster, Hale recognizes this in the excerpt below, just enabling employees to develop themselves will not necessarily provide one with the status of, say, 'SuperLeader'. Indeed, it may be interpreted as a weakness:

> You can't tell people what to do. They have to come to the conclusion themselves that something is a good solution. And for that to work, they have to have some kind of self-knowledge. They have to be able to reflect on and be open to changing yourself. *On the other hand, it may appear as if I have no demands when I don't tell them where they should be heading.*
>
> (Hale, headmaster)

The latter is indeed what Hale himself experienced: after putting his coaching ideology into practice, one of his subordinates described him as 'spineless' because he was seen as incapable of making decisions and standing up for a clear conviction (Wenglén and Alvesson 2008). In practice, managers seem quite aware of the dangers or limits of becoming a facilitator of growth. Rather than picturing growth leadership as a good in itself, some see it as a balancing act where too much autonomy granted to the subordinates should be avoided:

We should be coaches and help to self-help. We should not solve every problem that the co-workers have but give them the tools so that they can solve matters themselves. Then they grow. But this a balancing act between how much to help and how much one should refrain from helping.

(Barney, branch manager at a bank)

So the ideal of growing people indirectly cannot always be sustained in practice. Janet, a career employee at a local office of the Swedish Public Employment Service, nicely captures the tension between direct control and indirect control:

I am no administrator – I like to build things. It suits me. I look forward to laying the ground for something new and letting people grow into it. Develop into it.

(Janet)

This passage includes three ideas. First, Janet emphasizes that she likes to 'build'. In order to build, the leader forms a picture of what the garden could look like and starts to work towards this vision. However, part of the building process is beyond the direct control of the leader. This leads into the second idea of *laying the ground*. As we have seen, the leader as someone who facilitates growth, does not work directly with their employees but with the ground under their feet. The good soil is that on which productive plants (ideas, talents) grow and unproductive plants perish. The last idea is *to let people grow*, which is implicated in the second, but which cannot be reduced to it. Indeed, helping people grow often implies a direct intervention in the lives of employees, which we might see in line with bonsai gardening: a form of gardening in which plants *unnaturally* grow according to the ideas and aesthetics of the gardener. Relevant in this context is the distinction between enabling growth through the removal of barriers (weeding), and enabling growth through active improvement (as in bonsai gardening). The leader as facilitator of growth tends to picture him- or herself as the first, sometimes in order to escape the negative image of the authoritarian leader, but can in practice quickly slide over into the second, guided by personal or organizational ideals and objectives.

We shall follow Janet a bit longer. One of the ways in which she claims to help her employees grow is through appraisal interviews which, she says, also give meaning and pleasure to managerial work as an end in itself:

I enjoy the appraisal interviews, but they are very time consuming. [. . .] In Marlene's case she has been sick, felt unsure and stressed . . . [but] she's very able. I took her on an internal transfer from Hillthorp and have tried to develop her out of her insecurities and away from stress. It's just great to see how well she's doing.

For Janet, the appraisal interview is the best instrument to facilitate growth among her subordinates and as such is a central leadership practice. This is why she insisted that we should observe some of the interviews. The following exchange is taken from one of the appraisal interviews we have attended, between Janet and an employee, Paul:

J: Do you have sufficient time to complete your work?
P: It works OK.
J: Does Margaret help? Talk it through with you?
P: We have a little group and it usually works well – and we can discuss various alternative forms of collaboration.
J: I'd like to use you as a sounding board during the reorganization. The *job and development guarantee* will change – phase 1 will be more about coaching (of applicants): we'll be working with people from other offices. Phase 2 will be about workplace internships. We'll need someone to pilot this through. This is something that could be a challenge for you.
P: Sounds exciting!

So here we have an example of Janet claiming to create the conditions for Paul to grow by offering him a new task and area of responsibility. We immediately encounter the double-edged nature of facilitating growth: although aimed first and foremost at the betterment and improved interests of the employee in the long run, it may also entail cutting down or closing off that which is deemed undesirable. In other words, although the appraisal interview has a superficial element of positively developing the individual, it also contains elements of performance control. Such interviews can have a near examination-like quality and in effect are a practice where managers strive for disciplinary power over employees (Townley 1997). After all, it is managers, in this case Janet, who set the challenge. It is in this sense that enabling growth in an organizational context can rarely be separated from weeding, pruning, nurturing, staking and cutting practices that enable the manager to choose one form of growth above another. Recognizing the (partial) control element in the gardener's work allows us to appreciate that at the workplace the leader's attempts to develop or 'grow' employees will always entail an element of control. To put it another way, the direction in which employees develop will be circumscribed by the extent to which such development is consistent with and supportive of managerial and/or organizational objectives.

Judging from interviews with her subordinates, Janet is quite successful in getting the balance between direct and indirect control right. Picking up on the theme of employees gradually returning to work after a period of ill health, one interviewee, Carol, expressed her attitude towards Janet in the following terms:

> Janet and I have had a lot of contact the whole time. In the period I've been sick we've met each other once a week. It's felt very good. I don't think another boss would have given that amount of time to help me back to getting fit. [. . .] She has been very supportive and worked in a very solution-focused way. She has really listened, and tried to get me to think about finding my own solutions. She's also got me to think what is good or bad for me.

Similar views were volunteered by Marlene when asked to comment on her relationship with Janet:

> It's very good. She's helped me get a job here and understood my health situation. She's understood my potential, what I've done earlier and that I was more or less forced to work here. She tried to put things right for me. And then she understands that I like things to be organized and well ordered. She needs people like that: she's got too many visionaries and dreamers!

But it does not work for everyone. George, manager of a group of systems developers at an IT firm, has similar ambitions of developing people as Janet. He doesn't possess the technical expertise of his staff and therefore sees instead the need to lead through authentic and transparent relationships. He says:

> I'm quite sure that they think that I am open and that I am very inviting. I'm like, I tell them about my private situation and I say what I can and cannot do, and so on. And I hope they have caught that.

This view does not, however, align with how his staff sees his leadership or their view of the role of leadership more generally. George's efforts, rather, are seen as an unwarranted intrusion. The activities of George, when it comes to developing the workforce and the group are mainly seen as a nuisance – 'a very irritating factor' as one of his subordinates remarked. In this case, the need for personal development, feelings of commitment and joy are attributed to the work content. George is liked best when he does nothing in terms of trying to influence and improve his subordinates. They view development as coming from their work assignments, not from managerial interventions. Any form of 'facilitation' is seen as undesired interruption.

UNPACKING THE METAPHOR: MEANINGS OF 'GROWTH'

Let us briefly summarize what we have discussed so far. First, we have seen that the idea of the leader as facilitator of growth has become a popular figure in many contemporary theories and fashions of leadership. This idea is very attractive: SuperLeaders, authentic leaders and coaching leaders help employees in fulfilling their potential, make organizations successful, and have high moral standards. Second, we looked at some managers who see themselves as facilitators of growth in their managerial practice. In their accounts we recognized some of the ideas from the literature, notably the importance of self-knowledge among employees and the wrongs associated with authoritarian forms of leadership. However, we also noted how the ideal of facilitating growth in a 'pure' form can hardly be sustained in practice. In the case of Janet the image of a growth facilitator was linked to more direct forms of intervention and control.

So far we haven't asked what 'growth' actually means. Who or what grows and in what sense? Finding an answer proved to be far from straightforward. When we asked Janet what she means by 'growth' we did not get much of an answer. When pressed in a subsequent interview on what, precisely, she meant in her earlier statements by the expression 'growing', Janet explained that this concerned her, as a leader, '. . . giving her co-workers assignments that were a challenge. Growing meant allowing them to reach and use their full capacities'. In turn, this entailed co-workers 'taking on more responsibility'. The closest she comes to naming the form of growth she's after is, unsurprisingly perhaps, 'personal growth'. This is exemplified in the following reflections made to us informally about one of her employees, Alf:

> Alf hardly did anything previously. When I tried to get him to take on new duties he complained – he even went to the doctor's to report high blood pressure. It took a month to slowly talk him through it. Now he seems happier, and is doing new things. *He has even grown as a person.*

But what does it mean to 'grow as a person'? We did not get any clear answers to this question from Janet, or any of the other managers we have interviewed.

Turning to leadership theories of growth does not help much. Leadership literature on growth is rarely more specific than distinctions between, for example, 'technical growth', 'management growth' and 'total human growth' (Deegan II 1979). Here growth does not mean much more than 'better' or 'more': becoming *more* technically skilled, becoming a *better* manager or a *better* human being. The meaning of 'more technically skilled' is often the easiest to understand, especially if subordinates are clearly using certain techniques in their work. But the more fundamental connotations of personal growth, like becoming a better human being, are rather vague. Rather than addressing questions of this kind, most books that preach growth-fostering leadership quickly move to the level of method (like questioning techniques, goal setting, etc.) without asking what growth might entail. One catchy example of this is called the 'GROW technique', a popular acronym in the coaching literature that suggests a route towards growth: establish the Goal, check the Reality, consider all Options and confirm the Will to act (Parsloe 1999).

The term 'growth' seems to function as an almost empty signifier, much like the term 'excellence' dominates higher education institutions (Readings 1996). Still we might distinguish some different meanings of growth in leadership discourse. The first use of growth is akin to Immanuel Kant's motto of the enlightenment: *sapere aude*, 'dare to think'. Understood along these lines, growth and development denotes the move along a trajectory towards some sense of maturity, autonomy or rationality. Robert Wenglén (2005) has conceptualized managerial learning in much the same way: as a move towards becoming wiser, or at least less stupid. How viable such a view is in the performance-oriented working life of the contemporary workplace is a matter of conjecture. It is more likely, therefore, that the notion of maturity is connected more or less to instrumental ends connected with organizational performance (as we have also seen in the case of Janet). Nonetheless, the ideal works well rhetorically. After all, who doesn't like to be wise and autonomous?

The growth trajectory may also be seen in therapeutic terms. Referring back again to Janet's exchanges with Marlene and Alf, we can read these as acts of therapy. The essence of leading in the therapeutic take is that of making followers feel better about themselves. In other words, growth is seen as the reduction of neuroticism or the easing of a personal handicap. What is being targeted here is people's self-esteem or anxiety level rather than any movement upwards on a learning curve. Of course, the motivation behind adopting a growth-focused leadership style might also be a form of self-therapy: the practice of developing one's employees instils the manager with a sense of inner contentment that confirms a sense of his or her identity as a manager or at least is a source of job satisfaction.

Most of the takes on what growth and learning mean are connected with the instrumental ends of the organization for whom the leader and the led work. This is acknowledged when growth refers to the function or role that subordinates are supposed to perform. Janet mentions this third possible meaning of growth in one of the interviews:

> inviting my co-workers to develop, to take on new challenges – to take a step towards *growing in their role*. What this boils down to is providing a means for them to acquire both functional and social competencies.
>
> (Janet)

The 'growth' of technical skill clearly falls into this category, as well as becoming knowledgeable about one's field. It may also refer to developing the requisite skills to manage one's emotions. In customer service occupations, such as the Swedish Employment Service where Janet works, one's relationship with those whom one serves requires knowledge and skills in terms of managing one's emotions – one should exhibit emotions that are consistent with maintaining a productive relationship and these need not be at all the same as the emotions that the employee actually has as the encounter unfolds. Yet this is something that has to be learnt and can require considerable resources of identity work to perform successfully if one does not identify with the task at hand.

These three possible meanings of growth can certainly be recognized in both literature and practice. However, we would like to suggest that the vagueness of the precise meaning of growth partly explains its popularity. This leads us to a more sceptical discussion of the turn to growth in leadership discourse. Despite the fact that we may distinguish between different meanings of growth, it is rarely possible to pin these meanings down in actual conversations. The vagueness of the term, we would like to suggest, has a particular function. The different connotations of growth together paint a rosy picture of working life. This enables managers 'doing leadership' to legitimize their role and to carve out a positive identity space. We propose to understand this mythologically: as the restoration of man's fall from grace.

SCEPTICAL DISCUSSION: GROWING INTO THE GARDEN OF EDEN

Listening to managers, Janet included, one could easily get the impression that organizational effectiveness (or financial growth) follows logically from personal growth. In none of our interviews have we heard someone say that 'it was bad for the company, but at least it made John grow as a person', nor the reverse, 'it made the company grow, a shame though that we had to force Elisabeth into practices that are at odds with her personality'. This applies not only to subordinates but also especially to managers themselves. In virtually every contemporary leadership book we read that leaders must develop themselves before they develop others: 'You simply have to be the best of who you are', advises Jo Owen (2005: xiii) in his book *How to Lead*, in order to become the leader your organization needs. Similarly, Bill George (2003: 5) in his bestseller *Authentic Leadership* tells us that 'We need leaders who have a deep sense of purpose and are true to their core values' (saint-like qualities, in other words, see Chapter 4 in this volume). Business now pursues 'the new bottom line', which amounts to pleasing the heart and soul of the employee (Renesch and DeFoore 1996). We thus encounter a rather wonderful world in which the personal growth of leaders *and* subordinates coincides with financial growth of our organizations *and* their moral well-being.

The picture that emerges is that of paradise. It paints the picture of a sacred space that is uncontaminated by the crude laws of the real business world and bureaucracy: a Garden of Eden, or delightful and peaceful place, in which leaders and followers are happy and realize their potential while being productive. The image of personal growth that we find in leadership discourse often alludes to a pleasurable kind of work that is uncontaminated by the harsh demands of civilization. Work is now basically play, just as it was for God, says the theologian John Hughes (2007: 226). In the Garden of Eden, employees under a 'gardening leader' do not suffer the pain of toiling at the soil or industrial work: the leader as facilitator of growth protects a space in which people freely explore their talents and spirits. As we have noted, this comforting image is especially popular in gospels on knowledge work and the creative industries. Of course, this picture is too good to be true. Very few people feel that they are commuting to paradise on a day-to-day basis. Still, one might ask if there is at least some truth in the paradise-like image of personal growth and unconstrained play in the workplace.

For people working in the creative industries or in some other post-industrial environment – still a small percentage of the world population but these are the people who buy business books and attend leadership development programmes – the nature of work has indeed changed. They are 'empowered' and have the freedom, but which is also an obligation, to manage them-selves to a large extent. Optimists see them happily moving up in Maslow's pyramid, paving the way for others to follow the same route. However, such optimism misses the complexity of these new forms of work. Indeed, people that manage to blur the boundary between work and life, as contemporary business lingo often prescribes, often feel stressed rather than spiritually uplifted. Furthermore, one might ask if there is a price to be paid by those who do not climb the pyramid. For example, who will take care of the kids while the parents are busy with their personal growth? More fundamentally perhaps, who is doing the much more mundane industrial work needed to sustain the post-industrial life of a happy few? A more nuanced version of self-growth in the workplace is therefore called for.

The obvious danger of the self-growth fantasy is that it places the burden fully on employees, even those aspects that are beyond their control. This is well demonstrated by the case of women leaders who have the illusion that they have the power to change things that are in fact system-level features (Bendl 2008). Furthermore, it is not at all clear whether self-managing employees really have the space to grow into their spiritual or authentic selves. As Axel Honneth (2004: 467) notes,

> more and more the presentation of an 'authentic self' is one of the demands placed upon individuals, above all in the sphere of skilled labour, so that it is frequently no longer possible at all to distinguish between a real and a fictitious self-discovery, even for the individuals concerned.

We have also seen this in our case material: managers, like Janet, often decide the direction or parameters for 'self-growth':

> some people are negatively disposed to their work and developments in the office more generally. This reflects itself in their behaviour. They need even more fertilizer. We can distinguish between those who are positive as flowers and those who are negative as weeds. Some have a low level of self-confidence and don't dare to do things. They need a lot of fertilizer. Others don't want to do things – they are sitting around waiting for their pensions.
>
> (Janet)

What we see is that the fantasy of controlling the world by controlling oneself becomes itself an important control mechanism that can free managers from many of their responsibilities, or more generally, a way for organizations to maximize work input from their employees. Indeed, in most cases that we have studied, the manager him- or herself is not suffering less from the burden of self-management. Fully in line with the leadership theories discussed earlier in this chapter, managers are also supposed to find their true selves, or develop their potential, before they can effectively help their followers grow. This present-day version of the 'leading by example' dictum is often experienced as very demanding.

Earlier we noted that the term growth is often used in unspecific ways, both in leadership literature and management practice. We would now like to suggest that much of the talk about growth in organizations is unspecific for a reason. It not only refers to a particular 'soft' (or post-heroic) leadership style, its task is also to conceal and dispose of the hardness that no form of instrumental action can do without. The thin line between the embracing mother and the strangling mother allows us to use the growth metaphor and believe in it. We *like* to believe in the embracing mother, even if our quest for better performance contains elements of strangulation of ourselves and those in our surroundings. In reality, as some of our illustrations also show, underneath and within the growth metaphor we still find elements of more authoritarian forms of leadership. These elements direct us to what Zygmunt Bauman has called 'a gardening state', which usurps

> the right to set apart the 'useful' and the 'useless' plants, to select a final model of harmony that made some plants useful and others useless, and to propagate such plants as are useful while exterminating the useless ones.
>
> (Bauman 1991: 38)

This 'right' is certainly much less visible in forms of post-heroic leadership, but it hasn't disappeared. Indeed, part of the point of a business discourse on self-growth is to *make* it less visible. The leader as gardener suggests more than letting people grow according to their inner potential. He or she may also be understood as actively shaping their employees in the image of the organization. This brings us to our last section, in which we also discuss some more pejorative connotations of gardening.

GARDENING BEYOND THE FACILITATION OF GROWTH

The leader as gardener does not need to be connected to facilitation of growth. Indeed, the gardening metaphor has also been used to highlight more violent leadership practices, like separating the weed from the plants, or cutting and pruning. Shakespeare has highlighted both the care and the iron hand of the leader as gardener:

> Tis an unweeded garden/that grows to seed; things rank and gross in nature/Possess it merely.
>
> (Shakespeare, *Hamlet*, Act 1, Scene 2, 135–137)

With this quote from *Hamlet* Shakespeare introduced the imagery of a garden to craft an account of deterioration, death and decay in Denmark under what he saw as the doomed and malignant leadership of Claudius. The implicit idea here is that a well-kept garden depends on a delicate balance between the rule of nature and the tender care of the gardener. Without the latter, the former will take over leading to withering, overgrowing and decay. The suggestion is that bad rule leads to rotting and dead gardens, a general state of affairs underscored by the famous declaration from Marcellus to Horatio (*Hamlet*, Act 1, Scene 4, 67) that 'Something is rotten in the state of Denmark'.

Some of the elements we see in Shakespeare's use of the gardening metaphor we also see in recent writing on business leadership. For example, Dunford and Palmer (1996: 103) have grouped a number of writings from popular management texts that draw from what they label as the 'horticultural' metaphor. Their particular focus is how the metaphor represents downsizing in various ways including scything, pruning, shedding, chopping, getting rid of deadwood, slash and burn and mowing. These of course can often be read in different ways – in the context of popular management discourse and its general indifference to matters of power, domination and the effects of managerial prerogative on people leads one to infer that downsizing is inevitable and necessary and that to suggest otherwise would run counter to the laws of nature (or at least good gardening practice). The power of these metaphors and their allusion to nature has the effect of concealing the oppressive and inhuman nature of downsizing suggested in alternative accounts of the phenomenon as a leadership practice (Grey and Mitev 1996).

Gardening generally has both aesthetic and functional purposes. Simply put, a gardener whose endeavours are focused on growing flowers in an appealing landscape is largely motivated by aesthetic ambitions. The garden is an agreeable place to relax or be, as well as create – and the garden can be understood as an end in itself. Other gardeners will be more interested in growing fruit, herbs or vegetables. Although there may be some aesthetic aspects here, the main aim is, rather, that of production for final consumption as food of what is grown. This may, of course, also extend to commercial flower growing. In other words, the garden is a means to an end. This contrast between aesthetics (gardening as an end) and consumption (gardening as a means) is also reflected in approaches to human resource management, and by implication leadership (Legge 1978; Townley 2004).

The idea that human resources, like plants, can be regenerated as humanistic ends in their own right is a central idea in the concept of sustainable work systems (Docherty *et al.* 2002). The notion of sustainability, here obviously a metaphor from ecology, explicitly rules out work intensity as a means to improved performance. Instead it focuses on the requirements for developing a work system in the long run. Sustainable work systems are counterposed to intensive work systems. The latter are those that consume resources generated in the social system of the work environment. The interaction between the individual and work has a negative balance between consumption and regeneration and is characterized by exhausted work motivation, stress, long-term sickness absence, ill-health retirement, workplace downsizing and closure. In contrast, sustainable work systems develop by regenerating resources, add to the reproduction cycle and are consonant with long-term convergence between stakeholder interests.

The notion of consuming human resources, often motivated by short-term appeals to budget constraints or appeasing the demands of finance capital, has a clear analogy to the vegetable gardener seeing her garden as a means for securing short-term harvesting ends, often without due regard to the soil in the longer run. In contrast, the notion of sustainability has, for the ethically serious human resource professionals, a profoundly aesthetic dimension. This is also evident in our empirical material, particularly in the case of Janet who, in interviews, expressed a strong belief in the desirability of a healthy workplace.

As well as a distinction between aesthetics and consumption, the gardening metaphor also denotes, as previously argued, a distinction between growing or developing on the one hand and cutting-back and control on the other.

The centrality of these two dimensions within gardening practice suggest that we can unpack the metaphor as set out in Figure 5.1 and arrive at four distinct types of gardening work and gardener role as second-order metaphors: the landscaper, the pruner, the crop-rotator and the harvester. In terms of

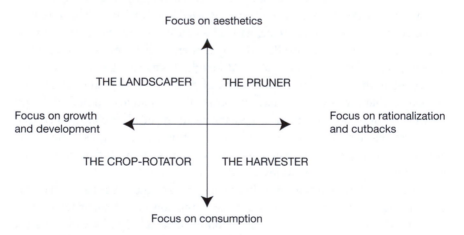

Figure 5.1
Unpacking the gardening metaphor

leadership practices and identities, each of these can be associated with specific leadership practices and specific channels for exercising leadership influence. We are not suggesting here that these are necessarily leadership styles which are enduring and somehow associated with traits or personalities. Rather, they should be seen as possible *enactments of leadership* (Weick 1979) that will vary according to the context. Such enactments are potential outcomes of the everyday struggle of managerial work and the need to maintain productive and meaningful relationships with subordinates and superordinates alike. In other words, leaders move in and out of different communities in their everyday work, a situation argued by Handley *et al.* (2007) as necessitating managers to adopt different identities as they navigate their way through the respective leadership challenges that they are confronted with.

The point is that these different connotations of the leader as gardener can all play out within a leadership as growth-facilitator identity. To illustrate this we briefly return to Janet who, as we have seen, sees herself as a facilitator of growth. An illustration of landscaping is that of Janet's ambition of leading a healthy workplace. This is reflected in her explicit commitment to employee health as a managerial objective. This also expressed itself in what, in an interview, she considered the highlight of the year:

> The highest point is that we have achieved a really low level of sickness absence and worked positively in terms of promoting wellness and good health. That has been really, really important in my view particularly in that we have been able to see a concrete result. Where there are sickness absences these are not due to work-related absences, but due to illnesses.
>
> (Janet)

Of course healthy employees contribute to the well-functioning of the organization but Janet goes further. She sees employee health also in *aesthetic* terms; as a desirable end in its own right, in much the same way that a gardener sees a flower display. This is not just a matter of performing identity work as a gardener or an HR professional (perhaps in an HR-hostile organizational context); it also about image, that is, displaying what one has supposedly achieved to others, notably one's peers.

As we have seen, Janet also displays an apparent willingness to promote growth and development for instrumental ends, which – in our terms – is to enact leadership in terms of the second-level metaphor as a crop-rotator. But in other situations she is also perfectly willing to use developmental means as a carrot for eliciting desired behaviours, an enactment of leadership that we would describe as pruning in that she is prepared to release staff who are not contributing to the common good of the office. This is illustrated in the following exchange, observed at a meeting between Janet and her opposite number in charge of an adjacent office, Karen:

Karen: Good. I've got a new person Anna-Maria. A really talented girl.
Janet: I have Harriet. She is difficult: afraid of everything. She's going to cognitive behaviour therapy. She went into the disabled applicant's group in August. I've said she must do the therapy or find another solution elsewhere – outside the office.

Examples of the final leadership enactment, that of the harvester, are less discernible in our case material. It can be recognized in more extreme versions of business process re-engineering whereby organizations are exhorted not to automate, but to obliterate (Hammer 1990) with a clear focus on business processes rather than tasks or functions or people. People are mere robots as sub-units within a wider machine totality, rather like plants that add nothing to the profitable production of the garden. Plants, like those led, are seen as infinitely malleable and expendable (Willmott 1994). This does not correspond with the language that self-proclaimed facilitators of growth use. Key elements of the enactments of leadership within the metaphor are set out in Table 5.1.

Table 5.1
Enactments of leadership and management

Leadership enactment	Landscaper	Pruner	Crop-rotator	Harvester
Example of leadership practices	Improving the work environment	Withdrawal of incentives from poor performers	Encouragement of functionally justified competencies	Increasing performance through greater work intensity and rationalization
Channel of leadership influence	Interest in personal career progression of staff (as a carrot)	Discouragement and replacement of 'dead wood'	Formally sanctioned training programmes (as a stick)	Threats of downsizing
Discourse	Empowerment, skills and growth	Control, jobs and costs	Empowerment, skills and growth	Control, jobs and costs
Management logic	Development as an end in itself	Releasing staff who don't add value	Development as instrumentally desirable	Headcount reductions to cut costs
Business ideology	QWL	Lean production	HRD	Downsizing

SUMMARY AND CONCLUSION

In both popular management literature and daily talk, leadership is often portrayed as an idyllic activity: good leadership produces shiny happy people and an organization under good leadership appears as an idyllic place to live. Not unlike, as we have noted, the Garden of Eden. There are at least two ways to understand the importance of linking leadership to an idyllic garden (and also a romantic English garden). At first sight, we can conceive this as an escape fantasy. In the Garden of Eden, the harsh realities that civilization brings have not yet kicked in, which is why it is often represented as a tranquil and peaceful state in contrast to the grey, bureaucratic reality of everyday organizational life. Where organizational actuality usually implies personal struggle, frustration, and conflict, the Garden of Eden fantasy might be understood as a way of coping with actual organizational reality. Thinking of an idyllic leader-gardener, present or non-present, or thinking of oneself as a leader-gardener, can be a form of consolation.

In this chapter we have argued that there is more to it. In order for leadership to function, it must be represented in idyllic terms: after all, nobody will follow a leader, or believes in a form of leadership, that is portrayed or represented in negative terms. It is therefore important to build an image of leadership that makes it possible to believe in it. The growth discourse in leadership does this remarkably well: not only is fear of authoritarian leadership effectively neutralized, because s/he merely makes people explore their potentiality, it also alludes to morality, creativity, play and authenticity – in contrast to almost everything that we associate with the harsh realities of pre-industrial and industrial work.

Yet behind this seemingly benign and innocuous facade of the gardener, her work and the Garden of Eden lies a darker side. As with the gardener and her pursuit of growing vegetables for efficient economic exchange and ultimately consumption, the leader in organizational life may see nurturing her employees in similar terms and engage in similar practices in the ruthless pursuit of organizational objectives. In such cases she would foreground the bottom line and subservience to financial interests through increased work intensity. We have shown that the growth-facilitator doesn't just entail watering, sowing seeds, applying fertilizer to lead to productive growth in the more general sense. Pruning, dead-heading, weeding and so on in what are clear analogies to practices of organizational rationalization, cutbacks and downsizing never really disappear. In the end, the idyllic picture of the Garden of Eden that we can detect in the growth- and gardening ideology in leadership discourse crumbles with other connotations of the very same metaphor.

NOTE

1   http://thinkexist.com/quotation/the_growth_and_development_of_people_is_the/150752.html.

6

LEADERS AS BUDDIES

Leadership through making people feel good

Stefan Sveningsson and Martin Blom

There are two things people want more than sex and money – recognition and praise.

Mary Kay Ash

INTRODUCTION

CONTEMPORARY BUSINESS AND PUBLIC SECTOR organizations are frequently portrayed as unstable and contradictory. This makes life in organizations occasionally complicated and difficult. It gives rise to conflicting expectations and demands. Ethical problems, worries, stress, a sense of lack of meaning, feelings of insufficiency are not uncommon. It is often suggested that an increasing number of people in organizations experience work-related stress and anxiety which makes them ill. In addition to the impact this has on the individual, there are the organizational issues to consider, for example, long-term absence, the impact of reduced productivity, unrealized organizational objectives, and the financial impact, for the organization as well as individuals affected by problems.

Based on the assumption that employees that feel good are better equipped to manage stress, anxieties, uncertainties and change, a variety of managerial means has been developed as ways of improving employees' well-being, many of which focus on employees' feelings and emotional status. We see this for example in the rather recent development in the emergence of therapeutic culture, emotional management and coaching. Targeted in this development is the presumed well-being of organizational members, their emotional status, self-esteem and self-actualization, often also described as important means for increased motivation and performance among employees. Many modern ideas of *leadership* are consequently intimately interwoven with this development as Western (2008: 94) points out: 'Therapeutic culture has had a huge influence on how leadership is enacted in the workplace, and how emotions and subjectivity are managed and organized'. An outcome of this development is an increasing body of literature suggesting that leadership activities should target peoples' need for recognition and praise. The renaissance of these ideas and concepts has its intellectual roots in many of the relationship-oriented behavioural ideas of effective leadership developed during the 1950s (Yukl 2006). Conceptualized as considerate and/or participative leadership, these ideas are sometimes said to involve a radical shift in understanding leadership in organizations, from command and control of employees to issues of motivation (Western 2008). In contrast to the classic idea of leaders as commanders (see Chapter 7 on the leader as commander), leadership also came to mean privileging employee social and psychological well-being and welfare. These ideas, intimately related to the Human Relations movement (e.g. Mayo 1949) suggested that more employee participation is beneficial in order to get happier workers and improved productivity. Fuelling and maintaining employee motivation is a key issue in this development and leadership researchers took up the notion of consideration as a way of understanding what triggers people beyond traditional command and control notions of role/task specification and expectations. In general, consideration involves leader concern for people and interpersonal relationships.

A relatively recent expression of these ideas is a popular stream of literature of post-heroic leadership that proposes that leaders should aim to become 'servant leaders' (see Chapter 4, on the leader as a moral peak performer). Servant leaders are sensitive and emotionally intelligent, empowering subordinates by providing protection, belongingness and self-esteem. Through such actions leaders and organizations would gain subordinates' commitment, motivation and sacrifice (Greenleaf 1970). Particular expressions of consideration could be leaders paying attention to people by using a variety of actions including small talk, common courtesy, remembering people's names and saying good morning. These practices are regarded as powerful managerial tools for accomplishing motivation and commitment: 'In initiated business circles, for example, it is well known that a weekend of shooting, anniversary celebrations, garden parties, a day at the races and similar social events are crucial in framing important managerial decisions' (Sjöstrand et al. 2001: 12). A good leader also listens to organizational members. Listening means giving full attention to the person seeking attention and by listening leaders make people visible and significant. Other common suggestions include using powerful, positive language in everyday social interaction since that presumably makes people feel important and encourages employees to contribute with additional efforts and productivity. In this literature, it is usually suggested that leaders engage in small talk, listen and generally care for people in order to boost motivation and commitment among followers. In line with much writing on motivation emphasizing inherent needs (Maslow 1954) motivation here is thus related to concerns of recognition, affirmation, inclusion and similar elements, not seldom connected to how we look upon and define ourselves in various social settings, i.e. aspects of organizational culture and social identity (Ashforth and Mael 1989). Consequently, in more recent writings managers are expected to direct their leadership towards how people understand themselves (e.g. Alvesson and Willmott 2002). Thus, we see an increased acknowledgement and emphasis of values, emotions and morals in studies of leadership.

By broadly connecting to these ideas, we aim to explore in detail how managers from a variety of organizations and industries express a specific embodiment of relationship-oriented and considerate leadership as a way of making people feel good. As explained recently by a CEO for a large service company: 'A manager's most important task is actually to make certain that people feel good, since people that feel good also perform well' (Dagens Industri 2 2009: 17). We investigate how managers informally try to befriend and empathize with subordinates in order to reach their objectives, hence the view of leaders as 'buddies'. This leadership orientation means looking after people and caring for people and making sure that everyone feels good, conditions we routinely associate with what buddies ideally are supposed to provide. Hence, in the wake of a harsher, colder, more demanding and stressful working climate (e.g. Sennett 1999), we introduce leaders who talk about the significance of buddy-like relations as most crucial in leadership. In the following sections we discuss this leadership practice with real-life cases and critically examine this leadership practice and some of its consequences. The latter involves a discussion of the dependencies and limitations that might follow from managers and employees befriending each other socially and emotionally. While this development of leadership ideal might seem favourable for all those involved, our ambition is also to exhibit the darker side of this buddy-like 'feel-good movement' and show how the humanistic ideas rather than empowering people can endorse victimhood and reduce individual autonomy (for leaders as well as followers).

LEADERS AS BUDDIES – ILLUSTRATIONS

In this section we will listen to managers from a diverse range of industries (such as telecom, high-tech electronics, food production, real estate, insurance industry, higher education and public services) that suggest that a significant aspect of leadership involves getting their people to feel good. An important character in the chapter is John Gentle, a former manager in the publishing industry and at present CEO of Insurance Ltd. As with other managers in this chapter Gentle positions himself as a buddy by building strong bonds with people in order to facilitate good feelings, motivation, and trust:

> If you go down the hierarchy what is it that people need? They need genuine consideration and that doesn't cost anything more than half an hour of your time. I have been successful in downsizing by the very reason that I've won the confidence of the employees in a genuine way.

Next we examine forms of leadership, all of them related to acts one would expect from a buddy: cheering, including, safeguarding, and being there for the people. These forms are all aimed at making people feel good, but they also include a variety of additional objectives and different means in order to accomplish these. First we turn to leadership as an act of cheering people.

CHEERING

Being cheerful is a common theme when managers conceptualize their leadership. Gentle often comes back to how important it is to make people feel good by paying attention to seemingly trivial and everyday matters, talking of his leadership as consisting of 'ordinary and smaller gestures' that 'are very significant'. This include naming people at meetings, greeting people on anniversaries and positively recognizing people whenever meeting them in the organization. These forms of encouragement assure, according to Gentle and other managers, that people feel good. He explains:

> It is important that people feel good and that you are responsive to people. You have to be nice to people. When Lucy felt a bit down the other day we handled the situation well. I received an invitation to a dinner, and it's important to attend those because you can push the company a bit. I felt that I didn't have the time to attend so I sent her and her husband instead. That didn't cost anything and she was very grateful and happy. This is exactly the kind of small matter that can be used in compensation without troubling anyone else. You gain a lot with that. Small and simple tricks that is hugely important.

When arriving at Insurance, Gentle restructured the organization in ways that relegated some senior managers to lower hierarchical positions. In order not to reduce motivation and commitment among these, Gentle regularly summoned them to exclusive resorts in order to discuss (what were said to be) strategic questions. Gentle says that:

It is important not to take the commitment away from this group and by going away to a resort also to do some fun things, like playing golf and having a dinner; I want to VIP them and assure continued work efforts on their behalf.

In general, the managers we have studied often emphasize how their leadership of cheering people and making them positive and happy also benefits the organization in terms of increased motivation and commitment. A manager in a bank, Michael, said that: 'I always keep track of people's birthdays and similar things as part of my leadership because I know that it makes people feel good and increases commitment'. A CEO for a large recruiting company said recently that leadership means 'caring for the little things', putting 'a little sunshine in people', 'providing confirmation by giving attention to people' and that it is generally important the leader engages in 'cheering' (Dagens Industri 2: 2009). The idea is that by keeping people happy by cheering and greeting, the company receives their loyalty and commitment in return. The objective behind this leadership process is to strengthen and assure motivation and commitment among subordinates.

INCLUDING

Second, many managers suggest that a central aspect of their leadership is to make sure that subordinates are cared for in terms of opportunities to participate in meetings and other sessions that ideally create well-being among the invited. Gentle talks about making people feel good by inclusion:

To have personnel meetings with everyone attending is important. When we have had a board meeting we shall have a meeting for the employees not later than 10 days after that. We've had one at which I joked a little with the janitors. I think they should be part of those meetings because they tell me they feel a little left out since they are at the bottom of the hierarchy. We brief people so that they feel included and get the possibility to be part. That makes them really happy and that's important. I participate in order for them to feel significant.

Here Gentle emphasizes how leadership requires making people feel included and significant in order to make them happy, also highlighting the informality by jokes. This is also stressed by other managers. One of them, Varnsen, an R&D manager at a high-tech electronics company (who we also briefly encountered in Chapter 4), emphasizes the importance of inclusion:

I experience myself as kind. I want everyone to be looked after. Nothing disturbs me more than when someone doesn't feel good. When someone ends up being 'outside' [the group] I get pissed. Everyone has a value and we all deserve respect. In that respect I'm rather kind, leadership to me is to make people take pleasure and feel valuable in the group.

The feel-good element is here regarded as most significant in the leadership process since 'nothing is more disturbing' as when that doesn't work. Neville, a manager in a global telecom company, says similarly that:

I'm emphatic in my style; I often keep away from and avoid just pushing things over people. I want to have a consensus view about what we're about to do so that everyone is along with the ideas, everyone is in the boat and knows where we are heading, that's my leadership.

In general, managers' talk about inclusion and making people feel significant is a way of making people get along with ideas, tasks and directions that they (the managers) have decided upon. The objective of this form of leadership act is to try to assure commitment by making people part of a larger task or mission (ideas) such as the company's business objectives or general direction.

BEING THERE

Some leadership activities focus on how well-being can be accomplished by being present and listening and 'seeing' subordinates. Janet, a manager at the national unemployment agency (the reader has met her before in Chapter 5, on leaders as gardeners), describes how she tries to see her employees:

I have a basic view that if my staff feels good then both employers and job seekers will get the best service. I prioritize my staff in all respects. I always have an open door. I'm here for them. I am well aware that I see my staff so often that I see it when they are not feeling good. I have my eyes and ears open for the overall atmosphere, ill-feeling, incidents and I respond accordingly.

Janet suggests that leadership is a matter of being able to sense how people are feeling. This is achieved by being present with 'the door open'. This view of leadership is backed up by Ollie (a manager in an R&D department in a global telecom company), who elaborates upon the necessity of caring for subordinates by sensing moods:

> I know this thing about being responsible for people. I listen to people, I sense moods. I've had this thing about responsibility for people. I'm working to make my employees feel good. I want to back them up, but it always has to be good for the company.

As some other managers, Janet and Ollie direct their leadership acts to the working conditions of their subordinates. A CEO for a large consulting company says:

> Our business model builds on making the customer feel good and an employee that is seen leads to a good working climate and work efforts. We had a unit that went quite bad. But then suddenly they made a terrific result and then I bought a rose to everyone which made them extremely happy.
>
> (Dagens Industri, 2 2009: 17)

Leadership is here exercised as an act of watching and being vigilant and observant about people's well being. The ambition behind making friends with and caring for people in terms of being there, watching and listening is partly to promote loyalty with and commitment to the organizational objectives.

SAFEGUARDING

A form of leadership, as expressed mainly by our middle managers, is to be able to care for subordinates by acting as a sort of shield between organizational levels. A manager in a global food company, Jones, talks about his leadership as safeguarding the recognition of subordinates' opinion in relation to senior management by providing them (the subordinates) with a voice. This assures that his subordinates feel good:

> I don't try to answer questions. If management [senior bosses] wants an answer I will ask them [his subordinates]. I'm that facilitator between [my subordinates] and senior management and they [his subordinates] are feeling good because they've got a voice in the upper echelons. Making sure that they get recognition.

Similarly, Erikson, the dean of a department at a Swedish business school, explained that his most important leadership activity was to look after his subordinates by protecting them from inappropriate control efforts from more senior managerial levels:

The most important aspect of my leadership is to protect people from senior managerial efforts aimed at increased control, because . . . that will only lead to that people will not feel good.

The idea of protection in order to maintain well-being is also expressed by Ollie, who says that one of his most important leadership tasks is 'to protect my people from the stupidities of top management'.

We can here note that the possibility of looking after followers is contingent upon the prospect of guarding their voice and interests, to assure their say among top managers, and to protect them from detrimental control, time-consuming activities and unpopular bureaucratization efforts. The act of leadership is here targeted at the working conditions of the subordinates and the objective is to make sure subordinates are heard and not overrun by unpopular decisions, i.e. to stand up for, represent and protect your comrades.

COMMENT

Although these forms of leadership may overlap to some extent, we think that the illustrations point to a variety of fairly distinct behaviours among the managers. Cheering amounts to enthusiastically paying attention to seemingly trivial details. Inclusion refers to recognizing everyone's efforts and contributions; no one is left unheard. Safeguarding suggests that leadership is a matter of protecting subordinates from the idiosyncrasies of senior level managers. Being there means being mentally and physically 'present' in order to spot any emotional disturbances in the atmosphere and act accordingly. These are leadership practices that, according to our managers, ensure that people feel good. Arguably, the assumption among most managers above is that buddy-like affiliations are productive for workplace behaviour and may reduce ill-feelings. By trying to act as buddies, the managers signal an ambition to care, help and build relations with subordinates. Leadership is here a matter of looking after people in order to create bonds and interdependencies that presumably make people work harder and get along with managerial change initiatives.

Going back to Gentle, we can note that his leadership acts create social bonds, while at the same time make people more willing to run that extra mile for him and the organization:

What is it that you [as a leader] want; well you want positive employees that raise themselves and work harder and are more positive. It's about that; getting people in a better mood.

This can be compared with how Janet talks about how important it is for her subordinates to feel good in order for them to provide her customers with the 'best possible service'. Similarly, Ollie describes how he wants his subordinates to feel good 'in the name [i.e. interest] of the company'.

In sum, the common denominator among these forms of leadership is the ambition to make people feel good by being considerate, informal, inclusive, attentive, and equal. In addition to acting on what the managers think is a generally humanistic leadership style, the objective is also to increase motivation, commitment and loyalty to the organization. Hence, the 'buddyfication' of hierarchical relations typically facilitates or enables tough managerial decisions and action. In the next section, we discuss and try to contextualize the idea of the leader as buddy.

BROADER ASSESSMENT OF THE USE OF THE METAPHOR

Significant when it comes to leadership is to acknowledge the multifaceted and multilayered cultural and social context within which it takes place. In different organizational settings and cultures, we tend to look upon leadership in different ways. As pointed out in Chapter 2, context is vital: leadership may, for example, be different depending of whether we study assembly line mass production or knowledge intensive firms, or whether we study small entrepreneurial businesses or large bureaucracies. The contextual sensitivity also concerns the occupational/professional, hierarchical and more overall societal level as well as different organizational situations such as growth and expansion or maturity and consolidation. In short, context matters when we discuss leadership.

Based on this notion, it is important to first emphasize that we have mainly studied Swedish managers in Sweden, even if a large part of them work in multinationals with several nationalities above, below and around them. Consequently, a more or less distinct Swedish perspective of management might frame the narratives (see for example Jönsson 1996). Based on this it could be suggested that the relatively egalitarian view of hierarchies and strong informality of superior–subordinate relations in Sweden makes our managers more reluctant to position themselves as authoritarian and excessively formal (compare with what Alvesson suggests about Swedish managers' passion for 'coaching' in Chapter 4). In addition, Swedes are often portrayed as relatively pacifistic and equal (e.g. gender). It is difficult to disregard this geo-ideological context in view of how our leaders describe themselves as relatively informal and equal, soft (anti-authoritarian), supporting (not giving the 'right' answer/ direction upfront) and considerate towards their followers. Hofstede (1980) makes a difference between masculine and feminine national cultures and suggests that Sweden belongs to the latter category. Masculine cultures refer to competitiveness, aggressiveness and self-assertiveness while feminine cultures refer to cooperation, mutuality, social relations and caring for others, In masculine cultures, managers are expected to be more task and performance oriented, while the leader-ideal in feminine cultures is expected to be more consensus seeking and relationship oriented. Most interestingly, however, is that even if seemingly aligned in particular with popular conceptions of 'Swedish management', the concern for followers' well-being and comfort seems at least to some extent an international phenomenon (see discussion on international leadership fashion below).

Second, the organizational context frames managers' tendencies towards developing buddy-like leadership behaviour. Several organizations in our study could be characterized as knowledge-intensive in that they include highly qualified subordinates occupied in complex and intellectually demanding tasks that require a substantial amount of autonomy (Alvesson 2004). These organizational characteristics tend to leave managers with a stronger supporting (as opposed to directing) role, and recently the subordinates' comfort and well-being have had a tendency to become a priority. It is sometimes suggested that leadership in these kinds of organizations is a matter of creating a strong sense of 'we' and thus a social belonging, or identity (Ashforth and Mael 1989). In addition to this, the study also involves service industries where the employees' interaction with customers is seen as a vital aspect of the perceived quality of the service (Hochschild 1983). In order to keep the employees happy (and subsequently, more service minded), leading them like a buddy might make it easy for managers to influence the mood and maintain a high spirit.

Related to this, it is also important to acknowledge the significance of organizational culture and its impact on what is perceived as appropriate leadership behaviour. A friendly and sociable organizational environment is often important in order to attract and retain employees (see for example Alvesson 1995). The specific situation an organization is facing could be significant here. A firm that is in need of high retention of employees (e.g. IT-specialist during the heydays of Internet development, with several competing employers trying to headhunt the same talents) might be more favourable towards (and perhaps more suitable for) buddy-leaders, who seem to make the employees' well-being and satisfaction their main priority. This can be contrasted with a firm in need of consolidation and work force reduction, where tough decisions 'have to' be made, and human suffering and despair is expected and often regarded as 'inevitable', hence low expectations of buddy-like behaviour (even if it is regarded as needed by many employees).

Third, leadership ideals and ideas are part of an international and changing management fashion. A supportive, caring, friendly and people-oriented leadership style has been in fashion for some time now and it is important to consider that much talk about subordinates' well-being is an expression of fashionable impression management, whereby the managers try to come forth as modern and up to date with the latest norms of how to do good leadership. After all, there are good reasons to believe that managers, as other resourceful groups in society, want to portray themselves as facilitators of 'feeling good' rather than bad guys pushing people into discomfort. Perhaps there aren't so many who want to be perceived as authoritarian bullies (and thus politically and morally incorrect) in a society that increasingly celebrates the therapeutic norm of providing people with comfort and self-esteem. Important to note, however, is that many of our managers also were characterized by their subordinates as being egalitarian and buddy-like. Based on this it thus seems as if leading as a buddy (rather than being idealistic expressions disconnected from what is happening in organizations) also is an activity recognized and encouraged by their subordinates.

Thus, the use of the leader-as-buddy concept emerges in parallel with a growing interest in coaching, therapeutic and related kinds of post-heroic leadership elements that provides ideological back-up to contemporary managers. In general, the individualistic, narcissistic, therapeutic society of today – with booming opportunities for life coaches, feel-good consultants, self improvement advisors, etc. – seems to provide a fertile breeding ground for this type of leadership ideal (Western 2008). Ideologically, it also provides a fashionable, progressive alternative to yesterday's industrial, hierarchical, raw, non-enlightened and inhumane forms of corporate leadership.

UNPACKING THE METAPHOR: VARIETIES OF BUDDIES

Previously, we identified four forms of leadership aimed at making people feel good by acting as their buddy. In this section we will examine these forms more conceptually by illustrating the variety of buddy-leadership (presenting four 'sub-metaphors' based on combinations of the four leadership forms discussed above) and more explicitly connecting to the leadership literature.

THE PARTY HOST

Managers in this chapter are strongly inclined to make subordinates' encouragement and belonging their priority; subordinates should be treated in a cheerful and inclusive way making them all feel happy and that they all belong to the 'party'. It is important to create a sense of exclusivity and recognition that makes people feel comfortable and cared for in various ways. By promoting an informal and friendly atmosphere (off-site adventures, golfing, surprise cakes, encouraging people by using their first names, and mingling around in the corridors) they try to support people, and maintain high spirits and motivation in their organizations, just like a party host would do in their efforts to look after their guests and keep them in a good mood. There are also some cases in organizational analysis where managers perform actual party-hosting, i.e. hosting dinners and receptions with the purpose of having fun (see Alvesson 1995; Fleming 2005). This is managers embodying the party host rather than the latter being a metaphor. In our case, Gentle talks of keeping people in a good mood and many managers explicitly claim that just being helping, empathic and aware of people's names seems to do wonders in terms of creating personal growth and well-being in their organizations (like 'good to see you again Mary', 'thank you Bob', 'Lucy, you're doing a good job', etc.). A good party host ensures that everyone feels a bit special and that no one is left unrecognized or forgotten. The party host draws on being cheerful, encouraging, and creating belonging and being present, the latter in order to see, listen to and acknowledge people. For instance, Gentle talks of recognizing people at meetings, naming people and making them cheerful when they don't seem happy. Managers also point to the significance of making everyone belong, making sure that no one ends up by themselves, in the corner or even outside the party. Like a good party host, as a leader, you try to control the stage, settings and atmosphere as well as guiding the experiences of the guests (followers) in a favourable direction. Who doesn't appreciate a good party host?

Although seldom explicitly expressed in this way, party hosting activities are well aligned with overall ideas of consideration and relationship-oriented leadership behaviour (Yukl 2006). Consideration for example, often suggests that leaders recognize and praise followers (subordinates in these cases) and relations-oriented texts usually include discussions of how leaders should encourage and support employees in order to build and maintain people's motivation and self-esteem (Yukl 2006). In our case we can see how this is illustrated by the way managers try to befriend their subordinates. Arguably, many of these acts (e.g. cheering, greeting and just being polite) are mundane and everyday activities performed by most people in organizations, but gain some special aura and powerful function when performed by managers in a 'leadership' context (Alvesson and Sveningsson 2003b). It is just not anyone expressing caring for people but their manager, and immediately subordinates are expected to feel better.

THE PSEUDO-SHRINK

During the last three decades or so the workplace has become an increasingly important site for personal growth, community and well-being. Following the Human Relations movement and Maslow's scheme on motivation, the idea of privileging emotions, group psychodynamics and self-actualization has become conventional in order to maintain healthy interpersonal relations and a rewarding workplace. Following a general broadening of the definition of 'illness', there has been a huge increase of counsellors, coaches, new age theorists/practitioners, feel-good consultants, and other pseudo-shrinks ready to assist organizations. As pointed out by Western (2008), leaders have not been immune to this development, hence we now tend to see the leader as 'therapist'. This development has subsequently made the leader in organizations become active in the management of emotions and (ill)feelings, hence the leader as 'pseudo-shrink'.

Managers in our case frequently suggest that it is important to 'be there' for your people and try to sense their mood by listening, observing and keeping doors open, all in order to be able to sense ill-feeling and problems among the people. Janet talks about leadership in terms of the significance of being able to 'see' any (organizational or individual) problem. Ollie also emphasizes his ability to listen and sense the mood in the organization. This implies close observation of peoples' behaviour and, like a shrink, trying to read emotional status among people in order to detect whether there any problems lurking below the surface. Just like shrinks are supposed to listen attentively and occasionally intervene in order to identify and correct a problem, managers here talk of their role as detecting ill-feelings and problems. Shrinks observe how people express feelings, try to understand patterns of thinking and emotional status, develop perspective on past events and current relationships, and try to clarify ambitions and aspirations for the future. Typically, shrinks should alleviate pain and suffering and add meaning and richness to life. Shrinks seek to increase peoples' mental well-being, and to act as a confidential and careful listener and speaking partner.

Inspired by the Human Relations tradition, the idea of actively listening in order to reveal problems is usually emphasized as a central element in relationship-oriented leadership behaviour (Yukl 2006), and often made a significant aspect of notions of 'servant leadership' (Greenleaf 1970). The servant leader listens in order to get to know and understand the concerns, requirements and problems of individuals as well as organizations. Writings on the significance of the mood of employees in service industries elaborate quite carefully upon how managers should aim at making people happy in order to maintain customer service (Hochschild 1983). Good mood facilitates the possibility to provide what customers would experience as good service. Managerial listening and sensing the local work place is thus aimed at the possibility to maintain a high level of customer service through the good feelings of the employee (Sturdy and Fleming 2003). But it doesn't necessarily stop with just keeping employees happy and in a good mood. Leaders as pseudo-shrinks aim at managing the emotional inner life of employees and thus part of how people understand themselves, their subjectivity and identity.

THE EQUAL OR 'ONE AMONG THE GUYS'

As suggested in the discussion about the significance of context in leadership, there are expectations on leaders that are contingent upon socio-cultural conditions, sometimes discussed as socio-culturally formed prototypes of what constitutes a (typical) leader and leadership (Lord 1985). Accordingly, everyone has an (culturally informed) idea of what constitutes a leader and good leadership. Who we experience as a leader is thus not only a matter of personal traits, but also how well someone fits in (look and behaviour for example) with our idea of what constitutes a prototypical leader (Hogg 2001). In a Swedish context, we often expect leaders to be informal and relatively open and participatory, not showing off or pulling rank in ways that would potentially hamper relations and subsequently, motivation. Managers are expected to relate to their subordinates in a way resembling how friends informally relate to each other and a sense of egalitarianism is promoted. People are treated as though they are at the same level. Consultation on an equal and open basis rather than confrontation is seen as typical for Swedish management hence the image of the equal that many of the managers above strive for (as opposed to the grandiose leader, elevated above the followers). The ideal of the equal aligns somewhat with exhibiting concern for people and interpersonal relation-ships in Swedish organizations where managers are less expected to express a direct, commanding or bullying style. To some extent the ideal of the equal also exhibits a participative leadership style in terms of managers using group meetings to improve communication, participation and potentially facilitating conflict resolution. There are writings about participative leadership and its poten-tial benefits in terms of decision quality, decision acceptance, high satisfaction and skill development among those involved (Vroom and Yetton 1973).

In our cases we can see how managers try to establish effective leader-ship by levelling with their subordinates and putting themselves on an equal footing. Managers also strive to create belonging, partly as a result of trying to put themselves on an equal footing and facilitating emotional bonding with subordinates. Inclusion is important and the leader's role seems to be, as

Varnsen puts it, to make everyone feel equally valuable. Especially, individuals or sub-groups that can be expected to be (or feel) left out (like Gentle's low-status janitors) are important targets for the leader's buddy-like recognition. Significant in this case is, however, the emphasis on the creation of a sense of meaningful belonging in terms of sharing and being part of a consensus. Managers' exhortations that everyone should feel that they belong indicate efforts to make people share meaning and values to some extent, i.e. organizational culture. Subsequently, this could also relate to the creation of a strong sense of 'we' in terms of in-group and social identity and, as Alvesson and Willmott (2002: 630) point out: 'By engendering feelings of belonging and membership, a sense of community, however contrived this may be, can be developed . . . Being a team member and/or a member of the wider corporate family may become a significant source of one's self-understanding, self-monitoring and presentation to others'. Community-making thus enables organizational control at the same time it ensures that the included people feel good.

Talk of belonging expresses a way of exercising a prototypically equal leadership facilitating sharing ideas, mission and directions set in groups. This amounts to including people and letting them participate in order to create sharing of ideas (not necessarily the same as exercising substantial influence). This is supposed to make followers happy and maintain a friendly organizational atmosphere. This is to some extent supported by qualitative research on participation (e.g. Kanter 1983) but in general it is difficult to unambiguously suggest that participation results in higher levels of satisfaction or performance (Yukl 2006). However, managers here suggest that community-making facilitates self-understanding in terms of the task of the group. They also indicate that community building decreases conflicts (such as less resistance to productivity raising efforts and other managerial change initiatives), based on the assumption that buddies avoid disappointing or backstabbing each other.

THE OMBUDSMAN

It is vital here to also be able to provide some protection in order to not disturb the core work of an organization with unnecessary demands. In many cases this protection concerns subordinates' working conditions. Subordinates in this chapter are often highly skilled and occupied in complex and intellectually demanding tasks that often require a substantial amount of autonomy (Löwendahl 1997). This is often claimed to encourage less formal managerial control and bureaucratization (Mintzberg 1998). Listening to the managers in this chapter, we can also note that leadership in these contexts involves looking after people in terms of safeguarding, that is, voicing concerns that are detrimental to autonomy and protect employees from ideas that somehow undermine creativity and innovation, the latter often regarded as crucial in knowledge intensive firms, even if other types of work organizations certainly also appreciate a reliable 'watchdog' or dedicated protector of their particular interests.

As we have seen earlier, many of our managers suggest that safeguarding subordinates' voice up to senior levels and protecting them from senior managers' control tendencies are central elements in their leadership. Jones says his subordinates feel good because he provides them with a voice at senior managerial levels. Erikson and Ollie say their leadership means protecting subordinates from control efforts and stupid ideas from senior managerial levels. This indicates an ambition to ally in a somewhat patriarchical way with those below, to gain (if only very local) leader status and respect among the group one is set to manage. On the basis of turbulence and a rapidly changing environment that creates worries and stress about work conditions and expectations, a leader can strive to balance this with stabilizing efforts such as voice and protection – an act not so much different from the role of an 'ombudsman'.

As is the case in most writings on managerial leadership, the objective behind acting as the followers' ombudsman, is the possibility to sustain focus on what (the leader thinks) is important (such as, for example, organizational effectiveness in terms of productivity, innovation and development) and at the same time earn the trust, loyalty and gratitude of the people you as a manager (to some extent) rely upon on a daily basis.

SCEPTICAL DISCUSSION

The idea that has come forth so far is that by buddying with people by looking after and befriending them, managers might increase productivity and effectiveness and facilitate organizational change. By facilitating a better atmosphere in for example the service encounter it is not unlikely that this leadership also supports less absence and fewer conflicts, possibly attracting and retaining employees. This is partly because of feelings of loyalty to the organization (i.e. the friendly managers). However, cheering, inclusion, safe-guarding and being there for each other all the time also creates strong social and emotional bonds between leaders and followers on an individual level. These personal bonds can tie people together in ways that sometimes benefit the official organizational objectives but sometimes work against them. We can also note that there are strong elements of mutuality in the leadership practices expressed by our managers, which is why the 'buddy-like' leadership practice also could be seen as a means for creating emotional interdependencies between people – leaders as well as followers.

LEADERS AS BUDDIES – A MEANS FOR GOVERNING SELF-ESTEEM

Throughout this chapter we have seen how managers exhibit strong convictions about showing openness, integrity, and honesty and being genuine when it comes to making people feel good (see also Chapter 4 in this book). Managers emphasize that there is no room for acting or role-playing in this leadership practice, hence no room for empty impression management. There almost seems to be an aura of altruism in some of the managers' characterizations of their leadership practices. Although one can imagine people partly pretending to act as a party host or any other of the metaphors above, the managers in our study suggest that this is a kind of leadership that demands authenticity and genuineness, pretending to befriend is not seen as a long term option (George 2008). Katz and Kahn (1978: 34) suggest that: 'Real skill in working with others must become a natural, continuous activity . . . in the day-to-day behaviour of the individual'. However, managers also emphasize the importance of paying attention to tactics and mundane details as a way of making people regard them as good leaders. In this latter position, managers use their leadership practices as tricks and play in order to primarily construct a favourable image of themselves as good and popular leaders that can be exploited for managerial identity work.

For example, Gentle talks of showing genuine consideration but this is also framed in terms of symbolic tricks in order to make people buy into him, his presumed style, and managerial agenda. To some extent the managers act as accessible, inclusive, trusted equals in order to create favourable images of themselves as leaders. The image of a buddy triggers strong, positive feedback through which the managers can emerge as nice and appreciated, perhaps even admired leaders. Subordinates come to like them and regard them as very significant for their own well-being because they appear to care for them and create such good moods. For example, many of Gentle's subordinates at the bank informed us about how they 'loved him' because of the way he positioned himself towards them in terms of making them feel good and looked after in a caring manner. In general, we like an attentive party-host that takes his/her job seriously and makes sure that we are not excluded, sees that we are always looked after and in a good mood. We also appreciate a present and accessible leader that is observant of our problems and ready to help us with them, and protects us from wickedness from above. And importantly, these leadership acts also make it (potentially) possible for managers to create a favourable image of themselves that can lever their own managerial identity work.

Important for this to work is of course that the positioning to some extent is confirmed by the followers. At least the managers presented in this chapter claim that their positioning is confirmed to a large extent, thus providing them with material for successful identity work and subsequently, a large amount of self-esteem and self-confidence. Gentle once illustrated his buddy-style leadership with a story about how he, at a special occasion (a dinner) actually remembered that one of his subordinates had a birthday:

> To everyone's surprise I raised and celebrated him [the subordinate] and after the speech he said 'how the hell could you remember my birthday at an occasion like this' and I think that's really fun and important. But it has to be done genuinely so that it is not perceived as something that is just needed as such.

Managers are frequently uncertain about the significance of their role as leaders and look for feedback from both superiors and subordinates. Buddyfication of manager–subordinate relations potentially creates positive feedback loops where the managerial identity as a (popular) leader could be maintained and possibly strengthened.

From a sceptical reading, buddy leadership can be seen as a means for governing leaders' as well as followers' self-esteem. It includes recognizing and confirming followers' presumed need for self-esteem and identity confirmation. At the same time it potentially supplies leaders with positive feedback that provides them with identity confirmation and self-esteem. Buddyfication thus facilitates mutual distribution of self-esteem and self-identity and managerial identity in particular. A potential risk with this is of course that managers go for popularity contests rather than make sure that subordinates do their job.

LEADERS AS BUDDIES – A VARIETY OF MANAGERIALISM?

Based on the significance of creating buddy-like relations for the maintenance of managerial identity, it is possible to regard this form of leadership as a compensation for loss of authority that, as discussed earlier, often follows with managerial work in knowledge intensive firms. By exercising leadership as cheering, inclusion, safeguarding and being there (in a broad sense), managers exhibit abilities to care for their people and their needs, and the conditions that generally make subordinates feel good as human beings. This makes it possible for managers to reclaim (or substitute) some of the loss of traditional authority that follows from managing self-sufficient professionals and experts. The loss is compensated by the ability to encourage, make people feel included, check on their mood and protect them and their interests – i.e. acting as their buddy. Besides being a potential source of managerial self-esteem, purpose and meaning, it also represents an increased involvement in and commitment to the broader lives and well-being of subordinates, or as Western (2008: 95) writes: 'A contemporary leadership/management role has shifted from leading an organization to managing the internal life of the employees'. This also relates to current trends that (perhaps over-) emphasize people management, processes, relations and informal networks in a variety of knowledge intensive and professional organizations. In much of the contemporary literature, the effective leader is often characterized as being psychologically and therapeutically skilled. Indeed, a common way to talk about leadership in many contemporary writings on leadership is to regard it as a therapeutic process. It is a matter of focusing on how individuals (leaders) get things done by socially recognizing others and making them feel included, acknowledged, successful and important.

From our cases of leadership we can see how the leader as a buddy comes forth as the key to the employees' well-being. Some would say that the self-governance of experts and professionals marginalizes managers to more administrative routine tasks. However, here we can see how a specific form of leadership, intimately related to writings of the post-heroic field, re-establishes dependency relations in favour of managers as a group of people and management as an organizational function. We can note how managers in this study reclaim authority by targeting people's well-being in general. This is also the case with much post-heroic writings on leadership. Although being seen as progressive and humanistic, much of these writings can also be seen as efforts to reduce the autonomy of professionals by targeting their well-being (emotions and identity). Rather than empowering subordinates, such as professionals and knowledge workers, so they become 'mini-heroes' in their own right (as some versions of post-heroic leadership suggest), the buddyfication of relations we see in this chapter reinstalls and reinforces subordinates' dependence on a few heroes, the big buddies. But even though labelled buddies these are still managers (it is, however, important to recognize that other relationships, such as those between peers, are also significant for a pleasant organizational atmosphere). From a critical perspective this is not unproblematic, since an exaggerated reliance on managers contributes to an overemphasis on and legitimization of managers' presence both in professional life and other contexts. This could produce unhealthy dependencies where employees' self-esteem and well-being are understood as contingent upon managerial symbolic activities and attention. Gemmill and Oakley (1992: 113) portray leadership as an alienating social myth that 'functions as a social defence whose central aim is to repress uncomfortable needs, emotions, and wishes that emerge when people attempt to work together'. Their basic concern was that 'in over-idealizing the leader, members deskill themselves from their own critical thinking, visions, inspirations, and emotions' (ibid. p. 117). In this chapter we suggest that this relationship tends to be *mutual*, i.e. not only do the followers restrict their autonomy in these buddy-like relationships, also the leaders become more fragile and strongly dependent on the followers' constant affirmation and positive, reinforcing feedback.

Another potential drawback or risk with the buddyfication of leader–follower relationships is that it is most likely problematic and stressful to suddenly switch from the big buddy to a role as the leader that has to make unpopular decisions, e.g. job cuts, replacements, etc. As French *et al.* (2009) argue, it takes a 'friend' to commit treason (disappointment or bad news can be expected from enemies). But is it fair to regard the buddy-like leadership ideals displayed in this chapter as mere instrumental managerialism? Is it, as demonstrated in the Hawthorne case, just a matter of increasing productivity by appearing to pay attention to the subordinates? We do not think so. In the case of John Gentle for example, our analysis suggests that his 'tricks' and manipulations are combined with an honest interest in people and wish to be liked, not just as a celebrated manager that gets things done effectively, but as a fellow human being. Being a buddy is therefore not just effective leadership, it is also regarded as 'the right thing to do'.

CONCLUSION

To conclude and summarize, we see four important aspects of leadership as buddying that besides fostering a pleasant organizational environment and amiable working relationships aims to reach managerial goals such as increased loyalty, productivity, effectiveness, support for managerial change initiatives, etc.:

- The *party host* is cheerful, inclusive, informal, considerate, nice and polite towards the targets of his/her efforts. It is important to ensure that everyone is part of a close-knit community. This facilitates a certain intimacy between leaders and followers that assures that people are happy and feel good (about work and their manager). This also creates social and emotional bonds that assure a certain loyalty and motivation among organizational members.
- The *pseudo-shrink* is there to help people, ready to sense any organiza-tional and/or individual problems, and to intervene in order to reduce or

mitigate risk or disharmony (and hence the expected output) in the workplace. This assures that people feel good since they know their leader keeps a caring eye at them, and as a result the organizational output is not jeopardized.

- The *equal/one of the guys* acts as a prototype for what is regarded as proper leadership within his/her specific socio-cultural context and represents/embodies what the organization regards as the right leadership. This enables trust and identification and increases the ability to represent the group as a leader (see 'ombudsman' below). Important here is not to distinguish yourself too much as a leader, but rather as a humble representative for the group (and to come out as the best of friends).

- The *ombudsman* ensures the voice and protects the interests of subordinates up in the higher echelons of the organization and ensures that his/her subordinates are not bothered with bureaucratic requests of doubtful value. By keeping detrimental control and bureaucratization efforts at bay leaders make it possible for their people to concentrate on their respective work (this is assumed to make them happy and feel good), i.e. focus on what is considered important for the organization/leader.

In many cases of so-called post-heroic leadership the managers, somewhat ironically, end up as being the 'heroes' after all, even if they appear in more humble versions as e.g. buddies – or perhaps super-buddies, the subordinates' most significant pal (at work, at least). They might not be as functionally skilled or knowledgeable as the employees they are supposed to lead, but nevertheless they are described as vital for the performance and success of the organization. Statements from subordinates such as 'We like him/her because s/he makes us feel good about ourselves' indicates how the managers still tend to be regarded as 'heroes' because of their presumed attention to the needs of subordinates. Mundane social activities (such as appearing to care for and befriend subordinates) are thus (to some extent) confirmed as being of significant importance for subordinates' well-being, and strong emotional bonds of mutual dependency between managers and subordinates seemingly follow these activities. However, these bonds of mutual dependency also risk undermining the autonomy of managers and employees alike since they become dependent on specific feel-good relations and acts, which are not necessarily connected to more substantial accomplishments. Put a bit ironically, something must be awfully wrong if the boss does not come by with a cup of coffee and an encouraging phrase like 'hello, how are you doing today, nice dress by the way' as he/she used to do every morning, i.e. act as a buddy. The pleasantries can, like the caffeine in the morning coffee, become a (social) drug. Although social affirmation and making people feel good and comfortable might sound progressive and humanistic, there is also a risk that it becomes an obsession and actually generates unhealthy dependencies and more fragile work identities, since we – managers and employees alike – all risk becoming addicted to pleasantries.

One could, of course, further balance the discussion somewhat by also critically discussing the alternatives to this 'new' friendly and jovial leadership ideal with its potential perils. More than 40 years ago, Blake and Mouton (1964) identified an exaggerated focus on productivity and task completion as another common leadership bias. In contrast to the risk of dependency and 'infantilism' of employees discussed above is a position where the manager pays minimal attention to the employees' well-being, social situation and development. That might indeed foster a more autonomous relationship between leaders and followers, but whether this type of 'detached' relationship really is desirable is of course always debatable (especially with the famous words 'no man is an island, entire of itself' in mind). Perhaps the leader's fraternization and involvement in making followers feel good could be viewed as another Scylla and Charybdis, where skilful navigation is needed in order to not end up in the perils of the extremes.

7

LEADERS AS COMMANDERS

Leadership through creating clear direction

André Spicer

INTRODUCTION

WE OFTEN ASSUME THAT in the workplace we can find inspiration, explore our inner self and gain a sense of fulfilment. However, not all organizations celebrate this kind of 'enlightened' leadership. In fact, an altogether harsher tone seems to be present in many workplaces. Direct force and 'micromanagement' continue to be woven into the fabric of the workplace. Aggressive and goal-focused behaviour continues to be rewarded and even expected from good leaders. The way we talk about our workplace is often replete with war metaphors. Given the continuing importance of military language, it should come as no surprise that not all leaders think of themselves in warm and nurturing terms. Some of the most well-worn clichés about leadership express quite a different reality. One example is 'You can't make an omelette without breaking a few eggs.' This phrase is used to indicate that a leader should be willing to undertake violent, messy and sometimes unpopular action. It is no surprise that this cliché has been variously attributed to a range of great figures including the French Revolutionary leader Robespierre, the general Napoleon Bonaparte, and the Bolshevik leader Lenin (who used the Russian variation – when you cut down trees, wood-chips will fly).

This hard-driving desire to achieve no matter what the consequences is also captured in another cliché about leaders frequently found in popular discussions. This is that leaders are alpha males who just cannot help themselves from gaining power and dominating any group they are part of. According to two executive coaches working in the area, 'alpha leaders' tend to have a high drive for success, high levels of stress and very low levels of self-reflexivity (Ludeman and Erlandson 2004; 2006). They claim alphas are oriented to action and love to have responsibility. They tend to be quite intolerant of vacillation and criticism from their subordinates. Indeed the hopes and wishes of others are seen as a barrier to achieving their goals. They are certainly not interested in nurturing the feelings and emotions of others as a 'gardener' or 'buddy' style leader might do. Indeed these macho leaders appear to gleefully reject many of the lessons of leadership research (and popular management platitudes) in favour of a harder or more action-oriented form of leadership. For them, 'winning isn't everything, it's the only thing'. And when anything, including other people, stands in the way of winning, they must be overcome. The emotional fall-out and damaged relationships that might stand in the way are thought to be an inevitable result of the alpha leaders' insatiable desire to achieve. Indeed, they have the quality of 'cyborg' leaders we will meet in the next chapter who perform in a machine-like fashion. There is certainly a danger here that we might think about there being an essential 'type' of leader who cannot help themselves and simply must assert their dominance. This certainly contrasts with most of our existing ideas about leadership that tend to emphasize its slippery, fluid and ambiguous nature. Nonetheless, this alpha image may be an attractive way for many leaders to present themselves. Acting alpha might serve as a way for would-be corporate warriors to convince others that they are made of the right stuff.

The idea that leadership requires difficult and tough action is a popular sentiment among leaders in the business world. In a recent article Jack Welch (the ex-CEO of General Electric) and his wife Suzy (an ex-editor of *Harvard Business Review*) argue that leadership is not about being a buddy:

> The next type of lousy leadership is at the other end of the spectrum: It's too nice. These bosses have no edge, no capacity to make hard decisions. They say yes to the last person in their office, then spend hours trying to clean up the confusion they've created. Such bosses usually defend themselves by saying they're trying to build consensus. What they really are is scared. Their real agenda is self-preservation – good old CYA.
>
> (Welch and Welch 2007: 88)

For the Welches, leaders are certainly not 'wimps'. Rather, they are bold characters who are able to stand up to their followers, even if they have to upset them. The leader needs to take decisions that might be unpopular at the time, but are ultimately good for the organization. In a previous chapter we have noted that Welch is frequently thought to have a saintly or messianic side. However, he also is frequently represented as taking harsh commanding decisions. Part of this involved a significant downsizing programme. He also famously instituted a system whereby he divided the workforce in three groups – 20 per cent of top performers who received generous additional benefits, 70 per cent of middle performers who got to keep their jobs, and 10 per cent of poor performers who were fired.

It might be easy to dismiss Welch's ideas about leadership as macho talk designed to appeal to an audience of lead-hearted management that does not reflect the leadership displayed by most middle managers. We could simply claim that Welch is a bully (an argument which Kärreman makes in a later chapter). Moreover, we could claim that firing people and distributing rewards is a task of management, not the kind of meaning-manipulation associated with leadership. For sure, being a commander today goes against the grain of many contemporary theories of leadership which emphasize humanistic approaches and place an accent on empowerment, involvement and engagement. However, contemporary management writers like Keith Grint (2000) remind us that many aspects of military life still characterize leadership in organizations. Indeed throughout Grint's book on the topic, he frequently draws parallels between military situations and the dilemmas that are faced by middle managers in organizations. The business press and broader discussions about leadership are infused with war metaphors. For instance businesses are locked in 'death-struggles' with competitors, CEOs are 'captains of industry', and mergers and acquisitions are 'assaults'. In our own empirical research, we noticed that military metaphors also appeared to abound. Some leaders claimed that leadership should involve commanding the troops. For instance, Klaus Wolfe, a leader in a large telecommunications equipment company, appeared to share some of Jack Welch's ideas about leadership. For him, leadership involved 'leading from the front'. This required him to make 'brutal' and 'pushy' demands on his followers. According to one of his subordinates, you should 'do what he says, his way, that's it!' Indeed, Wolfe did not advocate the same kind of regime of hire and fire that Welch seemed to favour. However, he did share the same regard for brutal honesty, an action orientation and the penchant for making great demands on their followers. The commander certainly shows a similar interest in using force, being direct and even forceful. These are characteristics also favoured by the bully-like leaders we will encounter in Chapter 9. However, unlike bullies, commanders' use of force is not simply about subordinating other people and ensuring our rule over them. Rather, force simply becomes a way for the commander to get things done in the quickest and most efficient way.

For Welch and Wolfe, leaders must be daring, willing to make harsh decisions, get everyone into line to achieve a common task and ultimately push towards victory. For many leaders this mighty task cannot be achieved through the kind of soft and cosy techniques that are so common among contemporary pop management theorists. Leadership requires steely coldness and hardness. It requires the leader to take the hard decisions and enforce social order. In short, it requires command.

In this chapter, we will explore what it means to look at leaders as commanders. Understanding leadership as command usually involves borrowing from the deep and rich language of leadership associated with military activities. It requires the business leader to see him/herself in military clothing. When a leader becomes a commander

> there is virtually no uncertainty about what needs to be done – at least in the behaviour of the Commander, whose role is to take the required decisive action – that is to provide the *answer* to the problem, not to engage processes (management) or ask questions (leadership).
>
> (Grint 2005: 1473–1474)

The commander's task is to define what needs to done, and get on and do it. In order to achieve this, a commander will typically rely upon 'coercive' or 'hard' power that involves use of physical force and imbalances of resources to induce someone to do something. To be sure, Grint contrasts commanders with leaders and managers. Furthermore, commandership seems to involve many of the ingredients usually associated with management such as hiring and firing. However, we noticed that some of the leaders we studied would often clearly relate commandership with leadership. Those who used this metaphor, saw leaders as engaging in warfare with competitors, seeking to win at any cost, undertaking strategic manoeuvres, defending the corporation from attack and enforcing discipline on the troops (see Amernic *et al.* 2007: 1853). Underlying this rich military language is the assumption that the leader is one who takes responsibility during times of violent threat and confrontation. Indeed much research suggests that organizations which must be highly reliable (such as the emergency services) often rely on command during periods of crisis (Weick and Sutcliffe 2001). This is because during periods of crisis they often do not have the time for excessive self-reflection or democratic deliberation. Rather, they need experienced and respected commanders to set the direction. Typically these commanders are characters who unilaterally enforce a direction and drive everyone to do it. They are often thought to be 'alpha male' (Ludeman and Erlandson 2006) characters who are willing to lead from the front and engage in battles with those who are not willing to fall into line.

In order to explore the metaphor of commander, I begin by looking in some depth at one leader – Klaus Wolfe. I then unpack the metaphor and consider some different variants of the commander. After doing this, I consider some of the reasons that leadership as command actually works. I then consider the wider applicability of this metaphor and outline some possible criticisms of it. The chapter is tied together with a conclusion that recounts the core argument.

ILLUSTRATION: KLAUS WOLFE

A striking example of a leader who saw himself as a commander is Klaus Wolfe.[1] Wolfe worked for a large multinational called Technocom. It provides high-technology software and applications for the telecommunications industry. Technocom is dominated by an engineering mentality. But recently it has had to develop competencies in other areas such as marketing and finance. As his Teutonic name suggests, Wolfe was originally from Germany. Just before we met Wolfe, Technocom had begun a substantial organizational change programme. Part of this involved the organization seeking to foster five core values: 'Our way of working – commitment', 'Leadership – trust and inspiration', 'Communications – openness', 'Decision making and rewards – empowerment', 'Organization structure and teamwork – clarity'. We were not surprised. These phrases sounded like the typical values which most contemporary companies try to nurture to make themselves more innovative and attractive places to work.

But Wolfe looked beyond the veneer of the mission statements and official values. For him, Technocom was a disorderedly and chaotic place. People did not do what they said they would do. They did not deliver programmes and they often would get bogged down in everyday detail. For instance, people at more junior levels of the organization did not seem to be particularly interested in the change programme. Instead, they were more consumed with day-to-day activities. The inaction of junior engineers upset Wolfe greatly. He told us that:

> I don't believe for a second that you are introducing a programme and that you're only talking about things; you must live it. If you don't live it as a manager you can do whatever programme you want, you will maybe also get some progress on the surface but in the end you will not move anything, not for a second.

For Wolfe, the culture change programme was simply empty talk – what he called 'the cultural tralala'. He believed that the only way you can get things done is to lead from the front. He had enough of talking about change. Instead he preferred to push for an action orientation. For Wolfe, you needed to 'do it' and 'live it' in order to lead your subordinates. This means that Wolfe placed great significance on leading through being a role model. This is his vision of leadership:

> I mean one thing that is leadership for me is you must be a role model and you must show, hey with every problem you can come across and I

think when I give that to the guys they will also give that to their people. It is a positive example that goes through the whole organization and negative examples in the same way

Like many other alpha male leaders, Wolfe thinks that it is his actions that count. He leads through simply doing. He illustrated this philosophy through a heroic story about how he personally delivered the development of a new product, and then with a team of trusted associates addressed issues ranging from logistical problems to a market downturn. In order to achieve this success, Wolfe acknowledges that he had to often act in a 'brutal' manner through 'reality checking' everything involved in his project and constantly 'pushing' the project. More concretely this is reflected in his day-to-day practices of leading. Instead of engaging in conjuring up broad strategic visions or devising complicated frameworks, Wolfe spends much of his time either in large all-employee meetings or working alongside software engineers to solve particular problems.

When we interviewed some of the engineers working under Wolfe, we were told quite a different story about 'leading from the front'. One subordinate described him as 'dictatorial' and 'authoritarian'. But instead of seeing these characteristics as a bad thing (as current pop management might lead us to expect), most of Wolfe's subordinates seemed to celebrate his commanding style. One praised Wolfe for the fact that he 'takes decisions'. This subordinate also seemed to admire how Wolfe is 'very energetic' and how he 'will jump around and shout' during meetings:

> He says what he thinks, he sticks with his decisions and, yes, things go wrong sometimes but he sticks with it. . . . He was here a couple of days ago, . . . he said 'Basingstoke you're doing this wrong, you have to sort this out, I'm not saying it because I want to put any blame on Basingstoke but because this particular part is going wrong and I expect you to shape up on this part'.

Despite the respect that some had for Wolfe's commanding approach, others felt far more uncomfortable. One follower described Wolfe's leadership style as 'Do what he says, his way, that's it! And the company changes to suit his way, whatever way he's at the time'. This employee has a kind of grudging respect for Wolfe's forcefulness, but he also recognizes that this insistence could be quite arbitrary at times. He was worried that Wolfe's demands would not be driven by a broad corporate oversight, but would actually change in order to fit in with his current whims. The other major concern that many of Wolfe's subordinates expressed was that his 'megalomaniac' approach stood in stark contrast to the sense of empowerment that Technocom was officially trying to nurture. Some felt this resulted in employees receiving mixed messages about how they should follow (should they just obey or should they try to be empowered employees who articulate new ideas?). Others thought that such an authoritarian style was dangerous because it concentrated too much power into the hands of one individual and removed the power of local sites.

In summary, Wolfe assumed that leadership involves imposing order on disorderly conditions. This can only be achieved through 'leading from the front'. Doing this sometimes required him to do fairly unpleasant things such as creating a sense of anxiety among his employees, demanding a lot from them, undertaking a punishing work schedule himself, as well as getting highly involved in the technical minutiae of people's work. Despite the fact these activities were often thought to be 'brutal' by others, they often felt they paid off in terms of quick delivery times and problems being surmounted. While this authoritarian approach seemed to inspire respect among some subordinates, it also engendered criticism – particularly because of the contrast with today's dominant assumptions that leaders should nurture and empower people.

UNPACKING THE COMMANDER

Wolfe's action-oriented approach, his attempt to create fear in his followers and his willingness to undertake 'brutal action' show some important aspects of a leader as a commander. However, there are a number of aspects of this metaphor that deserve further exploration. This is largely because there are different modes of command, and different ways people can engage in leadership by command. We would like to suggest that there is a range of different kinds of commanders: the one who leads from the front, the ass-kicker, the antagonizer, and the rule-maker. In what follows, we will look into each of these characters in some more depth.

THE LEADER OF THE CHARGE

One of the most frequent kinds of commanders we encounter in the field is the character who seeks to inspire the troops by leading the action from the front. They see themselves as gallant officers who instead of trying to cajole their troops from behind the lines are willing to charge head-on into the thick of action. They see themselves very much as people who lead through action. This was one of the central themes that ran through Wolfe's own story of himself as a leader. For him, leading involved difficult and daring action. We have already seen how he emphasizes that as a leader 'you must be a role model'. For Wolfe this involves actually acting out the behaviour that he hopes to see in his own followers. In a similar way to the cyborg leaders we'll meet in the next chapter, a commander like Wolfe sees himself as someone who is able to achieve very difficult tasks against adversity. We have already mentioned that he spent a significant amount of time telling us about his victory against the odds in getting a project up and running. He also tells us about his heroic willingness to take on difficult and daring assignments, often despite the best advice from his friends. Here is how he describes one situation:

> I was recruited by the CEO and what I found was a disaster . . . when we took over at that time, [Technocom was] a company without a strategy, without any planning, without any clear direction, some loose wishes . . . absolutely internal chaos in the test programme, doing badly in supplying Global Tech with platforms and having no discipline and no spirit, that is what I thought.

This steely attitude was also reflected in how Wolfe's subordinates spoke about him. They frequently talked about his punishing travelling schedule, his almost inhuman appetite for work, and 'serious drive'. These are themes that are also found in the cyborg metaphor. However, unlike the cyborg, their efforts are not largely inwardly focused on nurturing themselves as superhuman beings who are able to accomplish even the most awe-inspiring tasks. Rather, commanders like Wolfe focused on being very hands-on and engaged with others' work. For Wolfe, this involves rejecting what he saw as an abstract discussion of culture and personal development. Instead he devoted a significant proportion of his time to actually sitting down with engineers and working alongside them to solve practical problems. When he works with his subordinates, he claims he is able to lead by actually doing. Wolfe thinks that his own actions can easily be mirrored in the perceptions and behaviours of his subordinates:

> When I'm hyper nervous I see others getting nervous, if I'm cool even in the biggest trouble and I am silent and go and decide in a cool manner, it also radiates through the organization. So every panic in our organization is emphasized, every coolness, clearness is emphasized, every clear communication is transported to the people you are talking with and then the next level reaches it.

For Wolfe, acting in a certain way allows one to elicit the same behaviour in other people. Generally, this is not uncommon among managers. Similarly, a building site foreman in a UK firm claimed that:

You can only lead by example. In other words, besides working from 8 until 6, you don't turn up on site at 9 o'clock expecting the whole thing to [have been] churning away [since] dead on 8 o'clock, because we are all human. So you have got to lead from the front. Generally, I think, briefly that's leadership: to lead them from the front, to show by example and to motivate the guys into producing what you want, when you want it.

(Bresnen 1995: 504)

The assumption here is that the leader is someone who everyone looks up to, and their actions create a sense of social reality for the those whom they lead. Indeed, one well-known executive trainer called John Adair reflects these attitudes to leadership by claiming that 'the primal act of leadership is leading from the front in action' (Jones and Gosling 2005: 18).

THE ASS-KICKER

Sometimes commanders portrayed themselves as using more stringent means to motivate their troops. This often involved the leader talking about themselves as an ass-kicker who engenders a sense of fear in those who follow. One of the ways that Wolfe led was through building a sense that he always had a keen oversight of the projects his engineers were working on. To remind subordinates of this, he would often work directly with engineers on addressing projects and issues. As we have already mentioned, this reminded his subordinates he could lead from the front. It was also a physical manifestation that he was there, watching them, and willing to kick some ass if necessary. Recall how many of Wolfe's subordinates talked about his 'authoritarian' or 'megalomaniac' attitude and hinted at the concern and worry it created in a group. When Wolfe's principles were not followed, he was willing to show his wrath through what would often be considered highly unusual activities in the work place such as shouting and screaming.

Wolfe is by no means alone in creating a sense of fear in order to lead people. In a study of leadership on building sites, Bresnen (1995: 507) found one manager claiming that the 'men' should also be 'able to walk onto a site and say, "He's a fair man, but he's a hard man"'. This idea that leaders need to punish seems to be central to a lot of contemporary ideology about 'tough guy' or 'alpha male' management. Recall how Jack Welch would single out 10 per cent of middle managers who he deemed to be losers and they would subsequently be fired. For Welch the central benefit was the ability to create a sense of fear and anxiety amongst managers. Another top General Electric manager, Bill Conaty, reinforces the importance of creating fear amongst the workforce. During an interview, he told the journalist:

> There's nothing like a bit of anxiety and the knowledge that you're being measured against peers to boost performance. 'We want to create angst in the system,' he says. 'We have evolved from being anal about what percent have to fall into each category. But you have to know who are the least effective people on your team and then you have to do something about that.'
>
> (Conaty 2007: 66)

So it seems that creating fear through harsh punishment or threatening to fire people is thought to be a useful tool that can motivate people, create anxiety, and ultimately get things done. However, we should note that it is an approach to leadership which is rarely used in isolation. If a commander simply threatens their troops, then it is likely they would revert to a kind of learned helplessness whereby they cower and only comply with the letter of the law. The result is that real power will flow away, and the commander will only be able to lead their troops through direct force (Arendt 1958).

THE ANTAGONIZER

As well as leading the charge, creating fear and providing rewards, commanders also become antagonizers. They do so by directing the attention and vitriol of their followers towards an enemy. The commander leads by being clear who or what they are against. Think of when business leaders identify their core competitors in a particular market as needing to be weeded out and destroyed. For instance, in his attempts to reform an Australian maritime services company, the new CEO consistently referred to the threat of competition from ports in other countries that were more efficient (Selsky et al. 2003). Similarly, in his (ultimately failed) attempts to reform a public service broadcaster, its CEO consistently referred to the threats associated with globalization and increased international competition (Spicer 2004). If we look at some of the pronouncements of business gurus, we notice that they bear some striking resemblances. For instance, in their book promoting the virtues of business process engineering, Hammer and Stanton argue that leading the introduction of BPR programmes needs to be ruthless. They point out that in order to effectively implement BPR systems, those who oppose the system need to be rooted out and punished:

Nothing, however, speaks louder than dealing sternly with those who impede a reengineering effort. Leniency toward those who refuse to cooperate with the reengineering effort gives the lie to the leader's pronouncement about reengineering's critical importance. One reengineering leader we know was faced with a terrible dilemma. His oldest colleague in the company, a close personal friend, was not supporting the reengineering effort [. . .] At last, the leader had to take an extremely difficult step: He dismisses his friend. Personally wrenching though it was, this act had profound repercussions throughout the company; the universal conclusion was: this guy is serious. [. . .] If there is a single word that captures an effective leader's style, it is relentlessness.

(Hammer and Stanton, 1995: 41)

For sure, Hammer and Stanton are certainly not talking about the elimination of whole groups of people. But what they are doing involves antagonistically identifying a clear enemy – those who did not support re-engineering efforts. These enemies should be dealt with in harsh and uncompromising ways. For instance, if someone does not go along with the introduction of a BPR system, they should be fired – even if they are your best friend. Here the leader of the BPR change process is absolutely clear who he is against (those who resist BPR), and is also willing to take radical and unflinching action against these enemies. While it may sound disturbing, such approaches to leadership are actually fairly common throughout the business world.

THE RULE-BREAKER

The final type of commander breaks the official rules, and often seeks to establish their own rules instead. It involves leaders rejecting common assumptions about the rules and attempting to establish their own version of what is right and wrong, what is acceptable and unacceptable. If we return to Wolfe for one last time, we note that he prided himself on telling his subordinates what needed to be done – even if it was politically unpopular. Also recall that a number of his followers actually praised his courage for being able to say what was appropriate and what was unacceptable. We also found that making the rules was an important part of the leadership tactics of Paul, a senior executive in a large management consultancy firm. (We will come back to Paul in more depth in the next chapter – addressing the leader as cyborg.) In an interview, he claimed that he does not tend to go through the normal route of discussion before doing something. According to him 'sometimes . . . we don't want to wait. I don't want to just sit and wait until something has been coordinated with everyone. Because when it is so right to do, I can obviously not just sit and wait – let's do it!' He recognizes that it has become increasingly difficult to unilaterally set the rules (particularly after the firm was listed on the stock exchange). However, for him it continues to depend 'on how much power you actively take. I mean, you can do a whole lot yourself. Someone has to come to you and say "hey that's wrong", and that happens very rarely'. He realizes that attempts to actively grasp power and establish the rules often upset his colleagues. However, he claims it is a necessary part of running a high performing team:

> One of the other partners for example could come over and say 'hey I hear you do so and so. We hear that you are inviting your people to castles, and almost walk in the foot-steps of the royal family. What is that all about'. But I just say, 'well it is actually something we do on a Saturday and no one charges their time, so I don't see a problem'. So then I tell them that there is no longer a problem.

By ignoring the official procedures and setting his own rules, Paul claims he can support superior performance amongst his team. But he also argues that it is possible because they are so exceptional in their performance. He tells us of a visit to the champion cyclist Lance Armstrong he has planned for his team. He recognizes that this clearly breaks many of the official rules, and that it will be frowned upon by others in the group. However, he points out that it will be difficult to oppose because of the brilliant results which his team produced during the year. Like Wolfe, Paul prided himself on the fact that he avoided the official rule-book and constructed the rules himself. Both of these leaders did so even though they knew it would bring them into conflict with others. And both leaders did so because they thought that they were in some way exceptional.

MECHANISMS OF COMMAND

Leading from the front, ass-kicking, antagonizing and breaking rules are all different faces of the commander. But how do these approaches to leadership work, if at all? Are they simply the fantasy of corporate tough-guys who have received a disciplinarian up-bringing and watched too many Hollywood action films? Are they simply forms of management that rely on well established techniques such as manipulation of rewards? Or do these approaches to command work in some settings? In what follows, I will argue that although metaphors associated with command clash with some of our enlightened and humanistic ideas about the workplace, it can certainly work for a number of reasons.

Command proves that the would-be leader is willing and able to put themself on the line. This means they are willing to risk their reputation and their livelihood. This acts as probably the most obvious and cogent illustration that leaders believe in and are committed to the action that they undertake. They do not just strategize and plan. They actually want to engage in the task at hand and address the concrete problems that are faced by those they are leading. By doing this, commanders are able to send a very cogent and compelling message to would-be followers that they can actually do the job, and often do it very well. This means that they garner respect in the eyes of followers who recognize that they take a concrete and direct interest in the day-to-day tasks they are involved in. They do not just engage in empty talk and seek to create friendly environments as the gardener or buddy might do, but have a strict focus on the actual activities at hand. Recall the comments of Wolfe's followers. They are impressed with the man because he is willing to 'roll up his sleeves' and work with concrete projects with engineers. When Wolfe explains himself as a leader, he tends to foreground his own achievements by telling 'war stories' – a series of challenges met and overcome, objectives met. The focus of these stories is on tasks that were actually done, not relationships that were nurtured or similar issues. By engaging in the day-to-day tasks of the organizations, commanders can often garner a sense of respect. However, they can also create a significant sense of fear in their subordinates. This partially comes from a keen focus on the details of organizational life. But it also comes from a sense that if something goes wrong in these detailed arrangements, then the commander is not going to react with care and sympathy, but with a quick temper. Recall how Wolfe's subordinates spoke of how he would 'shout' during meetings when problems arose. This engendered a palpable sense of fear in his subordinates. When this was mixed with the respect he engendered from a close focus on the daily activities of the workplace, it often instilled a strong pressure on his subordinates – even when he was not around. They recognized that he 'knew his stuff', and that any mistakes or slip ups (no matter how detailed) would be punished.

In addition to instilling a mixture of fear and respect, commanders became seen as enforcers of collective standards. This often worked through leaders displaying they had skills and abilities that were actually respected by the people who are involved in undertaking a task. Richard Sennett (2008) points out that one of the central ways which craftsmen are able to lead their apprentices is through simply doing their task and acting as a kind of role model. The point is not to teach someone to be a craftsman; it is simply to be a craftsman. In this way, they become a kind of embodiment of collective standards of work. Leading through simply doing the tasks that are expected of one seems to work for a number of reasons. First, it provides a way of enrolling neophytes into a community of practice (Lave and Wegner 1991). In many ways the leader models what is valued practice. By doing so they act as a gate-keeper who introduces the led into a new world – whether it be the world of engineering, teaching or cooking. Leading through practice is vital because it is only through acting and participating in a particular practice that someone learns how to become a member of that community. This is where the second aspect of leading from the front comes in. By leading through doing, the leader is able to build up respect in the eyes of their followers. This is largely because one of the central things which is respected in any community of practice is the ability to not just to do the task, but do it well. Therefore leading from the front involves a perfect opportunity to show that someone can actually do the task, thereby garnering respect and recognition from the professional community in which they operate. The tragic results of when this is not in place can be seen when a leader washes their hands of the day-to-day practice and loses the respect of the people who are actually involved in the practices which sustain their organization.

As well as upholding common standards through action, commanding leaders are able to draw on the power that continues to be associated with images of harsh masculinity. This is despite the increasing feminization of many work environments with increasing importance being placed on facilitation, engagement and building relationships. Masculine management typically comes in the form of so-called alpha-male behaviour. This involves acting out a highly competitive and aggressive style of leadership. It may involve an attempt to stage highly public displays of punishment, rage and competition. For instance this might involve attempts to put on highly stage-managed instances of physical threat. While it is uncommon in the workplaces we studied, violence and fear continue to be a central aspect of many highly masculine workplaces that emphasize high stress and physical activity such as the armed forces, the police force, factory floors and restaurant kitchens. If we look at more familiar settings, we notice that modern leaders have found more subtle ways to create fear. One way some might seek to stage this masculine strength is through displays of bodily strength such as a gym-toned body, a vice-like handshake, or sheer stamina in undertaking work (Sinclair 2007). Other business leaders use more showy displays of physical strength such as competing in aggressive sports or engaging in high-risk physical pursuits. Such shows of simulated strength are frequently ineffective or perhaps seen as increasingly unimportant. However, it subtly endures in a whole series of substitutes for physical strength, including business suits which emphasize the strength of the body by widening the shoulders and giving pudgy figures a stronger more steely appearance. Another way commanding leaders try to emphasize their strength is by building a whole 'set' that aggrandizes themselves. Simple examples include middle managers who covet plush private offices with a large desk and sizable leather chairs. Senior executives typically seek to elevate their status by taking the top floors of office buildings, emphasizing their symbolic height, closeness to the gods and 'helicopter view' over the mere mortals below. Perhaps the most extreme example of such attempts to display force and strength in one's workplace is the 'sculpture' of two sharks eating each other which the infamous corporate downsizer 'chainsaw' Al Dunlap had on his desk for decoration. The message of this statue was clear to any visitor – the occupier of this desk is a vicious shark who can devour you.

Commanders also lead through the identification of enemies. This involves the leader making a clear demarcation between who is part of the group to be led ('the in group') and who is not part of the group ('the out group'). For instance, a leader trying to implement an organizational change programme might identify external enemies including other competing companies or other departments within their own firm. They may also point towards 'internal' enemies as we saw in the case of the leader's best friend who was fired because they opposed the BPR plan. Doing this has a number of distinct advantages for leaders. First, it can shore up the identity of a social group. We know that during times of war when there is a clear threat, a nation will often 'pull together' and become increasingly conformist and develop a sense of solidarity. This is because creating a sense of a group proves to be a powerful way of reinforcing the identity of those within a group. Existing work in social identity theory highlights how group identities are typically strengthened through the presence of strong 'out-groups' that a group develops its identity in opposition to (e.g. Tajfel and Turner 1986). Doing this can also make members of an in-group feel better about themselves (Oakes and Turner 1980). For instance external enemies are often represented as being morally questionable, evil or below one's own group in status. By making this separation, a leader is able to foster a sense that those within their group are good, morally superior and have a high moral status. As well as generally increasing the strength of group bonds and esteem, identifying a clear enemy helps a leader to reinforce a 'prototypical' image of the ideal group member. This can have definite advantages for the leader, particularly if they actually embody what is seen as the characteristics of the typical or even ideal group member. By being seen as this typical group member who is so different from external group members, the leader is able to shore up their position (Hogg 2001). This is because according to social identity theory, leaders of groups tend to be those who are the most 'prototypical' group member' (Van Kippenberg and Hogg 2003). As well as reinforcing their position as prototypical group members, identifying enemies allows leaders to point to external motivating aspects to justify their own actions. To encourage members of a group to do something, they can argue that if the group or organization does not do it, they will be defeated by an external enemy. This allows leaders to 'reify' the reasons for a certain action. This involves turning what might be a mixture of opinion, cliché and analysis into something that appears to be a thing-like threat with a very concrete form. This makes it very difficult for opponents to argue against.

DISCUSSION

Many leaders think of themselves as corporate commanders. This certainly grates against much of our contemporary ideas that leadership should be supportive, facilitative and inspiring. However, in this chapter we have argued that ideas about commandership still continue to characterize leadership discourse. Commandership is not just present in organizations; it is a distinct way of creating meaning, identities and expectations at work. It frames the workplace as a kind of battle group occupied by various troops.

The image of the leader as a commander may appear to be deeply unfashionable in today's corporate environment which emphasizes participation, care and engagement. It seems to ride rough-shod over the respect for the individual and therapeutic orientation that many leaders we have met so far in this book champion. However, being in command also appears to continue to be appealing to many managers. After-all, Ludeman and Erlandson (2004) claim that over 70 per cent of CEOs in corporate America fit their description of the alpha male. This more direct understanding of leadership may be particularly popular for a number of reasons. First, it allows the leader to put themselves in a heroic position. They can feel like a super-hero who is taking direct and bold action that is necessary. This means it helps the leader themselves to feel an intense sense of agency. They come to experience themselves as someone who can directly make a difference. Second, commanding leadership might also prove to be particularly appropriate in some situations. For instance, in situations of crisis or when there is a breakdown in order, people often feel desperate to take action and have a clear meaning given to an apparently disorderly context (Weick and Sutcliffe 2001). This often leads them to desire any kind of action that will give a profoundly complex situation some degree of meaning. By being clear and even harsh in their direction, the leader is able to attribute the kind of 'profound simplicity' that according to Weick and Sutcliffe, people seek at moments of crisis. But the intuition that commandership is appropriate during crisis situations is complicated by the fact that many organizations suggest that they are in a consistent state of crisis.

While leadership as a process of command has obvious and ongoing appeal for many, it also has some significant problems. The first, and perhaps most recognized of these problems is that it is, in most cases, highly unrealistic. This is because leadership is thought to be something that flows from a strong figure who is able to lead a group through social conflict. While this might be an appealing fantasy for would-be leaders, such a situation is fairly rare. There are some tasks such as fighting a fire, being in combat with the enemy or responding to an impending technical failure that involve urgent outcomes and dangerous situations which demand a strong figure and an absence of group conflict (Grint 2005). However, much organizational activity is far more humble and less exciting than this. Our own close studies show that leadership is rarely a heroic act of campaign and conquest. Rather, it involves a far slower and more everyday practice of negotiation, nurturing and agreement. This suggests that the main reality that the metaphor of leadership as commander takes on is either in the fantasies and espousals of leaders themselves (and sometimes their followers) or in fairly rare high-risk events such as crises when individual and collective routines break down. When such commanding leaders do appear on the scene, they may be tolerated or even lionized during times of crisis. However, due to their high pressure approach, many of their followers may wish for a return to 'normal business' and a more placid state of affairs. The result is that commanders may only be tolerated during a state of emergency and pushed to the side in more settled times. Perhaps nowhere can this be better seen than in the case of Al Dunlap. He operated as a well-known downsizer of a number of medium-sized US companies. In order to deliver significant increases in share prices, he engaged in savage downsizing exercises which radically reduced each organization's workforce. After using this formula in two companies, he moved to an electrical appliance manu-facturer. This high-pressure commander style began to show some cracks and eventually led to a stupendous downfall. But other commanders have realized that the best way to stay in control is to create a permanent state of emergency. For instance, Grint (2005) points out the Iraq war may have been partially used as a strategy to create a state of emergency that was used to justify the Republican administration's commanding leadership style. In the corporate world, some CEOs claim that their company is almost permanently buffeted by crises and therefore needs to be steered by their own firm hand.

The second major problem with understanding leadership as an act of command is that it is usually highly authoritarian. That is, it assumes there is a single individual who is empowered and knows best what to do. It also assumes that the forceful intervention of this individual is necessary in order to lead. This largely discounts any of the insights and value that might be created by followers. It also discounts the more everyday and participative methods of co-operation and coaching that we found espoused by many of the leaders that we studied. Indeed this authoritarian approach to leadership can often clash with the dominant ideas in firms and society at large that leadership should be participative, empowering and engaging. At best, this can create a situation within firms where employees received 'mixed messages'. For instance, one of Wolfe's subordinates pointed out that Wolfe's authoritarian style was in clear conflict with the more humanistic management approach which was the official line within Technocom. At worst, an authoritarian style can create alienation, disillusionment and even rebellion when followers compare it with dominant ideas they hold about how they 'ought' to be treated. For instance, when Australia's largest public broadcaster was taken over by an authoritarian leader called Jonathan Sheir it provoked widespread consternation, alienation and protest (Spicer 2004). At the height of these protests, a well-known broadcaster claimed that Sheir ran the organization like an army, and that the best organizations today were run like orchestras. In saying this, the broadcaster was pointing out the clear conflict between the ideas many of the staff had about how they felt they should be managed and the authoritarian ideas of their new director general. Needless to say, this conflict eventually became so great that Sheir was forced to resign and was replaced by a new director general with a less commander-like style. This kind of authoritarian approach can be highly masculine in tone and may frequently alienate women (and indeed many men) working in an organization (Fairhurst *et al.* forthcoming). For instance, the often violent and harsh approaches of many industries such as the military, policing, elite restaurants, the financial markets, engineering and law make them very unappealing for women. Indeed most of these sectors have recognized that they have a serious issue with attracting and retaining talented women. They also recognize that part of this is due to the masculine assumptions about leadership that dominate these sectors (Sinclair 2005). Indeed even within some of the most authoritarian organizations like the police force and the armed services, there have been purposeful and ongoing attempts to root out the kind of authoritarian assumptions about leadership that have dominated these organizations for years.

A third problem with understanding the leader as a commander is that it significantly blurs the lines between management and leadership. If we return to classic discussions about leadership, a lot of effort went into defining what exactly was unique about leadership vis-à-vis management. Classic responses typically point out that management often involves ensuring that an already established goal is efficiently carried out through the use of rewards and sanctions. Leadership involves the attempt to create these goals and motivate followers towards this goal through the use of inspiration, coaching, and transformational experiences (e.g. Kotter 1988). If we look back at what the commander does, we notice that there appears to be heavy use of what Kotter and others would consider to be 'managerial' techniques (such as the manipulation of punishments). By doing this, it means that the commander might give up some of the very tools and techniques that are essential to being a leader such as managing emotions and meaning.

The final, and perhaps most disturbing aspect of commander-based approaches is that they promote a masculine image of leadership. It assumes that leadership springs from the will and desire to dominate other people, and that this is achieved through a range of means that harks back to brute power and even violence.

CONCLUSION

Today leaders aspire to be buddies who create a cosy and friendly environment among followers, gardeners who seek to grow their employees, or saints who try to inspire their followers through their moral superiority. With the dominance of post-heroic theories of leadership, we expect to find workplaces teeming with enlightened leaders. In this chapter we have argued that some leaders do not take their job so lightly. Instead of seeking to inspire, nurture or counsel their co-workers some leaders use harsher techniques. They are willing to engage in sometimes harsh forms of command. The outlook of these leaders is best captured in the figure of Klaus Wolfe. At the beginning of this chapter, we argued he had very little tolerance for talk of cultural change. Instead, he was most concerned with action – that is, making sure that projects were often delivered against the odds. Far from being an unusual character, we have argued that Wolfe holds a set of assumptions about leadership that are actually quite widespread – that leadership involves command.

In this chapter, we have explored what it means to lead through command. We have argued that leadership by command involves seeking to lead from the front by getting involved in the action alongside their 'troops'. They often make hefty and direct demands of their followers and they are more than prepared to make direct use of punishments. In addition, they point out clear enemies at the same time as offering protection from them. Finally, they are willing to break established laws. Through engaging in these processes, the commander aims to establish a sense of social order – that is orderliness, which can then be used to drive towards victory over a well-defined enemy. Research suggests this kind of leadership can be quite effective during times of crisis or stress. However, it does come at a cost. This is because seeking to lead through command often can be unrealistic, clash with the humanistic values which dominate many organizations today, and alienate many women (as well as men).

Leadership by command may seem to be utterly at odds with the times. Some might claim that it is an unfortunate legacy of old male-dominated organizations that have a strong masculine bias. They might say these commanders are on the edge of extinction within the corporate jungle. While this may be an appealing thought, commanding leadership appears to be alive and well in contemporary organizations. Some would point out that while commanders are not always called for, they are absolutely vital during times of crisis when problems become critical and too much questioning and analysis would only exacerbate the situation (Grint 2005). Some would go as far as suggesting that authoritarian management styles are actually becoming more widespread (Ten Bos 2008). This can be seen in the immense popularity of a new wave of 'tough love' style management such as Judith Mair's (2002) call to 'stop the fun!' and embrace the rules and strong leaders who can enforce them. Perhaps leadership by command is not the past of organizational life. But rather it is part of its new, authoritarian future.

NOTE

1 I would like to thank Stefan Sveningsson who conducted the fieldwork this case is based on.

8

LEADERS AS CYBORGS

Leadership through mechanistic superiority

Sara Louise Muhr

INTRODUCTION

THIS CHAPTER IS ABOUT THE LEADER AS CYBORG. As an ideal this means that the leader appears as a supernatural creature transcending the border between what is human and non-human. Business leaders today are often said to operate in a fragmented and volatile environment, which demands a wide variety of skills and flexibility. These tough demands often tend to create the image of the strong and perfect leader, who can lead the company through the maze of opportunities and challenges. Leaders are supposed to lead the employees to maximize their potential and in this way be means to organizational profitability and success. Leaders carry a great deal of the responsibility for both success and failure and are often single-handedly credited (or blamed) for organizational results. The leader is therefore often constructed as a symbol of the organization, and the greater or more powerful he or she is, the better the organization looks. This emphasis on superiority and rationality makes them almost supernatural and superhuman. After all, we expect them to be rational, intelligent and always capable of producing a solution to get us out of trouble. The superior leader is thus expected not to fail; he or she must act with perfection. In other words the perfect leader appears as something, which transcends the border between human and not human – a cyborg.

The cyborg is then seen as a metaphor for the 'inhuman' aspects of leadership, and a cyborg leader is thus a metaphor for a leader who appears to be part man and part machine. He or she is inspiring and successful but also a mechanistic and sometimes self-centred and non-emotional rational being. A cyborg leader appears rational, calculative, competitive, and focused to a degree that makes them appear almost mechanistic and robot-like.

This type of leader might seem similar to the commander, which was discussed in the preceding chapter. However, where the commander is being direct and forceful in order to give precise directions, the cyborg sets new standards and expects his or her employees to follow suit. Where the commander is someone who wants to impose order, the cyborg breaks rules and sets new standards. The cyborg leader might appear strong and perhaps cruel like the commander. However, cyborg leadership is not performed in the military way of obeying orders, but in result-oriented, hard-working and independent ways that reflect the uniqueness and superiority of the leader. In this way, a cyborg leader is not just a strong character, but also someone who dares to set new standards. The cyborg leader simply believes so much in his or her abilities that they don't stop aiming higher. The chapter will in this way take a novel view on the strong and flawless leader and discuss those variations of superior leadership which turn mechanistic and perfect to an almost uncanny degree.

The cyborg as a metaphor for superiority is not new in organization studies (for some of the early contributions, see Wood 1998, Parker 1998, Parker 1999, Parker and Cooper 1998). In fact, science fiction and popular culture are seen by many to be both representing as well as affecting the way we perceive and conduct work and leadership (see for example Rehn and Lindahl 2008, Czarniawska and Rhodes 2006). The cyborg metaphor has, however, to my knowledge not been used to describe a particular form of leadership, and the use of the metaphor in this chapter therefore represents the acts of leadership we have observed in our empirical studies. Elements of cyborg leadership can be seen in many cases, but in this chapter, the characteristics of cyborg leadership will be shown in depth through mainly two cases, Paul and Lisa, who both, in different ways, conduct what I call cyborg leadership. In this chapter the metaphor of the cyborg therefore describes the action of managers in their endeavour to gain success for themselves and their organizational units. Cyborg leaders are therefore characterized as people, who sacrifice a lot in order to become perfect and skilful at their job – so perfect that they end up robotizing themselves, and although still being enthusiastic and inspiring, leaving a dehumanized impression. The cyborg leader in this way often ends up intimidating rather than inspiring their subordinates, something, which obviously contradicts the characteristics of the charismatic leader.

This chapter is thus about superior leaders and how they conduct leadership on their subordinates. In extension, it will also outline how cyborg leadership aspires to middle management, as middle managers often are the ones required to live up to the expectations of the cyborg leader. In this way cyborg leadership sieves through the hierarchy and can be seen in some form on most levels of the organization. In doing this I will first describe what a cyborg is, and then explain how it can be seen as a metaphor of how some leaders lead. Here, I will show how cyborg leadership is a metaphor for the perfect leader's extraordinary abilities as well as their gift of seducing followers. Empirical illustrations of two leaders (Paul and Lisa) are given to illustrate two key processes of cyborg leadership: expectation and intimidation. The metaphor will then be applied to the broader context of popular management texts to investigate where the notions of superiority stem from. These processes of superiority are then unpacked and I discuss different forms of cyborg leaders as well as their ability to possess a tireless supply of energy, being extremely self-confident, persuasive to the crowd of followers, and showing exceptional self-control. Finally, a critical discussion is initiated where the praise of superiority is questioned and discussed. Here it will be argued that perfectness and superiority might be inspiring and admirable up until a certain point where the same superior and perfect characters turn uncanny and even intimidating. The Achilles heel of the otherwise so invulnerable cyborg leader might therefore exactly be his or her self-absorbing superiority that leads to distance, fear or distrust between them and those they lead. So let's first return to the cyborg as it has been portrayed in science and popular culture.

THE CYBORG

The term cyborg, which is short for cybernetic organism, was originally coined by Clynes and Kline (1960), who developed the term to describe a being that is part human and part machine. In their particular context this was a being technologically altered to cope better with the conditions of outer space. Today, the term still refers to a creature that is part human and part machine, but is seen as less specific as it now more generally describes a creature that has any enhanced ability due to technology. The cyborg has therefore left the constricted context of outer space and is now a general symbol of how technology is transforming and maybe even transcending the human (Gray 1995). In popular culture, cyborgs are widely known from science fiction films, television series and novels. The perfected women in *Stepford Wives*, the cool cyborg Molly in *Neuromancer*, and the emotionless man-machines in the *Terminator* movies are just some examples. In these films and novels, cyborgs are most often displayed as mechanistic creatures, which, through technological improvement, have gained extra strength or are perfected to do a specific task. Their appearances are human, but they hold certain non-human advancements and thus transcend the border between what is human and non-human. All the creatures are simultaneously respected and feared and play in this way with society's discomfort with the increasing dependence on – and sometimes fear of – technology (Gray 1995, 2001).

In recent years the cyborg has also become a well-known metaphor in feministic circles characterizing a strong woman, who liberates herself from gender stereotypes. This trend started when Haraway (1991) wrote her famous *A Cyborg Manifesto*. In the *Manifesto*, Haraway discusses how the cyborg could inspire change and liberation from an oppressive system. She thus calls on readers to use technology to resist the conventional models that shape us as human beings in a patriarchal society. In this way the cyborg woman for Haraway is a creature with extraordinary and special abilities that can change the way women are perceived. By using their extraordinary abilities 'super women' can change both nature and culture and provide all women new opportunities – some might even say hope. Czarniawska and Gustavsson (2008) use Haraway as a point of departure when they argue that:

> the cyborg combines the traditional stereotypes with the visions of the new world, and the fear of women with the fear of robots. Like avatars, they might represent an ideal employee in that they are capable of inhuman efforts and concentration.
>
> (Czarniawska and Gustavsson 2008: 679)

In this chapter, the cyborg metaphor will not be limited to describe the female fight to break free of stereotypes. Here, it will be seen more generally as a metaphor for the way superior managers lead. By being flawless and successful, managers (both men and women) are actively learning how to use their alienation (coming from superiority), and the respect or fear others feel because of this alienation, as a leadership tool. So where Haraway uses the term to describe how women can break free of stereotypes, I use the cyborg metaphor to describe how some leaders are so flawless, rational and focused that they appear as if they were machines. By being perceived as superior and especially skilled, they stand out and are able to set new norms. Their superiority therefore inspires or maybe more correctly demands and disciplines subordinates to imitate and follow their successful behaviour.

The leaders' perfection therefore not only puts pressure on the leader him- or herself, but it also places demands on the subordinates who work under this superior person. Construction of superior leadership can be exploited in different ways and thus superior leaders conduct leadership in various ways. Common for this type of leader is, however, that being superior is the foundation for how others perceive them and also how they perceive others. They want their subordinates to become just as perfect, but how they do so varies. In this chapter I will discuss how the cyborg leader among other things leads by placing high expectations on subordinates while appearing flawless and intimidating themselves.

EMPIRICAL ILLUSTRATIONS

To illustrate processes of cyborg leadership, the chapter now turns to empirical illustrations. In this I will show how two successful leaders lead their subordinates by appearing superior and flawless. Paul, a partner in a large international consulting firm leads through great *expectations* of his subordinates. He is very successful and expects the same extraordinary ability from his employees. In this way, he is very enthusiastic and inspiring, but does not tolerate mediocre performance or even worse failures. Lisa is CEO of a large Danish knowledge intensive company, where she is one of the most respected and successful top managers. She shows exceptional work capacity and almost appears inhuman in her extraordinary accomplishments. This means that she has a flock of admirers surrounding her who adore her. However, she has problems showing people skills (i.e. being a 'buddy'), and for this reason she also receives criticism for being inhuman and cold by some of her subordinates. She thus leads her subordinates by *intimidation*.

PAUL – LEADING THROUGH GREAT EXPECTATIONS

Paul is partner in a large consulting firm and leader of one of the business units. The company has about 550 employees at the Danish office where Paul works, and there are about 50 people in his business unit. He is very successful and his unit is by far the most profitable in the firm. He is known for being one of the 'tough guys' who always lands the big projects. Making it to partner in one of the big consulting firms is in itself perceived to be an achievement of high status, but moreover he is one of the most prominent and dominating characters in the partner group. People know him, and he makes sure he is noticed. He is very confident about his success and does not hesitate to utilize this. He has developed his own very clear ideas of how to run his business unit, and even though it goes against the general line in the firm, because of his success he is 'allowed' to do so:

> I can just refer to my results and say, hey do you have a problem? But it's not only that. I would still do it my way even though things were different. It's the attitude that if something is important to me, and I really believe in it, then we also have to do it.

Paul runs his department as he sees best and does not care much about what is considered to be 'corporate' or 'standard operating procedures'. And even though the CEO wishes to equalize firm strategy, Paul has been very successful so far, and due to this, his independent behaviour has been tolerated. As one of his closest employees says about his independence:

> I think that there are rules that need to be taken somewhat lightly, especially in a big global organization. We have to have some entre-preneurial spirit: Someone who wants something different and does not take standing operating procedures too seriously. . . . And Paul does this much more often than anyone else here. . . . So he might not exactly unite the management group, but he certainly accomplishes things for our group.

Paul is perceived as a 'maverick'; a lone ranger, who does it 'his way' and is very confident in doing it his way, because he knows that no one can touch him. If people argue against him, he can easily neglect their comments, referring to the superiority of his department. He knows that he is successful and he has a theory of why it is so:

> I, as a leader in my position, can use my strengths to make sure that my employees are exploiting their strengths.

In the way he conducts himself as a leader, he is very focused on strengths, both his own and those of his employees. Through identifying these, he seeks to lead his department to excellence. He does not tolerate mediocre perform-ance. He expects the same excellence from his employees that they (and he) see in him.

> Why should we be at a *good* level when we can reach a much higher level of *excellent* performance? If you can get all the way up there, the poor performance is much further away. . . . Instead of just following protocols and methods, I want every individual to always have in mind what he or she can do even better.

Paul is not being modest about his achievements, quite the opposite in fact. He is very outspoken about his superiority. He sees himself as something the others should strive towards, and sometimes it even seems like he sees himself as super-human. And he very clearly expects just as much from his subordin-ates. He doesn't tolerate mediocre performance, as he perceives it as a sign of not putting enough effort into the job. He wants his employees to always be excellent performers and to take joy in being the best.

Paul has however a mixed influence on his subordinates. Some of them (especially the younger) adore him and think he is fantastic. They love the speed he brings to the group, all the special attention the group gets, and the special rewards (trips, dinners, shows) they see themselves entitled to. They love the glamorous and extraordinary feeling there is around the group and bathe in the success they have. Paul is enthusiastic, energetic and intelligent and they look up to him with great respect. As one younger consultant says about him:

> I am very proud of working in Paul's group. Paul is a fantastic leader. I've never met someone quite as inspiring. When I work with him, I immediately feel his energy and his passion for the job, and that is very contagious.

Others, especially the more senior consultants, have become increasingly suspicious about his leadership style and don't trust him to have integrity and true interest in the people. A consultant from a different group, who was recently promoted to the management team, has trouble deciphering Paul's way of being:

> I don't feel that he sees me as a person. I'm a resource, just a number, and that is beginning to get to me. Although he is definitely not the only leader in here, who treats us that way, I see him as exceptionally cold and calculative.

This is also very clearly expressed by a senior employee in Paul's group. She has worked with him for 12 years, and recognizes the enthusiasm around him. But she has also many examples of how he can switch between this inspiring energetic person to be read as a cold and manipulative person.

> He is completely driven by his own interests and has very little under-standing of what effects he has on others. He uses other people; they only serve his agenda. And that doesn't hold in the long run. He is kind of psychopathic. He is very enthusiastic, a good speaker and very good at motivating people, but at the same time he is completely unforgiving if people make the smallest mistakes. . . . I simply don't trust him.

Paul in this way has a very dominating leadership style, which gives him a lot of attention, adoration and respect among the younger people on his staff. But at some point this respect turns into a critical wondering about his methods and then to contempt for his harshness and perceived lack of empathy. He might be intelligent, enthusiastic and leading the business unit towards great success. But at some point the employees' perception of him changes. So although he seems to be able to seduce the new consultants, this lack of empathy and support damages his relationship to the more senior subordinates who lose trust in him. He thus conducts leadership in a very machine-like fashion. He performs at a superior level and without exception demands the same kind of excellence from his subordinates. He thus also sees his employees as parts of this smoothly operating machine of excellence and does not accept human flaws.

LISA – LEADING BY INTIMIDATION

The second example of a cyborg leader is Lisa. Lisa is placed in the top management of one of Denmark's largest companies and is therefore one of the highest ranking women in corporate Denmark. The company has almost 13,000 employees. Lisa has sole responsibility for strategy and branding, but is on a day-to-day basis 'only' managing a group of ten people. She made her career extremely fast and has been in a high-ranking position in several companies the last ten years. Lisa was headhunted into the company two years ago as part of a major restructuring plan. In this way, she was expected to turn the company around, occupying a position where the last two managers had failed. And Lisa has proven her worth. She has managed to change things and turn her group into a very successful unit. Besides that, Lisa has managed to give birth to four children. Lisa's story is perfect, almost impossible to believe – science fiction.

The way Lisa works is almost like a machine. She is capable of working extreme hours at the same time as having a large family at home. Although she could have had a very long – paid – maternity leave, Lisa chose to come back to work before the baby was even two months old. And even when she was breast-feeding a baby at home, she managed to control all her assignments.

> We didn't have anyone who could take over my projects. I was the only one who could run them. So I tried to stay on board and took part in meetings already after one month. I was away from work for two months and in that period I worked approximately one day a week from home. I had a good team surrounding me, so I managed to handle everything else over the phone.

The people she currently works with (as well as two former colleagues we also interviewed) see her as a person who never fails and is always available for business matters. Her skills are highly respected, but similar to Paul, her subordinates have different opinions of her as a person and a leader. But her perfection has a great effect on how her subordinates perceive her. One thing they all agree on is that, as she has been able to manage her life with a demanding job and four children (and a husband who works a lot as well) she is something special and they see her as a tough, almost higher being. Her story is fascinating, almost frightening, but in a strange way she makes it all seem so easy and casually states that other people could easily do as she does if they just wanted to. Her subordinates express this clearly in that they do not know how to act themselves when she is so 'perfect'. And understandably as she does not seem to have much respect left for people who can't handle it:

> I tease my employees a little if they say they think I'm tough, and tell them that they could do the same if they wanted to. The men also get paid paternity leave in this company, but they choose to go away on vacation with their wives and children.

So even though the men under her (her 'boys' as she calls them) have every right to take parental leave as they please, she teases them for spending it on 'holiday' with children and wives. For her, work comes first. One of her employees therefore expresses the impression that she never does much for pleasure. Her subordinates know that and almost feel embarrassed by prioritizing 'quality time' with the family instead of getting back to work as soon as possible.

Lisa's self-image is that she is tolerant and respecting the different priorities her 'boys' have. As she says, she is only teasing them. She laughs about how scared they seem to be of her. It doesn't seem like she is fully aware of the effect she has on them. So Lisa sees herself as a good example and a role model. However, Lisa expresses almost no emotion, which makes her really difficult to read. When she speaks it is thus very difficult to tell whether she is joking or being serious. She bears a professional expression on her beautiful face, even when she laughs, which makes it almost impossible to figure out whether she is joking or mocking. Her employees find it easy to communicate business with her, but they find it very difficult to discuss personal matters with her. To them, she appears non-emotional, almost non-human, like she is pro-grammed to run the business. But the minute a conversation leaves business matters her programme seems to break down, as she does not know how to handle personal issues. Thus professionally, they have a deep respect for her, but personally they seem to request more people skills from her.

Her employees seem to experience a clear line distinguishing her from them. They can never reach her level and they know it. She makes it seem so easy, but they don't really understand, which makes them feel inferior. They clearly respect her professionalism, but it is respect mixed with intimidation. They fear that unknown part within her, which is so different from their worlds. As expressed by one of her employees:

She is an extreme case. She sees people as machines only as input/output and doesn't care about the person inside. The relation between the leader and the employee doesn't interest her a bit. That frustrates me. They [the company] really have a motivation problem here, but nothing is done about it.

She is perceived to be different from other people in the organization – also from the other managers in the organization. Everybody knows of her and the way she appears to people. Some are impressed, but most express that they find the way she works incomprehensible.

BROADER ASSESSMENT OF THE USE OF THE METAPHOR

The cyborg metaphor itself is not common in management literature; however one of the basic elements, that of superiority and excellence, is by no means new. In the early 1980s, Peters and Waterman (1982), both schooled at McKinsey, began telling us how to manage a company and lead employees to excellence. The bookshops are now filled with management books revealing how to escape mediocrity and become an excellent and superior leader. For example John C. Maxwell (1999) gives us '21 indispensable qualities of a leader' to become the person others will want to follow. On top of that, several international leadership institutes offer courses in superior leadership. For example Bob Prosen, CEO of Dallas-based 'The Prosen Center for Business Advancement', writes in an advertisement for his popular management book *Kiss Theory Good Bye* that superior leadership entails, among other things, making sure that the leader focuses 'on results, not activities'.[1]

For some, there are few limits to our search for excellence. Leadership at this level is about becoming better and better. The leader must not fail. He or she has to be perfect and find his or her strengths. The magazine and on-line portal *Leadership Excellence* reassures us 'we shall not fail',[2] and the popular management guru Marcus Buckingham, author of *First, Break All the Rules* and *Now, Discover Your Strengths*, defines strength-based management (which Paul above implemented in his business unit), where the mantra is not to focus on improving weaknesses, but instead to focus on strengths and improve these to the level of excellent performance. In doing this, the leader is to break all the rules, not be restrained by protocol and procedure. This mantra of the business excellence literature seems to construct a discourse, which to a large degree seems to affect the high-handed cyborg leaders in their quest to construct themselves as superior overmen and revolutionize their businesses.

Some of the most famous and widely cited business leaders in history can also be said to hold cyborg qualities. This is probably due to the fact that through the media we hear more about the tough and successful leaders than the soft and caring (again of course with exceptions). Of these, Harold Geneen, Andy Grove, Henry Ford and John Sculley will be mentioned here to get a better grasp of what the cyborg metaphor means.

Harold Geneen, who in the 1960s and 1970s turned International Telephone and Telegraph Corporation (ITT) into a multibillion business, is said to have been one of the greatest businessmen ever. He was known as a super-accountant, with an extremely good memory and a way of dealing with numbers. However, he also penalized any deviation from expected good results. Thus, although he was known for his exceptional skills and strategic capacity, the *New York Times* said in his obituary that he 'stretched his people and his company to the legal limits, scarring the company's image to the point where it became a popular symbol of corporate arrogance and insensitivity'.[3] Among other things he was famous for the following quotes:[4]

- Performance is your reality. Forget everything else.
- Leadership is practiced not so much in words as in attitude and in actions.
- The best way to inspire people to superior performance is to convince them by everything you do and by your everyday attitude that you are wholeheartedly supporting them.

Like Paul, Geneen seemed to be a leader who wanted action and excellent performance. He was most likely very inspiring to those who followed him and undoubtedly very successful in what he did. But also ruthless to those who didn't follow him. The best way to inspire people is to convince them that you are right, but if they don't follow you, and if you can't convince them, there is no support. He was therefore a cyborg leader in the sense that he was exceptionally skilled and was considered a great leader. However, he was also called a corporate autocrat, who did what he pleased – also to his employees – as long as it benefited his company.

Andy Grove was one of the first employees at Intel, and was its CEO from 1987 to 1998. He was in charge of Intel when it experienced enormous growth in the 1990s and is said to be the one that transformed it from a minor memory chip manufacturer into the world's leading producer of microprocessors. As a leader he was extremely competitive, and was known to work by the motto 'only the paranoid survive'. In 1996, he published a book with that title as well. He was not known to be democratic and played rough with those employees who didn't align with the corporate way of doing things, and he was not afraid to take up fiery fights with troublesome rivals either. This style might have been fierce, but it is said to have led Intel to what it is today. And because of this success, he was allowed to be cold and calculative (Jackson 1998). Employees are a means to an end in cyborg leadership, also expressed by Henry Ford, who doesn't need any further introduction, but is known to have said the often cited words: 'Why is it every time I ask for a pair of hands, they come with a brain attached?'[5]

My last popular example is John Sculley, who was in the head of Pepsi during the so-called cola wars in the 1980s, where Pepsi and Coca-Cola fought a tough battle to be the world's biggest cola brand. As Sculley explains in his biographical book *Odyssey* (see also Alvesson and Willmott 1996), succeeding was something he had always believed in:

> We always believed, since the early seventies, when Pepsi was widely viewed as the perennial also-ran, that we could do it. All of us started out with that objective, and we never took our eyes off it.
>
> (Sculley 1988: 3)

He here describes a very determined form of doing business, setting a goal and accomplishing it at any cost. Pepsi was at that time called the marine corps of business and was known for their untraditional way of working. They generally appeared well-trimmed, tough and flawless, like nothing could beat them. And as he says about himself:

> If I was brash or arrogant on my way to the top, it mattered little to me. I was an imperfect perfectionist. I was willing to work relentlessly to get things exactly right. I was unsympathetic to those who couldn't deliver the results I demanded.
>
> (Sculley 1988: 4)

Complaining in Pepsi was at that time seen as inappropriate and gave the impression of personal failure of not being able to deliver. And many managers were replaced. If you didn't deliver still better results, you were fired (Alvesson and Willmott 1996).

Having said this, all leaders are obviously not all about excellence at any cost. As it has also been shown, for example, in the chapter on the 'buddy', a large body of literature comments on the need for leaders to show that they are human too. Based on all the material collected for this book as well as the general leadership literature, it seems like the cyborg leader is most common in top management. In order to be able – or more likely allowed – to develop into a cyborg leader, the leader needs to be so successful that they first of all get a high degree of freedom, and he or she needs a certain level of fame to make them object of (at least some of) their employees' idolization. In other words, the cyborg leader will probably be most common in hierarchic or bureaucratic companies, where the managers are not questioned as such and where there is a distinct distance between management and its employees.

The 'pure' cyborg leader might thus not be the most common leader type we meet in organizations. However, many leaders hold certain aspects of cyborg leadership or aspire to conduct such leadership. The popular literature above on excellence and stories of the tough and famous leaders naturally also inspire many lower-level leaders to try to strive towards the same level of excellence and rationality as for example Lisa and Paul practise. Although only a few leaders manage to reach a similar level of superiority, the cyborg metaphor is still relevant in order to understand the drive towards excellence and superiority, which most leaders can subscribe to. Displaying the extreme cases above thus makes it possible for us to unpack the metaphor and look at what such leadership means for both the leader and the subordinates. The discourse of excellence thus fosters certain mechanistic character traits, which are typical for the cyborg leader to adopt and perform, and which can be performed in more or less pure degree. In their pure form, these are extremely focused on performance and strategic insight, but generally lack a human and empathic aspect. Some of these traits will be unpacked below. In a less pure form, cyborg leadership also aspires to the middle manager in several ways. First of all, cyborg leadership is about having ambitions, setting a goal and aiming for that goal regardless of the costs. It is also about being competitive and constantly trying to be a little better. Thus cyborg leadership is not exclusively performed by the top manager, but also by the middle manager, who tries to emphasize his or her strengths, competes with his or her peers, and is focused on not failing and always doing his or her best. Cyborg leadership is in this way about impression management; that is, about giving the impression that you are the best at what you do, regardless of what you might do, and at what level that might be. To make explicit what cyborg leadership is about, the following will, however, concentrate on the more pure form of cyborg leadership. This makes it easier to explain the specific characteristics of the metaphor, but should not be seen as an expression of cyborg leadership only existing in its pure form.

UNPACKING THE CYBORG

Despite the central element of superiority, there are, however, great variances in how this superiority is performed in cyborg leadership. Without claiming to mention all possible versions, but to show the variety, I will here give a few examples of different forms of cyborg leadership: the charisborg, the technocrat and the perfectionist. Of course all three are ideal types. My goal here is thus not to draw specific boundaries between types, but to exemplify the possibility of various types. A cyborg leader can perform in a way that is similar to several or all of the ideal (sub-)types. Still, in most cases it will be possible to see one type performed more strongly than the others. The ideal types thus still serve an analytical purpose, which makes us understand cyborg leadership better. Our above examples of Lisa and Paul represent, as formerly mentioned, 'pure' cyborgs as they have the characteristics of all three ideal types. All cyborg leaders are, however, not as extreme as Lisa and Paul, and can be cyborg leaders by performing elements of only one or two of the types.

THE CHARISBORG

Leaders are often portrayed as charismatic individuals, who guide through their superior vision (Mio *et al.* 2005, Awaleh and Gardner 1999). Charisma and strong appearance distinguish the superior leader from ordinary men and women. This leader is a charismatic, energetic and emotional person, whom followers tend to 'idolize or worship . . . as a superhuman hero or spiritual figure' (Yukl 2006: 270). The followers of a charismatic leader are easily seduced by his or her personality and are thus likely to submit completely to the leader's superior abilities, and show devoted trust and unquestioning acceptance of the rightness and accuracy of their actions. However, the strong, rational and flawless leader can also have a different and less emotional appearance of superiority and perfection. This less-researched, so-called darker side of charismatic leadership (Padilla *et al.* 2007), is what I here call the charisborg. The charisborg is seductive and charismatic, but is not too emotional and empathic, which is often assumed about charismatic leaders (although well-known charismatic characters like Hitler were extremely non-empathic). Instead the charisborg is powerful and successful, and like both Paul and Geneen and Sculley, does not accept flaws or mistakes. He or she is inspiring and supportive as long as the employee does well, but ruthless and mechanistic when the employee performs badly. The charisborg is therefore charismatic in the sense that he or she has an ability to seduce an audience, but on the other hand ruthless in their means to reach a certain goal. On the surface, the leader therefore might appear charismatic, especially because of their skills in formulating unreachable goals as possible for a group led by them; however, when it comes to methods of reaching such goals, the charisborg – as any cyborg leader – is focused and possibly aggressive and doesn't compromise or tolerate failure.

THE TECHNOCRAT

Where the charisborg is most likely to be a top management figure, the technocrat can be 'anyone'. The technocrat is someone mechanistically devoted to the detail. He or she is extremely focused and like Geneen, for example, holds exceptional number skills, where they are able to see patterns and relationships that otherwise only machines can. They are admired for their skills and their leadership style is far less aggressive than the charisborg as they aspire to mimic behaviour rather than set expectations. Because they are so superior in what they do, they are natural role-models and their employees automatically try to copy their behaviours. The technocratic cyborg is typically more in line with the manager than the leader prototype – if one should stick to this distinction – but given their sufficient skills, the impression of superiority they give others can still lead to admiration and inspiration of subordinates, thus involving 'more than just management' control and command effects.

THE PERFECTIONIST

The perfectionist is a type somewhat placed in between the charisborg and the technocrat. The perfectionist, like the technocrat, is extremely focused on the detail. However, the perfectionist is not just a cyborg because of skills, but also because of a desire to be the best. The perfectionist believes in him or herself and is willing to sacrifice a lot to reach their goals. This type, therefore, does not accept failure and weaknesses, and will be someone that never does things half-heartedly. The perfectionist puts a lot of effort into being the best, and like Sculley, does not compromise with whatever it takes to bring them there. Such a person does, however, not only expect perfection from him or herself, but also from his or her employees. Employees doing well will be praised, but it will not take this type of leader much to let go of employees not living up to their expectations. This leader is focused on the job, not on the people they lead, and employees are therefore seen as means to an end. If the employees can't live up to their expectations, it is not difficult to let them go. Reaching the perfect result has first priority.

So what exactly is it that makes cyborg leadership work? What are these superior aspects of the cyborg leader? The cyborg leader performs leadership as a well-programmed leader superior to his or her subordinates, but not only by being 'better' or more 'intelligent'. Rather, like Nietzsche's (1995) concept of the overman, the cyborg leader is also someone who tries to break free of established rules and values to create something bigger; someone who tries to be some*one* bigger. The cyborg leader is an overman in the sense that he or she breaks the limits of what is 'normal practice' and creates new ways of being (or business). Similar to Nietzsche's overman, the cyborg leader thus has much more than just intellectual superiority.[6] As emphasized in popular management literature, a leader needs to create results and gain followers to be able to function themselves as norm-setters. Being superior therefore holds many different aspects, but it is especially unique to cyborgs. What can make them capable of achieving this status are the following four characteristics: (1) a tireless energy, (2) self-confidence, (3) seductive persuasiveness, and (4) self-control.

TIRELESS ENERGY

A cyborg leader holds the ability to keep working on a continuous basis, almost like a machine that does not need breaks. It appears as if he or she can carry on tirelessly for hours and hours without showing any signs of exhaustion. It is almost as if they have an unlimited source of battery power, which never reaches low levels. This tireless energy makes them possess an unbelievable work capacity that for the 'normal' worker seems almost inhuman. Even though Paul works a lot, and according to his colleagues always is capable of showing energy and enthusiasm, Lisa is a more extreme example of this. The way she handles her life as a mother of four children and her job at the same time seems most of all impossible to her colleagues. None of the employees we have interviewed, neither the ones who adore her nor those who are sceptical about her leadership style, understands how she makes this possible. They clearly see her as an overman due to this. But it also makes her appear machine-like to them, *something* rather than *someone*. They do not know her personality, only her abilities.

SELF-CONFIDENT

The ability to always identify novel, and successful, business ideas and solutions has a tendency to affect a leader in a way that makes them strongly confident in their own abilities (Howell and Shamir 2005). Or, perhaps, it is also the strong self-confidence that gives them success. Andy Grove's competitiveness and almost paranoid tendencies and Sculley's determination and focused way of working are examples of the self-confident cyborg leader. Also the empirical material points to the fact that the confident acting and strong belief in their own abilities gives leaders an ability to continue and see things through to an exceptional degree. They have strong convictions that what they do is the best way. They believe in one thing and stay focused – some may even say obsessed – with this one idea. The cyborg leaders in our cases in this way see their own superiority and want others to follow suit. But they also have problems with supporting subordinates who disagree with them. As the subordinates say about both Lisa and Paul, they want creative feedback on their ideas, but have a low tolerance for people who want to do things differently. In this way they want their followers to 'learn their place', and as long as the followers are with them, they are enthusiastic, supportive and inspiring. But when they either disagree too much or fail, the support risks turning into dismissal or ridicule.

SEDUCTIVE PERSUASIVENESS

A cyborg leader is someone who leads in a persuasive and seductive manner. They are excellent at image building and impression management because they, in Awaleh and Gardner's (1999) description of the great leader, are capable of extraordinary framing techniques and are thus able to craft rhetoric that seduces followers. They are not seductive and persuasive because of their charming and appealing personality like most charismatic leaders, but they are persuasive and seductive because of their extraordinary abilities and their authority. They are looked up to professionally, and very good at communicating their plans, and therefore appear seductive and persuasive. The cyborg leader might be an excellent accountant, but never the quiet type hidden behind numbers. In other words, the cyborg leader is more than just an excellent machine. Like Geenen, who was exceptional with numbers, the cyborg leader also has punch and a powerful personality. A cyborg is therefore not the grey machine in the background, but the beautiful, shining and intimidating man-machine. Cyborg leaders stand out from the crowd, not only because they are perceived to be intellectually superior, but also because they carry an aura of authority and excellence. They are someone employees want to follow because they lead to success. Everyone in the two case study organizations knows Lisa and Paul respectively. They are both brilliant speakers and can therefore persuade or seduce their followers not only by their performances, but also by expressing their plans in an attractive way. In seducing especially the younger employees they are both capable of mobilizing a critical mass of followers. The crowds of younger employees, who worship and look up to them, are key to their leadership style. Both Lisa and Paul play on inflicting feelings of shame and self-guilt on their followers to ensure unlimited support and desire to improve. Their appearance in this way produces a sense of shared mission and in the case study material above this is exactly what gives

Paul's and Lisa's departments a work-culture not seen elsewhere in their organizations. They both inspire their subordinates to be like them and hire them young, so they can train them to fit in with their strategy.

SELF-CONTROL

In this game of seducing and securing followers, cyborg leaders are also extremely skilled at not showing their own emotions, and their inner selves. They maintain a perfect façade, and seduce their followers with excellence and status. They never reveal the person behind the mask; they only give away the mechanistic outer. In this way, the cyborg leader seems invulnerable to outside attacks, and is so much in self-control that when attacked from the outside it does not seem to bother them. They keep their heads high and are capable of arguing against any personal criticism which just bounces off their armour. Both Paul and Lisa act in this way, but in very different ways. Paul is the enthusiastic, inspiring (some say manipulating) energetic person, who is able to be so enthusiastic about his own ideas that it is almost impossible to argue against him. At the same time he can turn around in a second to be vicious and aggressive towards failure or criticism, something which makes his employees think twice before they question him. Lisa on the other hand is always calm. Although her employees find her professional skills very inspiring, they have never seen her show emotion, as she does not want to see emotions at work. She does not show any, and she does not want to hear about her employees' emotional issues. She does inspire her employees professionally, but not in the enthusiastic way Paul does. However, both of them create this appearance of invulnerability and inhumanity, which also makes it very difficult for their employees to stay devoted to them as they obtain seniority. After a while, the employees start looking behind the mechanistic façade. They search for something more, a person behind the mask, a person they never find, however.

The cyborg leader in this way shows several aspects and levels of superiority, but they seem to have a foundation in narcissistic behaviour. As argued by Pullen and Rhodes (2008: 9) 'the narcissistic leader strives for personal success won through fierce independence, high visibility, upward mobility and the defeat of rivals'. The cyborg leader as illustrated by the above character traits thus has a tendency to be narcissistic in their extreme focus on their own abilities and business ideas. Neither Lisa and Paul nor Geneen, Grove, Ford and Sculley accept other ways than their way. They are successful and believe completely in their methods. Paul says over and over again that he knows that he is the best and that no one can do the job as well as he can, whereas Lisa thinks of herself as so indispensable that she can't find anyone to take over her assignments when she is on maternity leave. In this way, as argued by Kodish (2006), great leaders are in fact expected to be narcissistic due to their aforementioned 'larger-than-life' (self)image. In this way the narcissism of cyborg leaders can lead to both strong group relations as well as holding the danger to terminate these (Cluley 2008). The argument here is that the cyborg leader up until a certain point, through his or her self-centred way of being, is capable of creating a group around their success. The followers' adoration is at this point very important as their idolization and investment in the group distances the leader from the rest, which again reinforces the narcissistic character (Cluley 2008). Being superior thus calls for less superior people around them and cyborg leadership is in this way very much relational. And it only lasts if there are no critical interventions (Janis 1972). When the more senior employees for example start to question and be sceptical about work methods, the idolization and over-value of the leader is destroyed and feelings of self-guilt, frustration, anxiety and jealousy are created instead. Leaders' moderated narcissism can therefore be productive for team-spirit and performance, whereas excessive narcissism can lead to an unhealthy fixation on power, status and prestige (Kets de Vries 1985).

In this way, it seems that this mechanistic robotic behaviour is also the cyborg leader's Achilles heel. The lack of emotional empathy and 'people skills' makes their followers doubt their superiority when they gain tenure. From being worshipped and adored for their excellence, they turn incomprehensible and intimidatingly non-human. A good example of this is the famous 'downsizer' Al Dunlap often referred to as 'Chainsaw Al'. As mentioned in Chapter 7, Dunlap was famous for displaying two sharks eating each other on his desk. These were supposed to show his 'shark-like' behaviour. Dunlap, who was once celebrated as the best downsizer ever, destroyed his career by getting too confident in his own miracle-making. His attempt to increase the stock price of the company Sunbeam ended fatally and he was dismissed and never seen on the business scene again. After his fall it was said that his story was 'the logical extreme of an executive who has no values, no honour, no loyalty, and no ethics. And yet he was held up as a corporate god in our culture'.[7] Dunlap managed to build up an image of extreme competence and indestructibility. But it also seems that this image became his downfall. Believing too much in his own abilities and not caring about the figures or people he manipulated led him to build up a fantasy, that when it collapsed took him down as well. On this point the cyborg metaphor is similar to both the commander and the bully metaphor. The commander creates a sense of fear in order to lead and the bully manipulates and lures the subordinates under his domination. However, both the commander and the bully are more active in their intimidating form of leadership, whereas cyborg leaders intimidate more subtly through *being* superior, inducing shame among their inferiors.

The next section will discuss critically the cyborg leader's superior qualities, and pinpoint where on the continuum they change from being an adored (although also feared) leader who makes their employees work at an insane pace to an alienated inhuman creature, which induces incomprehension and potential failure.

SCEPTICAL DISCUSSION

A superior and perfect leader functioning as a role model might be what every organization wishes for. It is after all what all the popular management books and leadership courses preach. But is it all that good? Do we really want perfection and super-humanness in our leaders? Superiority creates respect, but sometimes superiority goes from being respectful to being intimidating. As we saw above, the imitation of a superior leader can easily turn into hatred of the inhuman leader. Something happens on this continuum of superiority, something that might be understood better in the light of what has been called 'the uncanny valley'.

THE UNCANNY VALLEY OF CYBORG LEADERSHIP

As Czarniawska and Gustavsson (2008: 670) indicate, one of the points that the science fiction film *Stepford Wives* (2004) is trying to prove, is that perfection is not attractive. Perfection scares us because it does not seem natural. This relationship between the natural and perfection is explored in the theory on the 'uncanny valley' developed by the artist and roboticist Masahiro Mori (see Mori 1970). Mori, who designed robots, claimed that robots could only resemble humans up to a certain point, after which they turned uncanny and frightening. In a similar way, I argue that this can be viewed from the other side, where humans can resemble robots (perfection and superiority) up until a certain point where they go from being admired and respected to being feared. There is in this way a certain point where the mechanistic capabilities become intimidating.

The superior leader can be seen as setting out as Haraway's cyborg on the quest for liberation and breaking free of the system. After all, superior leaders are said to be unconventional (Mio *et al.* 2005) with a vision that is radical and novel (Beyer 1999). Cyborg leaders like Paul and Lisa utilize this unconventionality to try to 'liberate' themselves as well as their subordinates from 'mediocre performance'. In this sense, like what Geneen, Grove and Sculley were all famous for, they want to improve human performance in general and lift their businesses from mediocre performance to excellent performance. This is obtained up until a certain level where they, through the impact they have on their subordinates, end up reinforcing the structures by their intimidating behaviour. At that point, they change from the liberating Haraway cyborg (or the successful and ambitious middle manager) to become the intimidating machine, which only reinforces his or her own rules and procedures and again locks up the employees in oppressive behaviour. This is the uncanny valley, that point where they change from being respected and adored (seen as a role model) to where they are intimidating and feared (seen as a limiting and oppressing character).

Is the cyborg leader, then, the leader of tomorrow, the future perfect? Is the cyborg setting us free or in fact locking us up in an eternal circle of improvement? The employees are told not only to work better and more productively. They are also told to enjoy excellence. As Paul said, being excellent compared to being merely good is a much more fun way to work. But in their search for excellence to satisfy the cyborg leader's demand, the employees turn into competition addicts – addicted to winning and to being the best. As the statements from the following employees (subordinates to either Paul or Lisa discussed above) show:

> The goal was to prove that I am good enough to my friends . . . But [it] probably just triggered my inner struggle to be good enough . . . I always have to prove to myself that I am good enough. I don't compete against others, I compete against myself.
>
> (John)

> Once, we had a diving competition, that should show who could swim the longest under water. One swam two lengths under water, so I thought 'I can do that better'. I swam almost three lengths, but when I was a few meters from the end, I blacked out and had to be carried up from the water. In this way, I have never given up on anything.
>
> (Martin)

> Working is like playing tennis. I want to win. Then it doesn't matter whether it has been a nice experience.
>
> (Michael)

In this way it can very well be questioned whether superior cyborg leaders in the pure form and their quest for excellence is always a desirable model. There is without doubt a certain point where the focused, inspiring and respected leader turns into an identity regulating control mechanism. The focus on superiority locks the employees into a game of being best and gives them the same intolerance of mediocre performance as their leaders communicate. The unquestionable superiority of the leaders forces the subordinates to be high performers as well. However, they can never seem to reach the same level of excellence. When the employees in this way always are surrounded by superiority and impossible expectations they tend to end up either pushing themselves so hard to the limit of what is humanly possible that they risk injuring themselves, or the leader sinks into the uncanny valley where he or she becomes intimidating. As we saw with Paul and Lisa's employees, none of them have yet actually managed to live up to the great expectations. The cyborg leader in its more extreme form is an impossible role model, and impossible to imitate. And this leads their employees to either push themselves to an insane competitive identity struggling to improve all the time, or it makes them realize that this is never possible and that they can just as well give up. The employees who give up on the imitation obtain a more careless attitude, and in fact a disrespectful attitude, which could lead to a termination of employment – either by a dissatisfied leader or a dissatisfied employee.

It does, however, seem that a certain level of superiority makes an excellent leader and a role model to follow (Awaleh and Gardner 1999). Therefore some level of cyborg leadership can be a desirable model. An above average manager can work in an energetic, reliable machine-like way denying specific human weaknesses and being intolerant to people not delivering. With this cyborg behaviour, he or she can push (or inspire) his or her employees to better performance. Therefore, what this chapter also tries to show, is that there is a certain level where this superiority instead of improving the employees rather destroys them as human beings as well. That is where the machine in the cyborg takes over and it becomes too uncanny. Although cyborg leadership in its extreme form as we saw it performed by Lisa and Paul is not common, analyzing leadership through the cyborg metaphor makes it clear that the search for excellence has a darker uncanny side, which is extremely important to understand in order to be aware of the consequences that the leadership discourse of excellence can have. Obviously, it is desirable for organizations to have great leaders that can lead subordinates to better performance, and cyborg leadership on the more moderate level can definitely be seen as desirable in most situations. After all, having focused and competitive leaders, who are concerned about always doing their best and never failing, must be said to be a positive achievement for organizations. However, it is also important to note the question whether this quest for excellence is also leading our workforce towards being an army of machines. Management literature has made a great deal out of the liberation from monotonous assembly work, and has cherished the liberation from routine work. But is the pressure for superiority again turning us into machines always pushing ourselves over the limit of what is humanly possible? Is the cyborg not merely a metaphor for the machine-rationality we meet at the workplace? Are we all turning into work-intensive excellence-seeking cyborgs?

CONCLUSION

In the search for excellence, the cyborg leader sets out by successfully breaking free of normal practice. In their success, they acquire a crowd of followers, and their way of being works as a norm-setting role model. The cyborg leader is respected and looked up to and in their superiority they make their followers perform better as well. Their self-confident success inspires others to imitate them and copy their success. Because of their superior performance, and often charismatic appearance, the cyborg leader naturally has several followers. No matter where on the human–machine continuum the particular cyborg leader is, he or she will, due to the way they stand out from the crowd, attract attention and other employees would want to be included rather than excluded in the group surrounding the cyborg leader. The followers are, however, due to the success of the leader, locked into a performance game struggling to gain membership to the group. In this way, the cyborg leader can be said to have a certain degree of control over the subordinates. Due to his or her central role as a role model and norm-setter, the subordinates get locked into an identity-regulating discourse of 'worshipping' the leader. The cyborg leader wants followers, narcissistically needs followers and in fact demands followers to be just like them. Paul demands the same excellence and does not tolerate one single mistake and Lisa knows she is far too superior to ever be copied, so to prove her powerful status she mocks her employees for not being able to copy her, forcing them to keep trying.

The cyborg leader is in this way far from the 'buddy' ensuring a good working environment, but is instead breeding excellence. As the commander, he or she might break a few eggs in the process, but, to use Nietzsche's metaphor, the cyborg leader leads the species to a higher rational state. In this way, the cyborg leader (at least in its pure form) can be said to be the 'overman' of business, who in an evolutionary manner leads the company to success. Geneen, Grove and Sculley all ruthlessly, focused and committed to success, led their employees to accomplish something extraordinary. But also as Nietzsche implied with the overman, the extreme cyborg leader like

Chainsaw Al often shows a radical self-importance or hubris, which makes it difficult for them to identify what is acceptable human behaviour. In this sense it is very difficult to say whether they are good leaders or not.

Lower levels of cyborg leadership can with much conviction be said to be beneficial. However, in the more extreme form they might end up lacking in people skills; skills that are certainly needed, if one asks their employees. On the other hand, could they have been so successful without performing this emotionally cold and mechanistic leadership style? And maybe a more relevant question is perhaps where on the continuum the cyborg leader should stop, or be stopped, to prevent them being transformed from a successful, skilful and admired leader to becoming uncanny and intimidating. However, is this at all possible, and who would be qualified to judge?

In fact, are we as academics in a position where we can judge whether this cyborg leader is good or evil? After all, when we think about it, who programmes these overmen, cyborgs? The answer is, that we in fact do so ourselves. It is the business schools and universities, which encourage superiority, which fundamentally create these performance-driven cyborg leaders. The best students take with them a drive to perform in their subsequent careers, where they continue to fight about assessments, evaluations, rankings and promotions. The successful leader has from the very beginning been regulated and directed by the norm-setting values of education and career. Business has always been and will always be about being the best and the survival of the fittest. If we are to improve, inferiority is not tolerated and not doing one's best is never an option. As Pedersen (2008) argues, our modern way of working demands that the employee always be fitter, happier and more productive.

NOTES

1 See: http://www.kisstheorygoodbye.com/thebook/.
2 http://www.leaderexcel.com/.
3 *New York Times*, published November 23, 1997, see http://www.nytimes.com/1997/11/23/business/harold-s-geneen-87-dies-nurtured-itt.html.
4 See: http://www.brainyquote.com/quotes/authors/h/harold_s_geneen_2.html.
5 http://www.quotesea.com/Quotes.aspx?by=Henry+Ford.
6 Nietzsche's overman has, however, been misunderstood and interpreted to be the foundation of the anti-semitism that led to the Holocaust and other terrible cases of racial superiority. I (as many others), however, don't believe that Nietzsche had this intention in his manuscript. Instead, I perceive Nietzsche's motive for the Übermensch was to describe a character that managed to overcome humanity, not as a racially superfluous master, but as a superior creature, who would constantly test itself and its opinions against the common sense of the world.
7 http://www.businessweek.com/1998/27/b3585090.htm, but see also http://www.businessweek.com/1999/99_42/b3651099.htm, both accessed on June 19, 2009.

9

LEADERS AS BULLIES

Leadership through intimidation

Dan Kärreman

'He was astonishingly rude to people'. Civil servants were shocked by his habit of abruptly getting up and leaving meetings when officials were in the middle of speaking. He became notorious within the building for shouting at the duty clerks, bawling at the superbly professional staff who manned the Number 10 switchboard and blowing up at the affectionately regarded 'Garden Girls', so called because the room from which they provide Downing Street's secretarial services overlooks the garden. When one of the secretaries was not typing fast enough for an angrily impatient Prime Minister, he turfed the stunned garden girl out of her chair and took over the keyboard himself.

THE ABOVE IS AN EXCERPT PUBLISHED in the *Guardian* from Andrew Rawnsley's book on Gordon Brown's years as Prime Minister in the UK. The allegations of abusive behaviour created a media debate around Brown's character and leadership style. Brown's antagonists used the allegations to demonstrate that Brown was unfit to lead, while protagonists used the allegations to frame Brown as complex man, capable of inspiring leadership despite his temper. This chapter, however, suggests that the shared assumption from antagonists as well as protagonists – that abuse, threats and displays of anger always is at odds with leadership – might be misleading and hide more than it reveals. Consequently, this chapter pays particular attention to the dark side of leadership.

The leadership literature, although vast, generally agrees with the common sense assumption shared by Brown's antagonists and protagonists and rarely admits the existence of the darker, or coercive, tools available for leaders and managers to get things done. This is odd, because, as common sense suggests elsewhere, carrots work well to motivate and persuade, but there is a reason the proverb adds sticks. It also stands in stark contrast to the literature on management control, where coercive forms of control have been recognized for decades – consider, for example, Etzioni's (1965: 651) concept of coercive control:

[t]he use of a gun, a whip, or a lock is physical in the sense that it affects the body; the threat to use physical means is viewed as physical because the effect on the subject is similar to that of the actual use of such means.

What has this to do with leadership? Most would argue that management control is hardly the same thing as leadership. In fact, some would argue that management is about maintaining operations and leadership is about transformational change (see for example Kotter 1990). However, matters are more complicated if one consults the literature on management control, which is reasonably in agreement that management control includes the exercise of power and influence in order to secure sufficient resources, and mobilize and orchestrate individual and collective action towards given ends (cf. Langfield-Smith 1997, Speklé 2001 for reviews). This is, of course, very close to textbook definitions of leadership, or, for that matter, the working definition of leadership for this book: 'asymmetrical relationships, influencing processes and situations where people in some kind of formal and institutionalized dependency relationship are targeted' (Chapter 2).

Leadership is an area which is covered by a vast literature. However, despite the amount of ink used there are, as pointed out in Chapter 2, several blind spots. For example, for mostly opaque reasons leadership research tends to focus on carrots and refrains from taking a closer look to the sticks available to presumptive leaders. Leadership research tends to have a soft focus, and circle in on charisma, character, and moralism (see the chapter on the saint metaphor for more on this). It is easy to have sympathy for this humanistic or humanitarian bias but it also denies us insight into the darker spectrum of the leadership phenomenon. After all, for every Churchill, Roosevelt, Gandhi and Mandela, there is a Hitler, Stalin, Saddam Hussein and Amin. If we accept the first set of names as archetypical leaders, we cannot possibly deny that the second set of names were also leaders, although in a different sense (Churchill's views on Gandhi also add ambiguity to the issue).

Can we deny this? Below, it is argued that the exclusion of morally challenged individuals is in fact a common idea in contemporary leadership research, and it is demonstrated why this is a mistake. The chapter advocates a descriptive, or sociological, perspective on the leadership phenomenon, rather than a prescriptive – or normative – perspective. Additionally, this chapter will also take a closer look at what usually gets lost or pushed to the margins in leadership research – threats, coercion, violence, shame, guilt and so on.

The literature on leadership typically suggests that leaders are generally supposed to do good. Ciulla (2004: xv) offers an example of this view: 'Managers and generals may act like playground bullies and use their power and rank to force their will on people, but this is coercion, not leadership.'

This is also demonstrated by the existence of the so-called Hitler problem in the leadership literature. There is an actual debate, still unresolved, whether Hitler can be viewed as a proper leader, since his deeds were mostly evil. The typical story line is nicely captured by a popular Swedish textbook on organization analysis, where it is explicitly stated that Hitler cannot be viewed as a leader because leaders by definition must do what is socially useful and right (Bruzelius and Skärvad 2004: p. 369).

This is not to claim that leadership always is constructed as doing what is morally right. In fact, perhaps the most popular and frequent distinction between leaders, the distinction between task-orientation and relation-orientation (Yukl 1988), does not explicitly target the moral dimension, and it can be reasonably argued that this distinction does not really touch on moral issues at all. On the other hand, the relation-orientation at least implicitly hints at an ethics of care, while the task-orientation perhaps points towards a more utilitarian understanding of leadership conduct.

Thus, we can say that the moral dimension is firmly established, at least implicitly, even in very basic understandings of the leadership phenomenon, and at least one of these understandings – the task-orientation – very well admits darker or coercive tools. Yet, probably for reasons that are fairly easy to understand, most leadership research tends to look away from the dark side of leadership, unless it is not being explicitly framed as dysfunctional or otherwise problematic. Again, to be clear, it does seem feasible to view the dark side of leadership as inherently problematic, but it deserves to be taken seriously as a matter of descriptive inquiry, at least so we know what practices are involved, how they function, and their consequences, before we start to condemn them.

Although the dark side of leadership clearly is overlooked, it hasn't been completely ignored. To be fair, there exists some previous work on the more sinister practices of leadership. Leaders have been constructed as petty tyrants (Ashforth 1994), abusive supervisors (Tepper 2000), and bullies (Einarsen *et al.* 2007, Harvey *et al.* 2007, Ferris *et al.* 2007), and the journal *Leadership Quarterly* dedicated a special issue on destructive leadership (2007, where also Einarsen *et al.* and Ferris *et al.* appeared). This chapter will follow the lead of Einarsen *et al.*, Harvey *et al.* and Ferris *et al.* and take a hard look at the bully as a metaphor for leaders.

Why would one use the bully as a metaphor for leaders and leadership? Obviously, there are other dark metaphors available: the sociopath, the rapist, the contract killer, the hit man, the backstabber, and the turncoat easily spring to mind. All of these metaphors resonate with certain organizational practices traceable to leader conduct. Those laid-off from company restructuring may wonder who put a contract on him or her, and who wielded the axe. The community damaged by a relocated factory may wonder how decision-makers can sleep at night. Anyone who has got lost in the moral mazes of modern bureaucracies, admirably documented by Jackall (1988), may feel entitled to ponder why loyalties suddenly ceased to exist and why allies turn up on the enemy side in turf wars.

However, although these metaphors resonate with actual reality and are also clearly metaphorical – it is safe to assume that very few are prepared to believe that leaders actually are contract killers – they all share the quality of being a bit too specific and narrow, to inform of practices that are too marginal for real leaders, and do not seem to be able to add anything important or illuminating to the kernel of truth about leaders. In this chapter, it is assumed that the bully is a metaphor that is better equipped to simultaneously add depth to our understanding of the leadership phenomenon, and illuminate darker practices that move people at the leaders' command. It is no accident that Gordon Brown was depicted as a bully, rather than as a sociopath or a thug. The use of the bully as a metaphor for leadership draws upon Cornelissen's (2005, see also Chapter 3) idea that the extension of a metaphor involves three generic steps: (1) developing a generic structure (2) developing and elaboration of the blend which comes from the interaction of two bodies of knowledge, and (3) then inputting the emergent broader meaning into broader theory. Below, the chapter continues with an outline of the generic structure of the bully, then proceeds to a discussion fusing leadership and bullying themes, and ends with discussion of the scale and scope of the bully metaphor.

In popular vernacular the bully is a person who pushes other people around. The dictionary that comes with Mac OS X Leopard defines the bully as: 'a person who uses strength or power to harm or intimidate those who are weaker'. The dictionary also informs us that bully can be used as a verb: to 'use superior strength or influence to intimidate (someone), typically to force him or her to do what one wants'. The execution of strength, force, harm, and intimidation are clearly activities that are not nice (but perhaps not necessarily morally wrong) and also clearly linked to the exercise of power. Leaders exercise power but it is clearly wrong and misleading to equate leaders with bullies. This link does, however, seem important and edifying, and justifies the view of leaders as bullies in a wider and more systematic sense, and not just as a metaphor that casts light over marginal or incidental leadership practices.

What and who is the bully then? In brief, the bully is persistently and systematically engaged in intimidating, malicious and stigmatizing acts (Einarsen 1999, Tracy et al. 2006). Hodson et al. (2006: 384–385) understand bullying as 'blatant emotional abuse by a superior . . . /or/ . . . subtle violation of interpersonal norms . . . that . . . inflicts "dignitary harm" on the victim, highlighting the role of hierarchy and subtlety'.

Unsurprisingly, the bully has a presence in the workplace literature, often to distinguish between harassment, which is legally codified, and other forms of abuse. Nelson and Lambert (2001: 84) argue that bullying is distinctive from harassment since

> its power derives not from violation of specific norms, but from the potential effects of bullying to intimidate, humiliate, coerce, and finally to silence those who fall victim to it. . . . The term 'bullying' also directs attention to a certain type of conduct and its effects in a way that is both familiar and trenchant.

Vega and Comer (2005: 101) also specifically differentiate bullying from harassment:

> Bullying is not about benign teasing, nor does it include off-colour jokes, racial slurs, or unwelcome advances that are the hallmark of legally defined harassment. Workplace bullying is the pattern of destructive and generally deliberate demeaning of co-workers or subordinates that reminds us of the schoolyard bully. Unlike the schoolyard bully, the workplace bully is an adult, usually (but not always) aware of the impact of his or her behaviour on others.

The bully thus has a broader and less conspicuous palette than the harasser. He or she targets specific persons, untroubled by gender, race and ethnicity. Anyone can be a victim. The bully is not necessarily informed by stereotypes, nor is he or she always driven by psychological motives, such as sadism. Anyone can be the bully. If anything, being a superior, 'a leader', facilitates bullying because it provides a natural pulpit and exaggerates and reframes behaviour that otherwise would have been viewed as benign in nature. A constant flow of negative feedback is easier to deflect if it comes from a peer, rather than a superior, and a constant flow of negative feedback will, at some point in time, cease to operate as informative and eventually diminish, demean and destroy.

ILLUSTRATING BULLYING

In organizational life, bullying may play out as in the example below, taken from an internal meeting at a management consulting firm. The company is a big firm – it has over 10,000 employees worldwide and caters to all consultancy market niches, but claims to be particularly strong at implementation. We meet the firm at one of its devices for managing knowledge: the competence group. The competence group is organized around a theme (for example database management, organization design, and, as is the case for the example below, management process) and consists of organizational members that gather regularly and exchange experiences about the theme. The meeting is fairly typical for competence groups. It consists of two lectures, one by a customer and one by a senior manager at Toptop. There are around twenty people in the audience, ranging from newcomers to senior partners. The mix is common for competence groups. The meeting introduces a new management process: Value management. The example is taken from the senior consultant's talk.

Mark has recently worked with a client company that uses value management, or so he at least claims. He suggest the client is very satisfied with the tool, but I [the author] must confess that the meaning of value management escaped me from his presentation. Mark describes the project but does not indicate the actual results delivered by value management.

This does not stop the participants from being enthusiastic about the idea. One of the junior consultants becomes sufficiently enthusiastic to suffer from severely clouded judgment. He asks Mark whether the firm is working on this, and makes clear in no uncertain terms how important he thinks this is, and his lack of patience with those who block initiatives of this kind. Unfortunately, he has completely forgotten that Jake, a senior partner, sits in the audience, and that senior partners may dislike to be bullied into action on vague initiatives with unclear upsides by freshmen with a tenure no longer than a year at the firm. Ominously, he has also forgotten that a senior partner may take offence at being painted as roadblocks.

Mark can't resist taking advantage of a situation with so much potential fireworks, and passes on the question to Jake, who makes clear what he thinks of cocky nobodies. He fires back in a sour and moody voice, and asks what the poor young fellow means, clearly affronted by the question. The young consultant, who slowly realizes that he is completely out of his depth, attempts to walk back his question, while struggling with his voice and the coherence of his speech, and with crimson rising at an alarming rate at his cheeks. Jake finally puts the knife in and finishes off the young consultant by vague references to policy documents that clearly are only accessible to members not likely to put their feet in their mouths. Mark, amused by the exchange, announces that value management is going to be inaugurated as a subject for a competence group the next day – hence showing that senior management indeed is on top of this question. Jake makes clear that he wants to change the subject. The only reminder of the incident is the crimson face of our young friend, which lasts the rest of the meeting.

In this case bullying is carried out through *humiliation*. Humiliation is achieved through making the target feel ashamed and foolish by injuring dignity and self-respect. Humiliation targets the victim's sense of self and social stature by denying him or her the right to proper place or voice. In a way, humiliation is an endemic feature of everyday life, and is likely to be inflicted upon victims without bad faith. However, the fact that normal life is rife with humiliating occasions also makes it useful for the bully, who thrives on drawing on the rich opportunities offered by everyday interaction.

The bully may look for several ways of humiliating the victim: the exclusion from a group, the undermining of a vocational or professional claim, and the rebuttal of the victim's assertion to be somebody. All are on display in the excerpt above. In a way, we are perhaps not surprised that the junior consultant is smacked down. In fact, we may even be entitled to think that the young man is asking for it. He is brash, cocky and out of line. On the other hand, there are lots of ways to deal with arrogance that do not include extended humiliation. One might wonder why the senior consultant finds it necessary to invite the partner to respond to the unfortunate comment, and why the partner chose to demolish the poor fellow, forcing him to a lopsided and mismatched question and answer session where the junior consultant gets crushed without abandon, and where the lasting remains of the encounter are imprinted on his reddened face for the rest of the meeting.

From a Goffmanesque micro-sociology perspective the encounter is baffling. After all, according to this perspective, social encounters are almost entirely geared towards avoiding these kinds of face-losing interactions, where the polite varnish of social structure is removed and hierarchy, raw power and naked authority rear their heads. On the other hand, this is perhaps precisely why the encounter is instructive for understanding the use value of humiliation. It denies authority, undermines voice, and establishes and confirms privileging power structures.

BROADER ASSESSMENT OF THE METAPHOR

There is a legitimate case to be made that bullying as a phenomenon is always repugnant and morally indefensible. Also, bullying as a leadership practice may generally be dysfunctional and destructive. This is how the leader as a bully is typically framed in the literature. For example, Harvey *et al.* (2007) view the bully as an archetypical destructive leader, and Einarsen *et al.* (2007)

depict the bully as a prime example of a failed leader. Generally speaking, these arguments are convincing, although there might be situations were bully-like behaviour is neither out of place, nor morally wrong, as, for example, in the occasional dressing down of a wrongdoer. Bullying may never make sense in the long run, but it is possible to imagine situations when bully-like conduct may have productive outcomes.

This is, for example, suggested by Ferris *et al.* (2007). They argue that bullying might be a strategic device for accomplishing positive outcomes in very specific circumstances. In particular, they point to the usefulness of understanding bullying as a way of engaging in organizational politics. Here, bullying can be framed as a way of advancing the agenda of a group interest, and not necessarily as an individual behaving as an egotistical jerk. Generally speaking, Ferris *et al.* indicate that bullying might be an effective tactic towards 'low maturity members' that might produce short-term gains for the organization, as well as for the bully.

It seems fruitful to expand Ferris *et al.*'s claims somewhat. There might exist typified situations where bullying may achieve desirable results. It may, for example, be useful when attempting to create a crisis mood to facilitate radical change. The literature on organizational change, for example, reliably informs us that people tend to prefer the status quo and resist change. Change is thus hard to achieve at least when no-one or nothing is rocking the boat. Bullying-like tactics may be a way of rocking the boat, goading reluctant and resisting organizational members to realize, or at least buy into the notion that a crisis is imminent, the status quo untenable, and swift action needed. Here, there are obvious parallels to the commander metaphor, developed elsewhere in this book. Both the punisher and the antagonizer types of the commander metaphor are likely to use tools and tactics that are tantalizingly close to bullying, if not the genuine article.

Ironically, bully-like behaviour is also quite useful when one wants to stabilize a volatile situation. As Goffman (1959) is fond of pointing out, most social situations are robustly controlled by etiquette and there is rarely a need for interventions to stabilize a situation. Having said that, social situations sometimes heat up, and leaders may think that stabilizing intervention is called for, even if it means engaging in bully-like conduct. In this sense, bully-like behaviour may be useful in upholding stability when the status quo is threatened.

Bully-like conduct may also yield productive results when superiors need to remind minions about relative differences in status. In particular, it may be useful in recreating and confirming status difference in otherwise egalitarian or symbolic-deprived contexts. The point here is not to engage in a discussion about the merits of a particular policy. The point is to remind everybody that there is a status hierarchy operating at the company, and also certain rules for how to speak in the presence of power. Humiliation may for example be an effective strategy for a leader with an under-represented gender, at least in a certain context. The author of this chapter once had a female ex-US army officer in the audience when he made a presentation of an earlier version of this chapter, and she explained how her instructors had been explicit in mentioning humiliation as a particularly effective way for female officers to get the proper respect and deference from their subordinates. In this sense, humiliation may be used to not only neutralize a perceived disadvantage, but also to elevate it into an advantage. Not only were you humiliated, but you were humiliated *by a girl.*

Finally, bully-like behaviour may be useful to enforce ideology, in particular when ideology faces countervailing forces and resistance. Such bullying is likely to happen at the margins and in a strategic fashion. History tells us that ideology is enforced through harsh means. The history of organized labour reminds us that most of the 'debate' between labour activists and employer representatives was hardly civil in the early days of unionization, and often deteriorated into outright violence. Of course, authoritarian parties all tend to have their paramilitary wing, set to scare the hell out of perceived enemies.

Obviously, this kind of obtrusive or hard enforcement is unlikely to happen in contemporary organizations in Western democracies, save the odd illegal alien-stuffed sweatshop. Here, the bullying is likely to be velvety, soft and unpredictable. It is not necessarily aimed to scare people. Rather it aims to make the victim reactive, defensive and fundamentally unsure what is going on. The resulting uncertainty makes room for the ideology, and creates a situation where it is unlikely to be rejected. This, in combination with the reaffirmation of relative status, may be all it needs.

Again, this section is not intended as a defence for bully-like behaviour. Rather it is intended as an exploration of potential productive outcomes, at least in the short run. It may be the case that bullying always is a losing proposition, at least in the long run. However, it is clear that short-run gains can be made and, of course, the world of business is an opportunistic place and not exactly known for patience.

UNPACKING BULLYING

The bully has several tactics at his or her disposal. The tactics have a common denominator, as demonstrated above. They all aim to undermine, coerce, exclude and silence. Below, two additional tactics, apart from humiliation, are highlighted: malice and intimidation. This is obviously not an exhaustive list but it highlights common and effective tactics that bullies put in play.

MALICE

Malice is the harbouring and execution of ill will, and the intention to do evil. Malice may be brought forward and cultivated in passionate ways, as you would against your nemesis or arch-enemy, but it may also be executed in a disinterested and cool way. There is no reason to believe that the bully has a preference for either form, but here I am going to exemplify malice of the second kind, the aloof and disinterested form. The case below, from a Danish professional service firm, illustrates malice through unofficially sanctioned forms of controlling gossip. This illustration is a special case of bullying as it portrays the leader as directly encouraging bullying at the workplace by hiring a person to be the object of gossip, thereby assuming that further bullying is controlled and encapsulated.

The leader applies a style similar to what Ribeiro *et al.* (1995: 43) called 'a vehicle for emotional ventilation'. The person is recruited not due to skills or experiences, but mainly on the basis of being bullied.

> The person does not understand that he/she is being a gossip target, and it makes the rest of the employees feel good.
>
> (Production manager)

The superior also notes that gossiping may add to social cohesion.

> Just as gossip can pull team members apart, gossip can also draw team members together. It is a managerial assignment to compose a team in such a manner that the right team members are drawn together. The 'gossip vent' plays an important part here. She is functioning as a kind of a virtual water cooler.
>
> (Production manager)

When prompted the manager gave the following reason for dealing with gossip in this particular way:

> malicious gossip can lead to employee turnover. We have experienced losing valued employees because gossip made the team atmosphere unhealthy and stressful. Even employees, who do not partake in the chatter, are influenced by the gossip and rumours.
>
> (Production manager)

Gossip has been shown to perform important collective functions, such as contributing to group cohesiveness (Tebbutt and Marchington 1997: 716) and thus contributing to unite a group (Noon and Delbridge 1993). However, as the manager notes, gossip may just as easily tear a group apart. To get a handle on this, superiors try to control this through obviously malicious recruitment strategies, although with an instrumental twist.

> Our main agenda is production effectiveness, and we are very dependent on manual workers who can work on shifts in a hectic environment with many changes. Our turnover rates are high which is why we will go to great lengths to keep the best [employees]. Those who have been with us for many years gain power, and are in many ways easy targets for gossiping. The dilemma we face is that those employees are also the ones with most knowledge. Those employees we'll like to keep. We therefore have to direct the gossip in other directions to maintain a healthy environment.
>
> (Production manager)

The excerpt shows clearly that the supervisor strategically divides his subordinates into valuable and less valuable employees. In relation to gossip, this means that a superior on purpose directs gossip at the less valuable person in order to ensure a healthy working climate for the remainder of the employees. In fact, he makes this strategic choice very well aware of the fact that it hurts the 'gossip target'.

> We are well aware that the person employed with the purpose of being the target for gossip might leave after a while. But we generally have a high turnover rate, and in many aspects we are not calculating with this person in regard to production effectiveness.
>
> (Production manager)

Thus, it seems that everything is done in order to benefit the company. The superior allows 'objective' utilitarian calculations to show which employees to care for and which not to care for, and the actions are excused with the argument that it benefits the rest of the organization – in particular its efficiency. We thus get the impression that people matter overall, but the singular individual is not noticed. Superiors in the organization therefore deliberately and methodically construct a 'victim', with the purpose of benefiting the organization overall. The person applies for a job with the honest intention of contributing to the organization, but has no idea what kind of contribution will be asked for. Of course, anyone hired to be the target of informal but systematic and extensive abuse will eventually quit. The manager is aware of this, but does not consider the feelings of the victim, but values how the person in turning into a victim can benefit the rest of the employees' working climate.

Hiring a 'gossip vent' is of course my own subjective evaluation. I do not discuss this in an open forum, and I don't put it down in my selection sheet – it would probably not be politically correct. But it works! I have been doing this job for many years, and over the years you learn.

(Production manager)

The gossip strategy is thus not something that is formally discussed in the organization. In a sense the manager may not know that he is engaging in malicious practices. But by making the excuse that it works, and by keeping it informal, the strategy is widely used in the company. And as an informal strategy, it can be much more powerful than a formal one. Superiors, who have been with this company for years, all use it, and this points towards a very well established informal strategy.

One of the interesting things of this case is the question it asks about the morality of utilitarianism. The practice of hiring a gossip vent can clearly be morally defended on utilitarian grounds (it creates more social good than it destroys) but it also means that one apparently can defend malice on moral grounds. This kind of malice is likely to be encouraged by the instrumentalized nature of the modern corporation. Perhaps 'encouraged' is the wrong word, but the modern corporation certainly does not offer good defences against this form of malice, and it even makes it possible to defend it.

INTIMIDATION

Intimidation aims to frighten or overawe someone into submission, and to make them do the intimidator's bidding. Intimidation mostly plays on fear: on threats of physical violence, or threats towards one's ability to support oneself. Intimidation is clearly at display in this excerpt from the film adaptation of the David Mamet play *Glengarry Glen Ross*.

Blake:	Let me have your attention for a moment. 'Cause you're talkin' about what . . . you're talkin' 'bout . . . bitchin' about that sale you shot, some son of a bitch don't want to buy land, somebody don't want what you're selling, some broad you're trying to screw, so forth, let's talk about something important. Are they all here?
Williamson:	All but one.
Blake:	Well, I'm going anyway. Let's talk about something important. (*sees Levene pouring coffee*). Put that coffee down. Coffee's for closer's only. You think I'm fuckin' with

	you? I am not fuckin' with you. I'm here from downtown. I'm here from Mitch and Murray. And I'm here on a mission of mercy. Your name's Levene?
Levene:	Yeah.
Blake:	You call yourself a salesman, you son of a bitch.
Moss:	I don't gotta listen to this shit.
Blake:	You certainly don't pal 'cause the good news is you're fired. The bad news is you got all you got, just one week to regain your job, starting with tonight, starting with tonight's sits. Oh, have I got your attention now? Good. 'Cause we're adding a little something to this month's sale contest. As you all know, first prize is a Cadillac El Dorado. Anybody want to see second prize? Second prize is a set of steak knives. Third prize is you're fired. You get the picture? You laughing now? You got leads. Mitch and Murray paid good money. Get their names to sell them. You can't close the leads you're given, you can't close shit, you are shit, hit the bricks pal and beat it 'cause you are going out.
Levene:	The leads are weak.
Blake:	The leads are weak. The fuckin' leads are weak? You're weak. I've been in this business 15 years . . .
Moss:	What's your name?
Blake:	Fuck you, that's my name. You know why mister? Cause you drove a Hyundai to get here tonight, I drove an 80,000 dollar BMW. That's my name. (To Levene) And your name is you're wanting. You can't play in the man's game, you can't close them? Then go home and tell your wife your troubles. Because only one thing counts in this life. Get them to sign on the line which is dotted. You hear me you fuckin' faggots.

(From *Glengarry Glen Ross*)

The excerpt above is often seen as one of the highlights of the film, itself regularly touted as a one of few films that 'gets' business life in general and life as a high-pressure salesman in particular. One of the striking things with the scene is how uncomfortable it is to watch – peeking in on a brutal dressing down of regular salesmen by a highflying boss from headquarters. Another striking thing is the realism the scene captures. Yes, there are exaggerations. If a manager actually used these words he or she would probably be sued, or at least forced into anger management sessions. However, the scene captures and lays bare the tense, anxious and emotionally charged atmosphere of the dressing down. And it only ever so slightly dramatizes it, as anyone with the flimsiest of business experience will testify. One might not have been on the receiving side of it, but one has witnessed it, or at least surely knows someone that has.

The basic premise of the scene is that the Blake character is there to put fear in their hearts. This is achieved by firing them. However, this is a pretty pointless move if you want to achieve results in some form. Thus, the intimidator does not only frighten and threaten. He or she also tells the victim what to do. The Blake character illustrates that this has two main functions: to establish status hierarchy, I'm a winner and you are losers, and to establish preferred core truths, real salesmen close, and winning is what it is all about. The intimidator may take pleasure in engaging in one-upmanship but he or she needs to envisage a route where the victims can redeem themselves.

There is more method in this madness. As pointed out above, bullying-like tactics may be a way of injecting a sense of crisis and urgency. One may suggest that this is what the Blake character attempts to accomplish in his speech, although it is clear that the subtext of that particular speech is much murkier than an ordinary run-of-the-mill 'barbarians at the gate!' speech from an executive in a financially distressed corporation. Regardless, intimidation may put the stone into motion, and may facilitate change.

The scene is illustrative but admittedly extreme and perhaps a bit too fictitious to translate well into organizational realities. In real life, intimidation is likely to be achieved through softer and less obtrusive means. Consider, for example the excerpt below, from a meeting between the CEO of an educational organization and the school managers. The educational organization is a private alternative to public schools with a radical pedagogic agenda in Sweden. The company was founded not long after the Swedish parliament decided to give way to these kinds of initiatives in the name of diversity. Now, after almost ten years in business, the company has had rapid, organic and successful growth, where most schools score high on national tests. The CEO is often described as charismatic by his subordinates. He is exceptional and they are loyal. They see him as the main architect behind the radical vision and how this should be reached. The excerpt is taken from a manager dialogue: meetings that the CEO frequently holds with school managers (the term 'principal' is not used).

Steve (the CEO) says that he wants to end the meeting with a short movie. The movie is shot by three girls in the 8th grade and deals with the subjects of physics, chemistry, biology and medicine. One of the girls eloquently plays the hostess, while the other two girls play reporters. The feature is an impressive production, although there is some giggling in the audience on a couple of occasions, where the editing and performances fall a bit short.

When the film has ended and the light is put on, Steve slowly moves to the centre of the stage. He says 'It's so moving' with a weak and tearful voice. I [The I here is a colleague of mine, who witnessed the scene] start to feel a bit uncomfortable since I suspect that his reaction is faked. The atmosphere, however, is emotional and silence roams the room.

Steve breaks the silence and asks, in a humble voice, 'how would you grade the girls?' At the same time he constructs a table on the whiteboard with three rows headed by an A, a B and a C. Mike is first out and answers 'A'. The next one in line attempts to problematize the exercise and says that it depends on the performances during the semester. Steve repeats his question, and now all the weakness and tears in the voice are gone. The manager makes another attempt to problematize the task, but is interrupted by Steve who, now with some steel in his voice, repeats his question. The manager yields and says 'A'. An additional tally of ten people give the performance an 'A', and Steve marks them all in his table. After a handful of straight 'As' more, a newly recruited manager hedges with comments on the grammar used 'but an A'. Another newly recruited managers says that he 'wants to break the pattern, but I can't'. 'I appreciate the comment', Steve says. The tune doesn't change until Liz's turn, who offers a 'B'. Steve marks it in the table without comment. The final four managers all say 'A'.

Steve says: 'OK, you all think that they deserve an A, do you think that they got it?' and continues, 'the consequence is that they don't need to attend any more lectures in Swedish'. Long story short, this means that they would get an A as the final grade for secondary school, although they still are one year short of graduating. One of the managers smilingly shares that she used to teach one of the pupils. Steve continues and raises his voice 'we get 50,000 per pupil and year, let's give them 25,000 and we take 25,000 and they can present something, whatever, next'. Steve's comment is greeted with thundering laughter. He sure knows how to play a crowd. Steve leaves the room, amidst the laughter, bellowing 'you can combine competence development with profitability'.

In this excerpt, intimidation is not achieved through fear, at least not manifestly so, but rather through the skilful construction of overawing power. Steve creates an atmosphere of submission not by physical threats, but through a combination of soft-spoken sentimentalism and forceful determination. The participants are lured into accepting that the students have created an outstanding performance by Steve's emotional endorsement, and his swift and decisive silencing of dissent or attempts to relativize the performance.

Is this intimidation? Yes. Two things are especially telling. First, the attempt by one manager to introduce context and other factors for marking the students is effectively stopped and silenced by Steve, without meeting further resistance. The second telltale is the manager who wants to dissent, but cannot. Here we can see the extent of Steve's success in creating submission. He has established his way, and he has got the participants to accept and support it, seemingly without cost. He can even afford to explicitly and gracefully acknowledge the submission and tolerate Liz's dissenting view.

Then, to demonstrate his superiority, and their foolishness, he dresses them down. Do they realize that the students have got a final degree and don't need to go to school anymore? Isn't this an opportunity for a wonderful business model? Although the comments are packaged in fun and laughter, their main message is clear. There is a reason that Steve is on top and the rest of the managers are not. Interestingly, this appears to be the sole lesson of this episode. It does not say anything about the practices and standards the schools should adhere to. It does not say anything about the pedagogies teachers should engage in, or the kind of students the schools should try to reach out to. In the end, it is about reaffirming Steve as top dog, and his skills in reassuring that it will stay that way.

The chapter on the cyborg metaphor demonstrates a third way to intimidate, by seemingly effortless superiority. The perfection of the cyborg scares and alienates the leader from his or her subordinates, yet manages to motivate and inspire them. Here, the intimidation rests less on what the leader does to the subordinates and more in the awe the subordinates project on the leader. Thus, the leader may intimidate, not only by being in the face of his or her subordinates, or by manipulating them, but also by just creating a plausible impression of perfection.

LIMITS OF THE BULLY METAPHOR

It is clear that the bully metaphor has its uses and illuminates certain types of conduct and practices. However, it is prudent to say something about its limits and shortcomings too. One of the main problems with the bully metaphor is that it over-emphasizes sustained use of intimidation, humiliation and malice. Although leaders may feel tempted, or pressed, to engage in such tactics, they are likely to use these tactics only intermittently and presumably with great care or under great duress. There are several reasons for this, not the least being that bullying in the long run appears to be self-defeating for anyone that aspires to lead. Nobody really trusts a person that delights in others' submission.

Of course, the clever leader may take his or her cues from Machiavelli, and delegate the actual bullying to surrogates, thus making it possible to stay above the fray. However, the bully metaphor does not help us to understand that kind of evasive action, and is thus quite useless to highlight such behaviour. Here, other metaphors are more informative, such as the benevolent dictator, or Machiavellian power player.

Another problematic aspect of the metaphor is that it might overstate the critical case against leaders. In a sense, the metaphor may just be too powerful and vivid, and block out other productive ideas on the leadership phenomenon. There is a historical parallel. The fascist cult of the leader cast a dark shadow on the leadership phenomenon for roughly 30 years, raising social taboos that inhibited productive thinking about the phenomenon. The bully metaphor might, in a similar vein, be said to cast leaders in an overly critical light. Having said that, this type of critique is a bit unconvincing. This chapter is based on the argument that we know too little about the interface between leadership and bullying, which makes it difficult to argue that this understanding is too dominant.

A more valid critique against the bully metaphor is that it might focus on the wrong type of critique of the leadership phenomenon. Although bully-like behaviour may be a salient ingredient in contemporary organizations, it may not curry the flavour that much. It may simply be the case that bullying is an unfortunate but rare and fairly inconsequential by-product of failed recruitment processes. Continuous bullying behaviour is likely to be frowned upon and looked down on in modern organizations. The problem with leadership in democratic countries is perhaps not so much out-of-control bullies roaming about but rather the addiction to authoritative persons, as explored by the saint and the buddy metaphors.

However, there are some indications that bullying as a leadership practice might be salient in and endemic to business contexts. For example, Ludeman and Erlandson (2004) suggest that approximately 70 per cent of American executives are of the 'alpha male' type, who, when pressured 'tends to shift his leadership style from constructive and challenging to intimidating or even abusive' (Ludeman and Erlandson 2004: 2). According to Ludeman and Erlandson's (2004, 2007) characterization of the 'alpha male' – driven, decisive, aggressive, competitive, impatient, prone to anger – the 'alpha male' seems to be a bully waiting to happen (see also Chapter 7). There is a thin line between being decisive or intimidating, charismatic or manipulative, or bold or imposing. The general point in this chapter is to suggest that 'successful' organizational action may, for example, come from intimidation rather than decisiveness, and to offer the bully metaphor as a way of understanding such behaviours.

CONCLUSION

The dark undercurrents of the leadership phenomenon – fear, loathing, exclusion, marginalization and so on – are under-researched and poorly understood. As pointed out above, some define this problem away and claim that by exploiting the morally questionable one ceases to be a leader. Thus, leaders are always doing what is morally right by definition. As should be clear by now, this is not a particularly useful idea. Organizations are rife with episodes where leaders, or people claiming to be leaders, use fear and other forms of coercive techniques to make people do things. To broaden and deepen our understanding of the leadership phenomenon, we need concepts and metaphors that capture and highlight such conduct and techniques.

This chapter has offered the bully as a metaphor to explore the dark side of leadership. In particular, it has highlighted how intimidation, humiliation and malice may be evoked as tactics for leaders to achieve desired results. Again, this is not to claim that this is an exhaustive list, but it is effective in highlighting how bullying operates in organizations, and what it may achieve. This move has its obvious risks for potential misunderstandings so let's clarify what is *not* suggested by this move. First, it is *not* suggested that all leaders are bullies. The premise of this book is that leadership is not one thing. It might not even be a thing, and is best understood metaphorically – as viewed as something else. Hence, what is suggested is that leaders who may engage in conduct that is bully-like, are best described by being understood as bully-like.

Second, it is *not* suggested that leaders are immoral or amoral. Rather what is suggested is that we are missing important clues on leadership by restricting ourselves to the moralistic understanding of leadership – that leaders by definition always do the right or the good thing, and that they disqualify themselves from being leaders by doing bad things. The argument is that it is preferable to be agnostic about the moral worth of leadership conduct. The moral worth of leadership conduct is a debate about morality, and not a conceptual debate.

Third, it is *not* claimed that bullying, or the tactics associated with bullying, is necessarily providing effective results. Put bluntly, that is an empirical question, and there are lots of reasons why bullying is counter-productive, as well as productive. But to think that bullying always is counter-productive, from an instrumental point of view, is a fantasy, and to look away from the way fear, humiliation, intimidation and so on shape behaviour in organizations is simply to look away from everyday realities for many organizational members. These feelings are artefacts, reactions to external probing, and this chapter humbly suggests that some of the probing may emerge from people we usually label as leaders.

10

COMMUNICATING LEADERSHIP METAPHORS

Gail T. Fairhurst

T HROUGHOUT HISTORY, LEADERSHIP HAS been a powerful idealization for society, serving causes both good and bad. Wars have been fought in its name, great science undertaken (countries have gone to the moon and back in its name), and some of us dutifully report to work each day with leadership as our primary goal. However, as powerful an idealization as it is, there is no simple explanation of its workings, nor its effects (Alvesson and Sveningsson 2003a; 2003b). It has kept writers, consultants, and researchers busy for decades now fueling an industry of advice and analysis, including books of this very nature.

Many have lost patience with this kind of activity because leadership research findings are often contested and shocking to some, and there is no universally agreed-upon definition of leadership. Until relatively recently, the latter was a cause of some considerable concern (Barker 1997; Rost 1991). Historically, leadership study has been dominated by U.S.-based leadership psychology and, true to form, psychologists generally believe that the answers to questions about leadership reside in the powerful inner motor all leaders supposedly have.[1] Moreover, most have done so using the discourse of science and the search for generalizable knowledge. The trouble is this inner motor has rather complex inner workings that resist the urge to generalize either because multivariate research produces too many qualifications and contingencies, or the advice from the business press can be obvious and banal.

But perhaps part of leadership's enduring complexity is also because the psychology model of leadership hasn't been road tested enough. By this I mean perhaps we should heed the lessons of more European and communication-based views of leadership.[2] Both focus on language and practices as leadership phenomena in their own right, not simply outcomes associated with the inner motor. Their concern is not with what language might represent, but what it is doing vis-à-vis the uses or functions to which it has been put (Potter and Wetherell 1987).

Metaphors are a powerful tool in this regard because, as the chapters in this book demonstrate, they can be used by leadership actors – designated leaders, emergent leaders, and followers – to understand and shape the world around them through influential acts of organizing. Even in those precise moments of communicating when holding oneself or another accountable for the actions taken, metaphorical language emerges in the labeling, explaining, and justifying of one path over another. Their remarkable power lies in the ability to create and privilege new understandings while obscuring others as they become the scaffolding around which thought coheres (Lakoff and Johnson 1980).

It is because they are so useful to leadership actors that they are useful to analysts as well. However, although it makes pedagogical sense to organize this book chapter by chapter each with a different metaphor, we must take care not to let metaphors reify behavior so that the fluidity with which leadership actors shift among metaphors is obscured. For example, how might the leader who is a commander also turn cyborg or gardener or saint? This is an important question. Some leaders may move easily among the metaphors, while others may choose to operate within a more restricted range; for example, those with a highly controlling style may find it uncomfortable to move beyond commander.

Thus, the primary aim of this chapter is to show how leadership metaphors, generally, and those in this book, specifically, serve as cognitive and communicative resources for leadership actors. Towards that end, it will be important to discuss the origin of leadership metaphors, how leadership actors may use metaphors, how they enter the communication process, and how leadership actors may or may not shift metaphors in their performances. This chapter then concludes with a discussion of follower metaphors and the implications of leader–follower metaphors for use in training and development.

WHERE DO LEADERSHIP METAPHORS ORIGINATE?

The answer to this question is that metaphors derive from systems of thought within society at a given time in history. The philosopher, Michel Foucault (1972; 1990), calls these systems of thought "discourses" and views them as the primary vehicles of culture. As historically grounded sets of ideas and practices, discourses shape and are shaped by how members of a culture see and act toward given phenomena. As we will see below, discourses can be organized and expressed in metaphorical terms.

To understand the historical anchoring of discourse, Foucault (1995) wrote about how the penal system in the West has evolved from punishment directed toward the body during the eighteenth century to punishment directed toward the mind in more modern times. The former discourse produces belief in and practices involving torture, while the latter subscribes to the merits of incarceration and suspended rights. To live during either time period is to be subject to the dominant discourses of the day – ways of thinking and acting toward phenomena that are made to seem quite normal.

For a leadership example comparing historical time periods, consider the Warren Bennis and Robert Thomas (2002b) book, *Geeks and Geezers: How Era, Values, and Defining Moments Shape Leaders*. Their focus is on two groups of leaders: those under the age of 30 or "geeks" and those over the age of 70 or "geezers." However, it is not the generations per se that interest these authors, but those defining events in which leaders and their cohorts come to share history and culture. Note also the specific metaphors attached to these groups: "geeks" are shorthand for "computer geeks," and "geezers" sardonically refer to "old people."

For example, "geezers" are products of an analog era whose tools and objects were the slide rule, record albums, and typewriters. Such tools prompt a linear and mechanical view of the world where experience is key. By contrast, "geeks" are products of a digital era and the profoundly transformative nature of its tools and objects such as televisions, computers, and the Internet. All of these encourage thinking around nonlinearity and living systems. As such, geeks possess a "beginner's mind" that supposedly delivers insight in ways that (geezer) experience does not.

In the same way that "geeks" and "geezers" are anchored in discourse, so are the leadership metaphors in this book although they may not be explicitly identified in this way. For example, many of the authors mention "contemporary society" and the interests that characterize it. From the leader as saint chapter (Chapter 4), Alvesson observes a "booming interest" in morality by society and business at large that has impacted on leadership. From the leader as buddy chapter, Sveningsson and Blom point to a therapeutic ethos in contemporary society that increasingly influences how leadership is enacted in the workplace. Huzzard and Spoelstra's leader as gardener chapter similarly notes the influence of the North American self-help tradition and its discourses of personal growth on the self-help literature on leadership. From Spicer's leader as commander chapter, Mr. Wolfe resides in the industrialized West in which the military-industrial complex has long been a combined presence, for example, in the ways that aspects of military life characterize organizational life and leadership (Grint 2000). In the leader as cyborg chapter, Muhr invokes modern cultural images like Schwarzenegger's menacing cyborg character in the *Terminator* and the automatons and robots of a modern technological society in which machines do wondrous things. Finally, in the leader as bully chapter, Kärreman refers to the dark side of leadership invoking culturally significant images like the "playground bully," but also "sociopath," "hit man," "backstabber," "turncoat," and so on.

In truth, metaphors abound in contemporary society, emerging not just from society at large but, as just alluded to, its self-help traditions. This includes the popular management industry, which of late has introduced such metaphors (and discourses) for leaders as "toxin handlers" of raw emotions (speaking of the need for emotional intelligence) (Frost 2003) and "alpha male syndrome" for dominating leaders run amuck (Ludeman and Erlandson 2006). Leaders as "heroes" and "visionaries" associated with new market economies have been around for a while now, but these are anchored as much in the scientific literature on leadership as the popular press (Bass 1985; Conger 1989).

Specific industries, professions, and institutions can also be the source of metaphors. For example, "playing God" takes on new meaning for doctor-managers who bring pathology not healing to administering (increasingly) integrated health care systems, and "patriarchy" redoubles with meaning in the Catholic Church and Islam, religions that worship masculine deities and actively bar women from significant leadership roles. Female leaders have been termed "queen bees" or "mothers" (Kanter 1977). Note also how several metaphorical discourses institutionalized in a business context, such as "journey," "game," "war," and "machine" (Clancy 1989), each have their leadership counterparts: "navigator," "team captain," "commander," and "controller" respectively.

Thus, leadership metaphors derive from a host of discourses marking contemporary society, discourses that members of that society are exposed to in varying degrees and as life's opportunities dictate.

HOW DO LEADERSHIP ACTORS ACTUALLY USE METAPHORS?

As Alvesson and Spicer allow in their introductory chapter, leadership actors may use metaphors in at least three ways. First, metaphors are, without question, powerful figures of speech because of their ability to shape meaning in novel ways (Lakoff and Johnson 1980). Their effect is to surprise, delight, and/or illuminate the listener. It is the reason that leaders have been urged for some time now to pay attention to their speech and story making abilities (Clancy 1989; Ibarra and Lineback 2005; McKee 2003; Shamir and Eilam 2005) and why successful leaders are "managers of meaning" (Bennis and Nanus 1985; Fairhurst and Sarr 1996; Smircich and Morgan 1982).

Second, especially when considered collectively, metaphors add dimensionality to a subject through their ability to portray it through many different lenses (Morgan 1997). For example, when leaders give extensive feedback, such an act might be seen as "gardening" because of its development potential, "commanding" because of its telling qualities, and/or "bullying" because of the emotional tone and so on. When analyzing their own or others' performances, leadership actors can thus better understand the range of positive and negative characteristics and consequences based on one view of their actions over another – just as Alvesson and Spicer have done with their multi-metaphor view of leadership with this volume, Gareth Morgan (1997) before them for "organization," and many others who have followed this rich path to analysis.

Finally, some metaphors derive their salience not just as a linguistic device or a lens to be applied, but as a means by which leadership actors actually construct and experience organizational life in relation to them (Smith and Eisenberg 1987). For example, consider Van Maanen's (1991) cultural analysis of Disneyland as a "smile factory." The "manufacturing of fun" appears nonsensical until one recognizes the cultural discourses that management deploys to produce these smiles. In particular, Disneyland is famous for its use of the metaphorical language of the theater, which effectively disciplines employees to be "members of a cast," wear "costumes" not uniforms, and carefully circumscribes their onstage, offstage, and backstage performances. To wit, once in "costume," one cannot deviate from the scripted role performance. Whether one is a Disney character or a member of a cleaning crew, all are subject to the formal rules, supervision, and (emotional) labor involved in such informal behaviors as smiling, pleasantry, and courtesy. The power of the "smile factory" lies in the ways in which Disney employees construct and experience their organization in relation to the theater (albeit with factory-like qualities) that, simultaneously, creates the Disney experience.

Thus, members of the same linguistic community can usually understand and linguistically deploy the theater metaphor, at least in general terms, but Disney employees will live it (or risk losing their jobs). From a managerialist perspective, the most successful Disney employees *internalize* or *master* the metaphor. The net effect of internalizing a metaphor is a set of well developed mental models for an actor in which the metaphor serves an organizing logic for specific ways of talking and acting in the presence of relevant others.

However, such mastery may be more or less difficult depending upon the individual, the metaphor, and the situation. For example, to the extent that leadership actors actually see their identities in terms of a specific metaphor, its use will be anchored in *patterned* behavior and the ways in which they *routinely* account for their actions – thus making it more resistant to change. Mr. Gentle from the Sveningsson and Blom chapter poses one such example in this regard.

Yet, it is also true that certain metaphors are more or less easy to master. For instance, leaders may have an easier time mastering the commander metaphor because the experience and desire for control is so central to the human experience. However, mastering the cyborg metaphor may be more difficult given the emotional and physical toll it can exact, however many *Terminator* movies one has watched.

Likewise, we may ask, what are the opportunities available to use a particular metaphor? Here the demands and tasks of the work context often circumscribe metaphor use such as we see with the affinity for the commander metaphor in crisis management, a routine occurrence in high reliability organizations (Weick *et al.* 1999). Strongly religious organizations might also self-consciously reject discourses of the night and bullying behavior antithetical to their established norms and values that are more likely to be rooted in "gardening" or "buddy" behavior.

To summarize, metaphors are linguistic devices, lenses for viewing the world, and a means by which leadership actors construct and experience the organizational worlds around them. Exactly how one comes to adopt one metaphorical discourse over another lies likely in the life stories of leadership actors and their exposure to, for example, successful bullying, autocratic, saintly, or nurturing role models and their respective discourses. It also depends upon the linguistic communities in which they reside and the norms established for specific metaphor use given the tasks they perform.

HOW DO METAPHORS ENTER THE COMMUNICATIONS PROCESS FOR LEADERSHIP ACTORS?

Bennis and Thomas (2002) observed that "geeks" and "geezers" each had a way of talking about their worlds. In interviews with both groups of leaders, each drew upon a different set of *themes*; their *metaphors, concepts of interest,* and *terminology* or *jargon* differed; and they posed different *arguments*. For example, impacted by the Great Depression and World War II, geezers told stories of hardship borne by their immigrant parents (themes). Their formative period was 1945–1954. They addressed the shaping role of the military in their organizations, as military concepts such as "chain of command" found their way into big business (concepts of interest and metaphors). Finally, for geezers hard work was essential to get ahead in this world, and the need to "pay your dues" was crucial (familiar arguments). Theirs was an era of limits, and their language use reflected such limits.

By contrast, the historical era for geeks was an era of options; their formative period was 1991–2000. The stories they told were not about making a living, but making history and having an impact (themes). Because geeks were born in an era of technology, growth, and globalization, theirs is not a search for a living wage as much as it is a search for meaning and identity (more themes). Gone was enduring loyalty to any organization, and in its place came the language of "entrepreneurship" and "entrepreneurial selves" in which the self became yet another "project" intertwined with one's career (terminology and metaphor).[3] Moreover, geeks increasingly argued for work–life balance as they often experienced or saw first hand the destructive effects of a parent's life given over to work and little else (familiar arguments).

That different story themes, concepts of interest, terminology, metaphors, and familiar arguments mark the language of geeks and geezers is common sense. But what we should not miss is that as historical eras play themselves out, it is the *collective experience* of its defining events, people, objects, tools, and so on that gives rise to ways of talking and seeing the world – in other words, *(cultural) discourse*. A really excellent way to think about discourse then is as a system of thought complete with its own *tool bag* of terms, concepts of interest, themes, familiar arguments, *and* metaphors for leadership actors to draw upon to describe, explain, or justify their place in the world at any given moment (Potter and Wetherell 1987; Wetherell 1998).[4] When viewed in this way, discourse seems much less reified and more "realizable," or likely to come to life, in everyday interaction and practices.

Metaphors are a particularly important tool in this tool bag given their ability to generate new meanings in figure–ground relationships where certain meanings are privileged and others are backgrounded or hidden. For example, writing about the appropriateness of metaphors of the night for the dark side of leadership, Kärreman argues:

> All of these metaphors resonate with certain organizational practices traceable to leader conduct. The laid-off from a company restructuring may wonder who put a contract on him or her, and who wielded the axe. The community wounded by a relocated factory may wonder how decision-makers can sleep at night.
>
> (p. 164)

To understand metaphors of the night as a culture member is to be able to argue for the relevance of such meanings when applied to other subject matter, in this case, the dark side of leadership. Night metaphors work well in unearthing this dark side, a topic often ignored in the leadership business press whose interests tend to underscore leadership's positive contributions to society. However, consider how the night metaphor also hides meaning. From Kärreman we see a rich array of dark images including a central emphasis on the bully (and a preference for agnosticism about the moral worth of leader conduct), but very little on how good and evil often coexist.

Similarly, recall Mr. Gentle and Janet, two managers from Sveningsson and Blom's chapter on the leader as a buddy. Both managers readily offer a philosophy in which they defend their efforts to make their people feel good. One gets the sense that their philosophies are identity-based and rather habitually argued given the variations on the same arguments they pose throughout the chapter. These arguments are part of their linguistic tool bags that they draw from as communicating actors, in this case, being interviewed by Sveningsson and Blom. In particular, note how Mr. Gentle repeatedly emphasizes "that people feel good and that you are sensitive to people" in the chapter (p. 99). He elaborates:

> What is it that you [as a leader] want? Well, you want positive employees that raise themselves and work harder and more positive. It's about that get people in a better mood.
>
> (p. 102)

From the same chapter, Janet's language game echoes that of House:

> I know this thing about being responsible for people. I listen to people, I sense moods. I've had this thing about responsibility for people. I'm working to make my employees feel good. I want to back them up, but it always has to be good for the company.
>
> (p. 102)

Buddy behavior and feel-good efforts by these leaders cast leadership, in Sveningsson and Blom's terms, as "an act of watching and being vigilant and observant about people's well being" (p. 102). Yet, the metaphor obscures the instrumentality of such efforts, in Mr. House's case to improve compliance and produce more, and in Janet's case "for the good of the company" as the single most important criterion dictating her show of concern. So the metaphors allow our leadership actors to argue persuasively for a particular way to lead, while minimizing the leaders' motives behind such efforts.

In summary, as members of society, leadership actors are exposed to the dominant discourses of the day. These discourses effectively function as linguistic tool bags by supplying actors with metaphors (for leadership and many other subjects), but also habitual forms of argument, terms, concepts of interest, and themes. Metaphors thus emerge here as one of a number of linguistic devices in these tool bags.

HOW CAN LEADERSHIP ACTORS SHIFT AMONG METAPHORS?

If we see the metaphors from the perspective of the discourses from which they originate, discourses that effectively function as tool bags for communicating actors, we can see how in theory, at least, this tool bag should be able to expand in the presence of multiple discourses. Are leadership actors exposed to multiple discourses? Without question, for as members of Western society, they have only to watch television or go to the movies any weekend to see images of the military, therapy, religion, technology, or the dark forces of human nature (sometimes all in the same film!) thus invoking their respective discourses. In so doing, it reinforces how all culture members may see and act towards a multiplicity of phenomena at any given time.

Television and movies notwithstanding, there are certainly many other more or less mediated cultural experiences, including work, psychotherapy, religious gatherings, military service, and so on, which expose leadership actors to a multiplicity of discourses and, by implication, multiple leadership metaphors. When leadership actors are viewed simultaneously as communicators and cultural inhabitants, shifting from one metaphor to the next can be done with relative ease to the extent that a discourse is made relevant by the situation and leadership actors become subject to its ways.[5]

However, recall our earlier discussion regarding the mastery of a metaphor and that one or more metaphors might be: (a) firmly anchored in a leader's identity and thus resistant to change; (b) more or less easy to master, for example, in the cases of the commander versus the cyborg; and (c) called for (or not) by the tasks and the work involved. These forces are certainly very real and should not be minimized. Yet, it is worth noting that whatever the forces at work to restrict the range of metaphor use (for example, commander), a leadership style might still involve a combination of compatible metaphors as much as a single one (for example, commander, cyborg, and bully).

So let's assume, for the moment, the relevance of multiple metaphorical discourses and personal predilections to use them given that, as a population, managers tend to be verbally skilled (Bass 1981). The more communicatively skilled the leadership actor, the more they should be able to creatively combine the language, arguments, and ideas surrounding each discourse. As such, metaphors might pair and cluster in both expected and unexpected ways. For example, we might expect the positive and negative leadership metaphors to each cluster together given the tendency of some to prefer consistency by typing one another as "good" or "bad." Thus, growth opportunities (gardener) given to employees might also be cast as feel-good experiences (buddy), and the consistent delivery of such experiences framed by leaders as their "moral obligation" to develop others might produce great regard and admiration for such leaders (saint). Likewise, the more authoritarian (commander) leader might at times resort to intimidating tactics (bully) and demand an over-the-top commitment to the job in time and energy for themselves and all who report to them leaving little time for life outside work (cyborg).

However, perhaps the more interesting metaphor pairs and clusters are the nonobvious ones. In pairs, the saintly commander can be the stuff of legend (for example, Rudy Giuliani during 9/11 or Warren Buffet of Berkshire Hathaway). But consider the saintly cyborg whose moral righteousness or selflessness is raised to extraordinary levels (for example, Mother Teresa, a strong-willed and tireless campaigner for Catholic causes and the poor), or even the gardening cyborg who is relentless about training and development and culling the "B's" and "C's" from the firm (for example, T.J. Rogers, the hard-charging CEO of Cypress Semiconductor).[6] Consider also the buddy bully whose signature is to lull a target into warm feelings before delivering the blow (for example, the Machiavellian leader) or, alternatively, "hug them until it hurts."[7] Consider also the commander buddy who rests and coddles the troops after a fierce battle (for example, U.S. Navy Tailhook commanders).

For metaphor clusters, consider the benevolent autocrat (commander) who sacrifices himself (saint) for key development opportunities for his people (gardener). Consider also the leader who uses feel-good experiences (buddy) to manipulate her people into doing what she wants (commander), and only what she wants, or risk dismissal (bully). Consider also the leader who consistently produces at peak efficiency (cyborg), one aspect of which is to develop his people (gardener) and make them feel good about themselves (buddy), so their own productivity levels may similarly be raised to new levels.

The complexity of human nature is such that it would be surprising if the most successful leadership actors did *not* easily shift within a range of leadership metaphors as situations dictate. Such an argument is consistent with the premise of many situational and contingency-based leadership theories, such as Hersey and Blanchard's (1993) situational leadership theory, Fiedler's (1967; 1978) contingency model of leadership, and House and associates' (House 1971; House and Mitchell 1974) path-goal theory.[8]

Having a number of leadership metaphors in one's repertoire gives leadership actors a great deal of mental and communication agility so as to better meet the demands of their jobs and the situations that they face. As such, these are good reasons to reflect on the metaphors' individual strengths and weaknesses as the chapters in this book have done. The book also raises questions as to viable follower metaphors and how metaphors generally may be used in training and development. Both are the subject of the discussion below.

DISCUSSION

While this book presents an interesting array of leadership metaphors to consider, no discussion of leadership metaphors would be complete without an appropriate set of follower metaphors. However, we must ask, why not begin the chapter (or the book, for that matter) in this way? The work of James

Meindl (Meindl 1993; 1995; Meindl *et al.* 1985) suggests an answer. Meindl argued that we as a society – a society of many followers to be sure – are enamored with the concept of leadership. The so called "romance of leadership" is a tendency to experience the world in leader–follower terms. Even when conditions are ambiguous, there is a tendency to see leadership as *the* driver of successful performance or primary reason for failure. As you might expect, the popular business press contributes enormously to this state of affairs.

One such outcome associated with society's love affair with leadership is a certain amount of leader centrism, that is, a tendency to focus primarily upon what leaders do – and this chapter and book, like the extant leadership generally, are no exceptions in this regard. However, drawing from Meindl's work, Uhl-Bien and Pillai (2006) argue for the social construction of follower-ship. That is, they are interested to know the attributions that followers make about themselves and their roles, especially because today's followers are much more multi-dimensional than merely being defined by their more subordinate status like sheep to the shepherd or cog in the machine.

For example, it is easy to imagine bullying leaders abusing followers who are mostly "victims" as most would decline the "challenger" role or risk job loss. Commanders would be keen to develop followers who are "good soldiers" not "deserters" or others whose performances are lacking. However, saint-like leaders might be most interesting to watch with follower "sinners," who might challenge them in ways that other "lesser deities" might not. Culture is also at work when hard-charging cyborg leaders produce a whole raft of cyborg "mini-mes,"[9] while those with weaker constitutions fall by the wayside. "Team" and "family" are also cultural forms driven by metaphor, and it is always interesting to observe followers who do not consider themselves "members" of either because there is such a discrepancy between the leader's rhetoric and actions. When these metaphors really take, however, it is interesting to see the effects of hierarchy minimized and the emergence of a kind of "partnership" take hold.

There are, of course, more situationally driven follower metaphors to consider, especially from the game of baseball. For example, when crises strike, one or more followers may "step up to the plate," or "take one for the team," which refer to the risk-filled nature of their performances and the possibility that it may be discounted, respectively. Crises might also produce followers as "hunker-down heroes" whose singular performance gets the job done for the work unit (Deal and Kennedy 1982). Ingratiating acts by followers towards leaders may garner the former a "suck-up" or "loyalist" attribution (think Dwight Schrute of the U.S. version of *The Office*). By contrast, some followers may become so central to a leader's success performance (in one or more areas) that they are accorded a special status, much the way former U.S. President

George W. Bush's campaign manager, Karl Rove, was designated "Bush's brain" on matters of politics.

The pairing of leader–follower metaphors is perhaps most useful in leadership training and development, including executive coaching in which the coach assumes a quasi-therapeutic role with one or more leadership actors (Brunning 2006; Gray 2006; Hunt and Weintrub 2007). Combined leader–follower metaphors cannot only offer up a more vivid depiction of contrasting styles, but prompt a greater reflexivity about power dynamics. For example, one key issue concerning Foucault's (1983; 1995) discourse is the ways in which it can discipline its users. The point to be made here is that discourse constrains leadership actors as much as it enables them. When we characterize discourse as a linguistic tool bag, it is easy to see how the size and nature of the tool bag (based on the creative potential of combining multiple discourses) allows leadership actors to be more or less strategic; as stated earlier, when successful they become "managers of meaning" and transformative agents (Bryman 1992; Smircich and Morgan 1982).

However, over time the use of metaphorical discourses suggests that leadership actors increasingly become passive receptors of meaning as much as they are transformative agents (Fairhurst 2007; Shapiro 1992). Discourse disciplines leadership to behave – turns them into subjects – so that they rather reliably talk and act within the bounds of what the discourse prescribes (Foucault 1983). One of the most obvious examples of the disciplinary effects of discourse is the way in which the organizations headed by the geezers who served in World War II went on to adopt many aspects of the military into organizational life, the most obvious being the notion of a "chain of command." These leaders were subject to disciplinary power of military discourse at a very young age. Its grip was still apparent when the war was over and the bureaucratic form began to seriously take shape, as the "commander" chapter by Spicer suggests.

Importantly, leadership actors may or may not be aware of the true extent of discourse's disciplinary effects. Training and development, but especially executive coaching, can serve as a powerful tool to prompt reflexivity in leadership actors about the choices they inevitably make, in line with their metaphors, over the inherent tensions of the workplace – people versus profits, open versus closed information sharing, public versus private performances, autonomy versus connection to others, competition versus cooperation in team dynamics, creativity versus constraint in problem solving, and many more.

For example, the cyborg might be invited to examine her disproportionate response to work–family tensions; the commander might be invited to examine his management of the autonomy–connection tension with capable direct reports seeking more autonomy; the buddy could be asked to review her orientation to open versus closed information sharing and the constant need to make others feel good in not-so-feel-good times; and the saint might be asked to consider the ethics of secret testing or "come to Jesus" (ideological) indoctrination for "sinners" who are pushing back against the system.

Likewise, followers might be asked to weigh the personal and physical costs of becoming a cyborg "mini-me" who mimics the cyborg leader versus that of a good soldier who works hard but seeks a certain amount of balance in life. Followers who become "loyalists" and "hunker-down-heroes" might also be asked to examine their expectations for noteworthy performances and the degree to which they are actually rewarded.

In coaching, key questions can be put to leadership actors. Leaders can be asked questions such as, "Are you aware that you come off as a bully at times?" "Is this metaphor one with which you want to consciously identify?" "What would it look like if you became more of a gardener?" "What kinds of conversations would you have?" and "How could you 'grow' people *and* profits simultaneously?" Likewise, followers might be asked, "Your leader is a commander and a bully, by all accounts, and you want more of gardener. How might you begin to have this conversation with him?" "What specifically could he do that would assist you assist him with meeting organizational goals?" "What metaphorical pairing best represents the kind of relationship that you would like to have with him?" "If your boss regularly uses metaphors like 'team' or 'family,' but her behavior towards you is more "cog in his machine," how might you communicate that the former sounds cliché and inauthentic?" "How best could you underscore the salience of a team or family metaphors?"

Individual coaching sessions could productively lead to team coaching sessions in which leader–follower pairs or work units might consider dueling metaphors that divide the work unit and create unhealthy rivalry, for example, "in-group" versus "out-group," or "the boss's A-team" versus "the B-team" or "lackeys." Team or work unit metaphors might be self-consciously considered for their aspirational qualities and the positive values they might introduce into the work unit's culture, much the way Steve Jobs ordered the "Jolly Roger" pirate flag to be hung above Macintosh headquarters in its early days to signal its rebellious nature toward industry giants at the time.

In short, coaching can produce the kind of reflexive discussion among leadership actors, individually or collectively, that not only prompts a more self-conscious use of metaphor and discourse, but also the ethics and values that form them. Training and development can then use healthy leader–follower metaphors to model and promote normative guidelines while pushing for reflexivity around the debilitating consequences of destructive ones.

CONCLUSION

The purpose of this chapter has been to underscore the importance of leadership metaphors, generally, and those in this book, specifically, in the communication process. Leadership metaphors are powerful tools that shape actors' influential acts of organizing. They emerge in cultural discourses that, in effect, function as linguistic tool bags in which metaphors, along with arguments, themes, concepts, and terms, reside. Seen in this way, leadership actors should be able to deploy multiple discourses, if made relevant and appealing as choices to them. At the same time, they might consciously avoid certain metaphors because of the values or ideologies they represent. When leader and follower metaphors are paired, they become an important tool in leadership development to the extent they can model healthy relationships and promote reflexivity about the destructive aspects of the leader–follower relationship.

NOTES

1 See Fairhurst (2007) for an extended discussion of the contributions of leadership psychology relative to a discourse-based view of leadership advanced in this chapter.
2 See, for example, work by Alvesson and Sveningsson 2003a; 2003b; 2003c, Barge 2004; Barge and Fairhurst 2008, Grint 2000; 2005; 2007, Fairhurst 2007; Fairhurst and Cooren 2008, Kelly 2008, Kelly *et al.*, 2006, Tourish and Vatcha 2005 and others.
3 See Bennis and Thomas, p. 10.
4 Potter and Wetherell (1987) and colleagues actually use the expression "interpretative repertoire" instead of "tool bag" that I am using here.
5 As later discussion will reveal, I am using the word "subject" here as Foucault suggested.
6 Jack Welch, former CEO of General Electric, is famous for grading employees as "As," "Bs" and "Cs" – and eliminating the "Cs" (Tichy 1997). T.J. Rogers and other CEOs have reportedly adopted this rubric.
7 U.S. President Barack Obama's chief of staff, Rahm Emanuel, reportedly recommended a "hug them until it hurts" strategy of recruiting Republicans into the Democratic Obama administration, thus increasing the presumed isolation of existing Republican lawmakers.
8 See also Yukl (2006) for a general overview of these theories.
9 "Mini-Me" was the character played by the diminutive actor, Verne Troyer, in the second and third Austin Powers movies: *Austin Powers: The Spy Who Shagged Me* and *Austin Powers in Goldmember*.

11

CONCLUSION

André Spicer and Mats Alvesson

ONCE AGAIN: THE (UN)BEARABLE SLIPPERINESS OF LEADERSHIP

IF WE WERE TO BELIEVE THE BLUSTERING statements of journalists in the business press, management gurus as well as many managers, we might come to expect that we can find leadership nearly everywhere. Everyone from a bored worker giving herself a pep-talk on the way to work in the morning ('self-leadership') to a middle manager telling various stories about corporate happenings over a cup of coffee become palpable instances of leadership. We began this book by noting that almost anything and everything appears to be a form of leadership in today's company. Moreover, everyone from the lowest functionary to the highest-level bureaucrat seems have become a leader, or at least a leader in waiting. This is particularly palpable with the rapid expansion of so-called post-heroic studies of leadership that lay particular attention on the distributed nature of leadership and train an analytical spot-light on the potential for leadership in even the most mundane activities. Alongside this intellectual extension of the concept of leadership, we have also witnessed a veritable practitioner obsession with leadership, increasingly also paralleled in certain academic groups. (The authors of this book are partly included here, but take a somewhat more cautious and sceptical position.) As we have already highlighted, leadership seems to be seen as a solution for nearly any kind of catastrophe or human failing. This has prompted the rise of what some have called 'leaderism' (O'Reilly and Reed 2010) which is a form of organizational control that places extensive faith in the training and facilitation of leaders. What all this amounts to is an excessive and widespread faith in the role of the leader in our organizations and society more generally.

At the same time as we have witnessed an astounding spread of faith in the notion of the leader, we have also witnessed an increasing fuzziness around what exactly is meant and indeed what we understand by the notion of leadership. Because leadership seems to become understood as nearly anything, it becomes increasingly tempting to think that it actually means nothing. One could argue for the word having different meanings and being used in different ways. However, most users of the term probably think there is such a 'thing' as leadership, although it may be defined in different ways. But such an idea is debateable. Perhaps there is nothing 'core-like' there? When potentially anything is leadership, identifying leadership becomes an increasingly difficult, if not altogether impossible proposition. This means that if we were to be asked for one word to describe what leadership is, it would be 'ambiguous'. This is because leadership is difficult, if not impossible to pin down. In prior research, we have found that there is sometimes a striking mismatch between leaders thinking they are doing leadership, followers thinking they are doing it, and when an academic researcher following them notices activities which would typically be associated with leadership (e.g. Alvesson 2010a; Sveningsson and Larsson 2006).

Such research is a minority. Most research assumes and, consequently, 'finds' leadership. More fuel seems to have been added to the flames by the recent, spectacular growth of leadership studies which has incorporated an increasing number of themes under the label of leadership. By naming anything and everything as leadership, it increasingly becomes nothing. Far from detracting the vast range of potential consumers from the topic, the ambiguity of leadership seems to have actually further whetted their appetite. It is precisely because leadership is so difficult to pin down that people have become so enamoured with it. This is because its illusiveness and slipperiness make it into a kind of sublime idea without form or shape that can almost become anything to anyone.

Of course the signifier leadership has a lot of company here: knowledge, strategy, culture, identity, and entrepreneurship come to mind. Language in general tends also to be slippery, much more so than we commonly assume. But this does not prevent us from here discussing leadership as a prime example of ambiguity. It is often used in order to signal something really important and substantial, but what this may be is increasingly vague and cryptic.

The ambiguity of leadership might be attractive as it can be used in almost any way and with a great likelihood that people hearing the word will nod approvingly ('yes, leadership is what we need'). It also can create some difficulties. In particular, feelings of uncertainty and anxiety can be prompted by being unsure what exactly leadership is and when one is engaged in it. Indeed some of the leaders who were involved in this study were profoundly uncertain about when they were leading and what leading actually involved (see also Carroll and Levy 2008). Reading the academic literature did not turn up any greater certainty. As we pointed out in the first chapter of this book, we found there was a profusion of definitions. Instead of clarifying (as a definition is supposed to do), these various definitions actually created a great degree of uncertainty around what exactly leadership is. The result was that anyone interested in the field of leadership faces a genuine sense of puzzlement about what is meant by leadership and what is involved in leading.

A METAPHORICAL APPROACH: A PARTIAL RESPONSE TO THE SLIPPERINESS PROBLEM

In this book we acknowledge the ambiguity of leadership. However we don't claim that just because leadership is a slippery category, we should give up our pursuit. This option is worth serious consideration. It is possible that we should avoid leadership talk altogether as it is so overused and seems to contribute to confusion. Nevertheless, we have taken a different path in this volume and tried to signal an awareness of, and a means for, handling some of the variety in leadership talk. We have argued throughout the chapters in this book that one way that leaders (really managers expected/claiming to do leadership), followers, as well as those who research them can understand leadership is through using a range of metaphors. Indeed, we have tried to tease out the various metaphors associated with metaphors of leadership. We have pointed out that these metaphors are not just innocent figures or speech or tools to add a little rhetorical spice. They are also models for thinking which people faced with the ambiguity associated with leadership use to negotiate their way through these tricky conundrums. Indeed, various metaphors become models for thinking that can shape how leaders think about what should be done and how they might go about doing it.

The central aim of this book has been to pursue the various metaphors that can be used to negotiate this murky universe of leadership. Drawing on our own empirical work investigating leadership, but also from wider considerations of the research and business press on the topic, we identified six broad metaphors that seem to be consistently used by many of the leaders (and wannabe leaders). These were the leader as saint, buddy, gardener, commander, cyborg and bully. We saw that each of these metaphors seemed to suggest different kinds of things which the (potential) leader should do: the saint should seek to inspire followers through their moral vision; the buddy should seek to cultivate good and friendly relations with their followers; the gardener should help their followers to develop and grow, the commander should lead from the front through strict, sometimes inspirational and sometimes perhaps even harsh action; the cyborg leads through relentless and often super-human performance exhibiting norms such as rationality and work discipline; and the bully should push their followers along through various forms of intimidation, including 'kicking ass'. As well as guiding leaders in how they should think about their own activities, each of these metaphors also provides a follower with a framework oriented to what they should expect of their leaders. For instance, a follower who thinks of the ideal leader as a buddy will inevitably expect and perhaps often see acts of leadership which involve leaders being friendly, encouraging and engaging. They will also be sensitive to deviation from this ideal. When there is a mismatch between the metaphors of leadership that a follower clings to and those their leaders follow, then there can be quite serious consequences. Confusion, disappointment and/or conflict may follow. In the worst cases, the result of a clash of metaphors is a breakdown in leader–follower relations. It is not common, but occasionally it is almost as if the followers and the leaders live in different universes – where each has radically different ideas about what constitutes good leadership and what the leader actually is doing (Alvesson 2010a).

An interesting aspect is how leadership is typically talked and indeed thought about in a positive light. We found the existence of some darker metaphors of leadership. However, it is more common to think and talk about leadership in largely positive ways. After all, who could not like a buddy who goes out of their way to make their followers feel good, a saint who embodies all the great values of the organization, or a kindly gardener who helps their followers grow? All these are highly positive images of what the leader does. Indeed, even when we found leaders who had an apparently more 'realistic' image of what leaders should do, they often presented this in a fairly positive light. For instance, leaders expounding the commander metaphor would often highlight the martial virtues associated with leadership such as strength, will and courage. Cyborgs would see themselves in terms of excellence, as almost superhuman characters who are able to lead through transcending the pedestrian efforts of their followers. Even the bully metaphor seems to have positive aspects to it – such as encouraging better performance from laggard followers. What we notice in most of these cases is an attempt to portray the leader as an almost sacred character who cannot be scared by the problems and detritus of everyday life (Grint 2009). Because of this almost sacred character, it as if we expect the leaders to be mainly good and positive characters, doing valuable, although sometimes for those not pulling their weight not entirely pleasurable, things. When a leader shows that they are subject to the same kinds of tensions, insecurities and inconsistencies as us mere mortals, it often creates a sincere sense of concern and perhaps even panic amongst followers. This desire to see the leader in pure terms can then lead followers to become very disappointed when leaders don't live up to espoused metaphors. They can experience a radical shift in perspective from seeing their leader as an entirely good character to seeing them as an entirely bad one.

But if we look beyond the surface of usual accounts of leadership, we notice that there are some interesting paradoxes lurking within many of the metaphors that we use to understand and engage with leadership. Indeed, throughout this book we have tried to highlight that there are paradoxes associated with each of the metaphors we looked at. Saints can become cult leaders. As pointed out in the saint chapter even the followers of Hitler, Mao and Osama bin Laden may have viewed these characters as moral peak performers standing for the ultimate good for their people. Buddies can become ineffectual managers who are more interested in making people feel good than actually ensuring the job gets done. Gardeners can become wannabe therapists who are more interesting in invasively exploring the early life experiences of their followers than hitting targets. Equally, many of the 'darker' metaphors of leadership which we explored can have potentially beneficial sides. Commanders can actually create respect for a strict focus on getting the job done and in particular in drastic situations (fire fighting, crisis management) they may be crucial. Cyborgs can get employees to look beyond their petty emotional concerns and limited commitment and instead focus on delivering the results. Even bullies can help to hold the group together and inspire commitment through firmly dealing with deviance and poor performance, thereby clarifying and reinforcing a sense of how things should be. Sometimes, of course, the bully can create a commitment to actually getting rid of him/her.

Understanding the metaphors we use to think through leadership therefore involves being able to recognize the ambiguities and uncertainties inherent in any metaphor. Doing this means putting aside many of the moral assessments which we usually have about metaphors of leadership. This means recognizing leaders are not simply all good or all bad. Rather they are more nuanced than they appear. Sometimes they also have a paradoxical character. In order to capture these paradoxes we need the kind of rich metaphors that we have outlined in this book. We hope that the exploration and recognition of these rich metaphors will help to advance how researchers study leadership, how educators teach leadership, how managers seek to lead, and how society engages with the question of leadership more generally. In what follows, we will look briefly at the implications for each of these groups in some more depth.

CONTRIBUTIONS

LEADERSHIP RESEARCHERS

The first group we hope this book will encourage to rethink some of their assumptions are researchers who are studying leadership. At the least, we hope that this book will push these researchers to revisit what are often blind comments on a rather clear and unproblematic view of leadership. Indeed many leadership researchers appear to continue to assume that leaderships is something which can be easily identified and captured in a survey. We have tried to point out that leadership is rarely so easy to spot. Rather, it is frequently very ambiguous and difficult to identify. In close-up studies, it is often obvious that what those intent on 'leading' are doing is much closer to management and administration. One can observe them for some time without seeing many actions that indicate leadership. In that sense, the so-called leader is perhaps best seen as a bureaucrat or senior administrator and the set of metaphors used in this book sidestep this. But as our focus here is on leadership our concern is how to try to capture this, in settings where what could be seen as leadership are to be made sense of. Here it is important to use a spectrum of concepts and ideas and refrain from the popular habit of using two versions of leadership and plugging everything into such a framework. Transformational vs. transactional or initiating structure vs. consideration come to mind as such broad-brushed divisions.

So we hope that by offering a series of metaphors, we will provide a way for researchers to begin to negotiate this ambiguity in a slightly more productive way. Second, by encouraging researchers to look at the metaphors that underpin how we think about leadership, we also hope to contribute to a growing body of studies that investigate the language of leadership (e.g. Fairhurst 2007; Kelly 2008). In particular, we hope that we have persuasively argued that leadership is a kind of language that can be more skilfully used. Moreover, the language of leadership not only informs leaders' talk, but also how they think about themselves as well as their subordinates. We should, however, be careful about not equating the talk of managers of how they lead with how to lead. After all, what people say, think and act may not all the time be aligned. Sometimes people talk more convincingly than they act; sometimes they do the opposite. But even though we should not be too quick to see popular language use as automatically forming organizations, the language of leadership is not impotent in shaping how many leaders (and indeed their followers) construct and reproduce the organizations they work within. We think that there is great scope to further investigate how the language of leadership works within organizations. Here we have looked at how the trope of metaphor works. It would be very interesting to investigate the operation of other tropes in leadership. For instance, how might we use simile, metonymy and synecdoche to think about leadership? We also might want to ask what would leadership look like if we placed more emphasis on more dissenting tropes such as anomaly, paradox and irony (Oswick et al. 2002)? Although we have certainly tried to begin doing this in the present study, there is clearly a lot more that needs further exploration. Perhaps one of the most pressing questions is what exactly is it that the language of leadership does not allow us to see. How does it mask important aspects of social reality such as domination, tiredness, exploitation and sorrow? How does it conceal, or at least discourage, us from seeing more subtle forms of influencing process than those that leadership vocabulary encourages (sometimes even disciplines) us to pay attention to. A vital step towards beginning to explore these aspects that have been masked by the language of leadership is problematizing the literature on leadership (see Alvesson and Sandberg, forthcoming). By engaging in this process of problematization, we hope to begin to unsettle some of our all-too entrenched assumptions about the necessity and goodness of leadership. Indeed, one of the most promising directions in studying leadership involves developing a strand of literature that is explicitly critical of the notion of leadership itself (for recent attempts see Collinson 2005; Alvesson and Spicer 2010). We hope that the broader spectrum of reference points for thinking about leadership offered in this book may also be helpful for this more critical project.

EDUCATORS

As well as making a contribution to research in the area of leadership, we also hope that our argument has some important implications for those educating leaders. Indeed, one of the striking things about business education in recent years has been the breathtaking expansion in leadership courses. While these courses were almost non-existent in many business schools 20 years ago, at least in part of Europe, today leadership appears to be the *plat du jour*. This means that instead of only getting on a series of courses in technical areas such as accounting, operations management and organizational behaviour, today's budding business school student seems to be interested in far more esoteric courses such as leadership. And they cannot be blamed for this. Many of the 'talent hunters' of large corporations seem to be obsessed with staffing their organizations with leaders (or at least that is what they claim – if they should succeed, they would face the problem of having far too many chiefs and too few Indians). The demands of large corporations seem to be backed by a whole set of demands in broader society for more leadership. Perhaps it is this widespread demand for leadership which has actually created the field of leadership studies as well as many of the text books which claim to capture the knowledge associated with leadership (including this one). Indeed one well-seasoned manager we were talking to exclaimed that academics studying leadership only seem to be doing this because there are many people who are willing to pay. Indeed, there is a huge potential market ranging from leadership-loving students to corporations who want to increase their leadership potential.

Perhaps the very first thing that this book aims to encourage is that we should become a little more circumspect about leadership in our teaching. We need to begin not from the position that leadership is something that can be unproblematically inculcated into willing recruits. Rather it is something that is difficult, if not impossible to pin down. Because of this, we all think that leadership education can offer a series of models which might help aspirational leaders to think through what it might mean to lead, how they think about leadership, and how their followers think about it. The central message we hope has been this – expand the metaphors your students think with. We hope that the central act of any form of leadership education will be disabusing wannabe leaders of a metaphor they may have become fixated on (after reading the biography of Nelson Mandela for instance). Instead, it is important that they develop a far less myopic vision of leadership through not only realizing the metaphor they themselves use to think through leadership, but also recognizing the other metaphors which might be at play around them. There are a whole range of tools and techniques which leadership educators can use to draw out these metaphors ranging from simple questions such as asking each individual in the class to think about which metaphor they might identify with the most (and indeed which one their followers might identify with). More complex and creative exercises could be used. For instance, you might ask each member of the class to write a short reflective piece about their own leadership style (or ideal). Then another member of the class would be asked to identify the metaphors that their classmate uses most frequently in their essay. Sometimes participants in a leadership course might find such literary exercises a little indulgent. To get around this, another technique is to ask participants to physically embody metaphors. This proved to be a very successful approach in a workshop looking at metaphors used in strategy processes (Heracleous and Jacobs 2009). This involved getting researchers to build a metaphorical representation of their organization using Lego. After they had constructed this metaphor, they were asked to explain it. Through doing this, they suddenly had to be clear about what their implicit metaphors were about how the organization operated and where it was going. A similar process might be done in the case of leadership. Doing so, we hope, might begin to bring to the surface some of the assumptions associated with leadership in an organization. As well as surfacing the implicit metaphors that followers have about leadership, educators might also encourage their students to challenge these metaphors. This would involve encouraging them to think more ironically about their own assumptions about what good and bad leadership is. A simple way of doing this might involve encouraging students to think about the limitations of a metaphor. This requires asking students when a metaphor ceases to work, what it blinds us to, and what some of the problems associated with the metaphor might be. Asking these kinds of questions might help to loosen some of the implicit metaphors which might have a stranglehold on people's minds. As well as considering the limits of a metaphor, students might also be helped by following the suggestion which Gail Fairhurst made in the previous chapter and mix 'dark' and 'light' metaphors. For instance, is it possible to have a friendly commander, a saintly bully or a cyborg gardener? By mixing metaphors in this way, students could begin to see the paradoxes and contradictions that lie at the heart of leaders and leadership. It may also help to achieve what could possibly be one of the most difficult feats of leadership education – unsettling the widespread assumption that more leadership is the solution needed to solve nearly any problem. Considering the ambiguities around leadership could push students to confront some of the darker and more difficult aspects of this dark art. Indeed it may encourage them to recognize that more leadership, in some cases, might actually be the problem rather that the solution.

An additional interesting task is to critically assess the set of metaphors used in this book. What are the pros and cons of considering this specific set? What is missing or what is represented in a debatable way? What alternative framings could be considered?

PRACTITIONERS

In addition to pushing for a different way of thinking about the education of leaders, we also hope that our interventions may bring managers some way towards other ways of thinking through their attempts to lead. We have already noted a number of times throughout this book that even the most functional of managers today seem to expect to be (or at least try to become) good leaders. We hope this book has highlighted that this is not just a matter of going on a few training courses, picking up fashionable leadership vocabulary or even having an influential coach. Instead, for us leadership is best thought about as mastering a set of lines of thinking and practice. This is facilitated by having access to a rich and varied language. The latter must engage with serious self-reflection. This guides what thoughtful managers and other leaders do and say when trying to lead. They have a sense of how to manage and frame meaning during acts of leadership. They have an understanding of the metaphors that are implicit both within their own language (and indeed thinking) as well as those of their followers.

Thus acts of leadership involve the tricky craft of seeking to actually surface and indeed work with the underlying ideas around leadership which float around in an organization. Sometimes this is easy – as aspirant leaders typically learn what kind of leadership gets noticed and then simply act this out. However, most managers work in far more tricky contexts where there is a complex variety of more or less espoused ideas about and templates for leadership (multiple metaphors) being more or less salient to varying degrees. Acts of leadership therefore become a reflection of the ability (or inability) to play with these multiple metaphors and productively put language use and action emerging from them together at the right place in the right time. Some people become too fixated with a specific metaphor and do not show enough flexibility in the metaphors of leadership they use. This fixation can prove to be the undoing of many leaders – particularly in pluralistic organizations where there are multiple, often conflicting, modes of organizing work at play simultaneously. There are often expectations on, or the need for, managers to provide moral examples, develop people, make tough decisions, and discipline people who are seen to strongly deviating from acceptable performance. Using multiple metaphors often also calls for being curious enough to know which metaphors those who are supposed to be being led hold. An important part of the work of leadership involves discovering this and seeking to create at least some kind of match. If this does not happen, then it is likely that acts of leadership, no matter how well intentioned or well executed, might misfire. A manager who thinks she is a buddy and concentrates on building close social relations and making people feel good, who works with people wanting a more forceful person to lead from the front will face problems. This will be particularly apparent if the metaphors informing manager and subordinates are not clarified or espoused.

In addition to awareness of metaphors and flexibility with the metaphors which are used, we hope that this book also encourages leaders to become a little less wedded to their treasured metaphors of leadership. This involves thinking more critically about their own assumptions about how leadership should be. We would like to suggest that doing this involves engaging with more dissenting tropes such as irony. All the metaphors we have suggested are intended to support an element of irony and, for the specific manager considering these, a dose of self-irony about his or her celebrated view of something as serious and pretentious as leadership. This means looking for the inconsistencies, limitations and ambiguities that are implicit in a manager's own acts of leadership. Perhaps recognizing these inconsistencies will not just drive leaders to develop a heightened sense of anxiety in the service of creating greater consistencies. Hopefully, it may allow them to think through the inconsistencies that are in fact a consistent feature of their own and others' behaviour. Indeed, it might allow them to recognize that managing and working with inconsistencies might be a central aspect of leadership as such. But perhaps more than anything, we hope that the reflection on these metaphors of leadership may loosen the spell that the notion of leadership has cast on many of today's managers. Indeed some suggest that one of the most important tasks for managers today might be putting aside many of the fantasies of leadership and returning to good old-fashioned management (Mintzberg 2009). As mentioned, most of our studies suggest that clear-cut examples of leadership action are rare. Indeed leadership is definitely marginal to managers doing administration and working with other people on a horizontal level. At the very least, we hope that this book encourages managers to reflect on whether the concept, and fantasy of, leadership is helping or hindering them in particular situations.

PUBLIC DEBATE

Finally, we hope that this book has some implications for wider debates in society. In particular, this book has set out to call into question the widespread mystique of leadership. We may reinforce this mystique through accepting the use of leadership vocabulary. Indeed we have used the somewhat debatable label 'leader', assuming that most managers at least some of the time do something like 'leadership' in one sense of another. Our questioning of the mystique involves the assumption that leaders are almost magical characters who can sort anything out. This has led to many organizations investing huge sums in leadership training programmes. Indeed, many national governments around the world have sought to tackle urgent social issues ranging from failing schools to climate change through increased emphasis on developing leadership capacity. This has gone hand in hand with an increasing psychic investment by people across the social spectrum in the idea and in some cases identity as leaders. Indeed being a leader for many of these people makes them into a good person. Conversely challenging leadership involves questioning their very sense of self. We have tried to unsettle this assumption that investing in leadership is always the best thing to do. One way that we have sought to do this is by questioning the images of leaders that seem to be deeply rooted in broader social discussions. In particular, we have pointed out that there appear to be multiple metaphors of leadership that float around in society. Moreover, we have hoped to highlight that not all of these metaphors are unproblematically good. We have argued that alongside more positive metaphors such as the friendly buddy there are also equally widespread negative metaphors such as the commander, the cyborg or the bully. Moreover, we have tried to show that there is also a darker side to apparently positive metaphors such as the saint. In addition, there are certainly some good sides to potentially negative metaphors such as the bully. By doing this, we hope to show that metaphors of leadership have a high degree of moral ambiguity and that one should avoid the naïve idea that 'good' leadership simply leads to 'good' effects.

More generally we hope that we have begun to ask whether leadership itself has become a metaphor that has got out of control in not only the academic and popular management literature but also in public consciousness.

Minimally, there is a risk that leadership is an idea and a solution that has been applied to too many settings and issues where it is largely inappropriate. This is particularly apt with the spread of what some have called 'leaderism' (O'Reilly and Reed 2010), the increasing assumption that more leadership is important to improving public services and society more generally. This creates a great hope in the potential of leadership, but it also can create great disappointment when leaders prove that they are only human too and cannot deliver on many of the great hopes that are invested in them. Perhaps it is time that we had far more modest expectations of leaders. One way to do this would involve ceasing to invest all our hopes and dreams in leadership. This would, we hope, rescue leadership from a kind of fantasy world and help us to understand it for what it is. It would help us to see leadership in the real world that is plagued by inconsistencies, contradictions and paradoxes. We hope that the metaphors we have looked at in this book and our approach emphasizing ambiguity and the need to develop more realistic expectations of leadership are part of undertaking this important task. Perhaps this may mean that when leadership is appropriate it will be carried out in more thoughtful and better functioning ways.

REFERENCES

Alvesson, M. (1995) *Cultural Perspectives on Organizations*. Cambridge: Cambridge University Press.

—— (1996) Leadership studies: from procedure and abstraction to reflexivity and situation. *Leadership Quarterly*, 7(4): 255–285.

—— (2002) *Understanding Organizational Culture*. London: Sage.

—— (2004) *Knowledge Work and Knowledge Intensive Firms*. Oxford: Oxford University Press.

—— (2010a) Leadership – alignment and misfit of images in leadership relations. Working Paper Department of Business Administration, Lund University.

—— (2010b) Leadership and organizational culture. In D. Collinson, A. Bryman, B. Jackson, K. Grint and M. Uhl-Bein (eds) *Handbook of Leadership Studies*. London: Sage.

—— (2010c) Self-doubters, strugglers, story-tellers, surfers and others. Images of self-identity in organization studies. *Human Relations*, 63(2): 193–217.

Alvesson, M. and Billing, Y.D. (2009) *Understanding Gender and Organization*. London: Sage.

Alvesson, M. and Blom, M. (2009) Less leadership? working paper. Department of Business Administration, Lund University.

Alvesson, M. and Kärreman, D. (2000) Varieties of discourse: on the study of organizations through discourse analysis. *Human Relations*, 53(9): 1125–1149.

Alvesson, M. and A. Spicer (2010) Critical leadership studies, working paper, Department of Business Administration, Lund University.

Alvesson, M. and Sveningsson, S. (2003a) The good visions, the bad micro-management and the ugly ambiguity: contradictions of (non-)leadership in a knowledge-intensive company. *Organization Studies*, 24(6): s. 961–988.

—— (2003b) Managers doing leadership: the extra-ordinization of the mundane. *Human Relations*, 56: 1435–1459.

—— (2003c) The great disappearing act: difficulties in doing leadership. *Leadership Quarterly*, 14(3): 359–381.

—— (2008) *Changing Organizational Culture*. London: Routledge.

Alvesson, M. and Willmott, H. (1996) *Making Sense of Management: a critical introduction*, London: Sage.

—— (2002) Identity regulation as organizational control: producing the appropriate individual. *Journal of Management Studies*, 39(5): 619–644.

Amernic, J., Craig, R. and Tourish, D. (2007) The transformational leader as pedagogue, physician, architect, commander and saint: five root metaphors in Jack Welch's letters to stockholders in General Electric. *Human Relations*, 60(12): 1839–1872.

Andriessen, D. and Gubbins, C. (2009) Metaphor analysis as an approach for exploring theoretical concepts: the case of social capital. *Organization Studies*, 30(8): 845–863.

Arendt, H. (1958) *The Human Condition*. Chicago: University of Chicago Press.

Ashforth, B. (1994) Petty tyranny in organizations. *Human Relations*, 47: 755–778.

Ashforth, B. and Mael, F. (1989) Social identity theory and the organization. *Academy of Management Review*, 14(1): 20–39.

Avolio, B. and Gardner, W. (2005) Authentic leaderhip development: getting to the root of positive forms of leadership. *Leadership Quarterly*, 16: 215–338.

Awaleh, R. and Gardner, W. (1999) Perceptions of leader charisma and effectiveness: the effects of vision content, delivery, and organizational performance. *The Leadership Quarterly*, 10: 345–373.

Badaracco, J.L. (1998) The discipline of building character. In *Harvard Business Review on Leadership*. Boston: Harvard Business School Press.

Barge, J.K. (2004) Reflexivity and managerial practice. *Communication Monographs*, 71: 70–96.

Barge, J.K. and Fairhurst, G.T. (2008) Living leadership: a systemic, constructionist approach. *Leadership*, 4: 227–251.

Barker, R.A. (1997) How can we train leaders if we do not know what leadership is? *Human Relations*, 50: 343–362.

Bass, B.M. (1981) *Stogdill's Handbook of Leadership*. New York: Free Press.

—— (1985) *Leader and Performance: beyond expectations*. New York: Free Press.

Bass, B.M. and Steidlmeier, P. (1999) Ethics, character, and authentic transformational leadership behavior. *Leadership Quarterly*, 10: 181–217.

Bauman, Z. (1991) Living without an alternative. *Political Quarterly*, 62(1): 35–44.

Bendl, R. (2008) Gender subtexts reproduction of exclusion in organizational discourse. *British Journal of Management*, 19: S50–S64.

Bennis, W.G. and Nanus, B. (1985) *Leaders: strategies for taking charge*. New York: Harper & Row.

Bennis, W. and Thomas, R. (2002a) Crucibles of leadership. *Harvard Business Review*, Sept, 39–45.

—— (2002b) *Geeks and Geezers: How Era, Values, and Defining Moments Shape Leadership*. Boston, MA: Harvard Business School Press.

Bess, J.L. and Goldman, P. (2001) Leadership ambiguity in universities and K-12 schools and the limits of contemporary leadership theory. *Leadership Quarterly*, 12(4): 429–441.

Beyer, J.M. (1999) Taming and promoting charisma to change organizations. *The Leadership Quarterly*, 10: 307–330.

Biggart, N.W. and Hamilton, G.G. (1987) An institutional theory of leadership. *Journal of Applied Behavioural Science*, 23: 429–441.

Blake, R.R. and Mouton, J.S. (1964) *The Managerial Grid*. Houston, TX: Gulf.

Blanchard, K. and Waghorn, T, (1997) *Mission Possible*. New York: McGraw Hill.

Boden, D. (1994) *The Business of Talk*. Cambridge: Polity.

Boleman, L. and Deal, T. (2003) *Reframing Organizations: Artistry, Choice and Leadership*. San Francisco: Jossey-Bass.

Bresnen, M.J. (1995) All things to all people? Perceptions, attributions, and constructions of leadership. *Leadership Quarterly*, 6(4): 495–513.

Brown, M. (1998) *Richard Branson: The Authorised Biography*. London: Headline.

Brown, R.H. (1976) Social theory as metaphor. *Theory and Society*, 3: 169–197.

Brunning, H. (2006) *Executive coaching: Systems-psychodynamic perspective*. New York: Karnac.

Brunsson, N. (2003) Organized hypocrisy. In B. Czarniawska and G. Sevon (eds) *Northern Lights*. Malmö: Liber.

Bruzelius, L. and Skärvad, P-H. (2004) *Integrerad Organisationslära*. Lund: Studentlitteratur.

Bryman, A. (1992) *Charisma and Leadership in Organizations*. London: Sage.

—— (2004) Qualitative research in leadership: a critical but appreciative review. *Leadership Quarterly*, 15(6): 729–769.

Bryman, A., Stephens, M. and Campo, C. (1996) The importance of context: qualitative research and the study of leadership. *Leadership Quarterly*, 7, 3: 353–370.

Burns, J.M. (1978) *Leadership*. New York: Harper and Row.

Calder, B.J. (1977) An attribution theory of leadership. In B.M. Staw and G. R. Salanick (eds) *New Directions in Organizational Behaviour*. Chicago: St Clair.

Carroll, B. and Levy, L. (2008) Defaulting to management: leadership defined by what it is not. *Organization*, 15(1): 75–96.

Chemers, M. (2003) Leadership effectiveness: functional, constructivist and empirical perspectives. In D. van Knippenberg, and M. Hogg (eds) *Leadership and Power*. London: Sage.

Chen, C.C. and Meindl, J. R. (1999) The construction of leadership images in the popular press: the case of Donald Burr and People Express. *Administrative Science Quarterly*, 36(4): 521–551.

Ciulla, J.B. (2004) *Ethics, the Heart of Leadership*. Westport, CT: Praeger.

Clancy, J.J. (1989) *The Invisible Powers: The Language of Business*. Lexington, MA: Lexington Books.

Cluley, R. (2008) The psychoanalytic relationship between leaders and followers. *Leadership*, 4: 201–212.

Clynes, M.E. and Kline, N.S. (1960) Cyborgs and space. *Astronautics*, September, 29–33.

Cohen, M.D. and March, J.G. (1986) *Leadership and Ambiguity: the American College President*. Boston, MA: Harvard Business School Press.

Collins, J. (2001a) Level 5 leadership: the triumph of humility and fierce resolve. *Harvard Business Review*, 79(1): 67–76.

—— (2001b) *From Good to Great*. New York: HarperCollins.

Collinson, D. (1992) *Managing the Shopfloor: subjectivity, masculinity and workplace culture*. Berlin: Walter de Gruyter.

—— (2005) Dialectics of leadership. *Human Relations*, 58: 1419–1442.

Conaty, B. (2007) Secrets of an HR superstar. *Business Week*, April 9.

Conger, J.A. (1989) *The charismatic leader*. San Francisco: Jossey-Bass.

—— (1998) Qualitative research as the cornerstone methodology for understanding leadership. *Leadership Quarterly*, 9(1): 107–122.

Cooren, F. (2001) *The Organizing Property of Communication*. Amsterdam: John Benjamins.

Cornelissen, J. (2005) Beyond compare: metaphor in organization theory. *Academy of Management Review*, 30(4): 751–764.

Cornelissen, J.P., Oswick, C.L., Christensen, T. and Phillips, N. (2008) Metaphor in organizational research: context, modalities and implications for research. *Organization Studies*, 29(1): 7–22.

Covey, S.R. (1992) *The Seven Habits of Highly Effective People: powerful lessons in personal change*. London: Simon & Schuster.

Czarniawska, B. and Rhodes, C. (2006) Strong plots: popular culture in management practice and theory. In P. Gagliardi and B. Czarniawska (eds) *Management Education and Humanities*. Cheltenham: Edward Elgar.

Czarniawska, B. and Gustavsson, E. (2008) The (d)evolution of the cyberwoman. *Organization*, 15: 665–683.

Dagens Industri (Weekend) 2: 2009.

Davidson, D. (1978) What metaphors mean. *Critical Inquiry*, Autumn, 31–47.

De Cramer, D. (2003) A relational perspective on leadership and cooperation. In D. van Knippenberg, and M. Hogg (eds) *Leadership and Power*. London: Sage.

De Rond, M. (2008) *The Last Amateurs: To Hell and Back with the Cambridge Boat-race Crew*. London: Icon.

Deal, T. and Kennedy, A. (1982) *Corporate Cultures: the rites and rituals of coprorate life*. Reading, MA: Addison-Wesley.

Deegan II, A. (1979) *Coaching: a management skill for improving individual performance*. Reading, MA: Addison-Wesley.

Den Hertog, D. and Dickson, M. (2004) Leadership and culture. In J. Antonakis, A.T. Cianciolo and R.J. Sternberg (eds) *The Nature of Leadership*. Thousand Oaks, CA: Sage.

Denis, J.L., Langley, A. and Cazale, L. (1996) Leadership and strategic change under ambiguity. *Organization Studies*, 17(4): 673–700.

Docherty, P., Forslin, J. and Shani, R. (eds) (2002) *Creating Sustainable Work Systems: emerging perspectives and practice*. London: Routledge.

Dunford, R. and Palmer, I. (1996) Conflicting uses of metaphors: reconceptualizing their use in the field of organizational change. *Academy of Management Review*, 21(3): 691–671.

Einarsen, S. (1999) The nature and causes of bullying at work. *International Journal of Manpower*, 20: 16–27.

Einarsen, S., Schanke Aasland, M. and Skogstad, A. (2007) Destructive leadership behaviour: a definition and conceptual model. *The Leadership Quarterly*, 18: 207–216.

Eisenberg, E. (2007) *Strategic Ambiguities: essays on communication, organization and identity*. Thousand Oaks, CA: Sage.

Endrissat, N. (2007) *Connecting Who We Are with How We Construct Leadership*. Basel: Pabst.

Etzioni, A. (1965) Organizational control structure. In J.G. March (ed.) *Handbook of Organizations*. Chicago: Rand-McNally.

Fairhurst, G. (2001) Dualisms in leadership research. In J.M. Jablin, L.L. Putnam, K.H. Roberts and L.W. Porter (eds) *Handbook of Organizational Communication*. Thousand Oaks, CA: Sage.

—— (2005) Reframing the art of the framing: problems and prospects for leadership. *Leadership*, 1(2): 165–185.

—— (2007) *Discursive Leadership: in conversation with leadership psychology*. Thousand Oaks, CA: Sage.

—— (2009) Considering context in discursive leadership research. *Human Relations*, 62(11): 1607–1633.

Fairhurst, G.T. and Cooren, F. (2008) Leadership and the hybrid production of presence(s). Paper presented at the annual meeting of the International Communication Association, Montreal, Canada.

Fairhurst, G.T. and Sarr, R.A. (1996) *The Art of Framing: managing the language of leadership*. San Francisco: Jossey-Bass.

Fairhurst, G. and Grant, D. (2010) The social construction of leadership: a sailing guide. *Management Communication Quarterly*, 24(2): 171–210.

Fairhurst, G.T., Church, M., Hagen, D.E. and Levi, J. T. (in press) Whither female leaders? Executive coaching and the alpha male syndrome. In D. Mumby (ed.) *Discourses of Difference*. Thousand Oaks, CA: Sage.

Ferris, G.R., Zinko, R. Brouer, R.L., Buckley, M.R. and Harvey, M.G. (2007) Strategic bullying as a supplementary, balanced perspective on destructive leadership. *Leadership Quarterly*, 18: 195–206.

Festinger, L. (1957) *A Theory of Cognitive Dissonance*. Evanston, IL: Row Petersen.

Fiedler, F.E. (1967) *A Theory of Leadership Effectiveness*. New York: McGraw-Hill.

—— (1973) The contingency model: a reply to Ashour. *Organizational Performance and Human Behavior*, 9(3): 356–368.

—— (1978) The contingency model and the dynamics of leadership process. In L. Berkowitz (ed.). *Advances in Experimental Social Psychology*. New York: Academic Press, 60–112.

—— (1996) Research on leadership selection and training: one view of the future. *Administrative Science Quarterly*, 41(2): 241–250.

Fineman, S. (1998) The natural environment, organization and ethics. In M. Parker (ed.) *Ethics and Organizations*. London, Sage.

Fleming, P. (2005) Workers' playtime? Boundaries and cynicism in a 'culture of fun' program. *Journal of Applied Behavioral Science*, 41(3): 285–303.

Fleming, P. and Sturdy, A. (2009) 'Just be yourself!': Towards neo-normative control in organisations? *Employee Relations*, 31(6): 569–583.

Fletcher, J. and Käufer, K. (2003) Shared leadership: paradoxes and possibility. In C. Pearce and J. Conger (eds) *Shared Leadership*. Thousand Oaks, CA: Sage.

Foucault, M. (1972) *The Archeology of Knowledge and the Discourse on Language*. London: Tavistock Publications.

—— (1983) The subject and power. In H.L. Dreyfus and P. Rabinow (eds) *Michel Foucault: beyond structuralism and hermeneutics*. Chicago: Chicago University Press, 208–226.

—— (1990) *The History of Sexuality: Volume 1*. New York: Vintage/Random House.

—— (1995) *Discipline and Punish*. New York: Vintage/Random House.

French, R. and Simpson, P. (2006) Downplaying leadership: researching how leaders talk about themselves. *Leadership*, 2: 469–479.

French, R., Case, P. and Gosling, J. (2009) Betrayal and friendship. *Society and Business Review*, 4(2): 146–158.

Frost, P.J. (2003) *Toxic Emotions At Work*. Boston, MA: Harvard Business School Press.

Gallie, W.B. (1955) Essentially contested concepts. *Proceedings of the Aristotelian Society*, 56: 167–198.

Gemmill, G. and Oakley, J. (1992) Leadership: an alienating myth? *Human Relations*, 45(2): 113–129.

George, B. (2008) *Authentic Leadership: rediscovering the secrets of creating lasting value*. San Francisco: Jossey Bass.

Goffman, E. (1959) *The Presentation of Self in Everyday Life*. New York: Doubleday.

Gouldner, A. (1960) The norm of reciprocity—a preliminary statement, *American Sociological Review*, 25(2): 161–178.

Grant, D. and Oswick, C. (eds) (1996) *Metaphor and Organizations*. London: Sage.

Gray, C.H. (1995) *The Cyborg Handbook*. London: Taylor & Francis Ltd.

—— (2001) *Cyborg Citizen: Politics in the Posthuman Age*. London: Routledge.

Gray, D.E. (2006) Executive coaching: Towards a dynamic alliance of psychotheraphy and transformative learning processes. *Management Learning*, 37: 475–497.

Greenleaf, R. (1970) *Servant as Leader*. New York: Paulist Press.

Grey, C. and Mitev, N. (1996) Re-engineering organisations: a critical appraisal. *Personnel Review*, 24(1): 6–18.

Grint, K. (2000) *The Arts of Leadership*. Oxford: Oxford University Press.

—— (2005) Problems, problems, problems: the social construction of 'leadership'. *Human Relations*, 58(11): 1467–1494.

—— (2007) Learning to lead: can Aristotle help us to find the road to wisdom? *Leadership*, 3: 231–246.

—— (2010) The sacred in leadership: separation, sacrifice and silence. *Organization Studies*, 31(1): 89–107.

Gronn, P. (2002) Distributed leadership as a unit of analysis. *Leadership Quarterly*, 13: 423–451.

Hammer, M. (1990) Re-engineering work – don't automate, obliterate. *Harvard Business Review*, July–August.

Hammer, M. and Stanton, S.A. (1995) *The Re-engineering Revolution: a handbook*. New York: Harper Business.

Handley, K., Clark, T., Fincham, R. and Sturdy, A. (2007) Researching situated learning: participation, identity and practices in client-consultant relationships. *Management Learning*, 38(2): 173–191.

Haraway, D. (1991) A cyborg manifesto: science, technology, and socialist-feminism in the late twentieth century. In D. Haraway (ed.) *Simians, Cyborgs and Woman*. New York: Routledge.

Harvey, M., Treadway, D.C. and Heames, J. T. (2007) The occurrence of bullying in global organizations: a model and issues associated with social/emotional contagion. *Journal of Applied Social Psychology*, 37: 2576–2599.

Haslam, S.A. and Platow, M.J. (2001) The link between leadership and followership: how affirming social identity translates vision into action. *Personality and Social Psychology Bulletin*, 27(11): 1469–1479.

Hatch, M.J., Kostera, M. and Kozminski, A. (2006) The three faces of leadership: manager, artist, priest. *Organizational Dynamics*, 35(1): 49–68.

Hensmans, M. (2003) Social movement organizations: a metaphor for strategic actors in institutional fields. *Organization Studies*, 24(3): 355–382.

Heracleous, L. and Jacobs, C.D. (2008) Understanding organizations through embodied metaphors. *Organization Studies*, 29(1): 45–78.

Hersey, P. and Blanchard, K.H. (1993) *Management of Organizational Behavior: utilizing human resources*. Englewood Cliffs, NJ: Prentice Hall.

Hochschild, A. (1983) *The Managed Heart: the commercialization of human feeling*. Berkeley, CA: University of California Press.

Hodson, R., Roscigno, V.J. and Lopez, S.H (2006) Chaos and the abuse of power: workplace bullying in organizational and interactional context. *Work and Occupation*, 33: 382–416.

Hofstede, G. (1980) *Culture's Consequences: international differences in work-related values*. Beverly Hills, CA: Sage.

Hogg, M.A. (2001) A social identity theory of leadership. *Personality and Social Psychology*, 11: 223–255.

Honneth, A. (2004) Organized self-realization: some paradoxes of individualization. *European Journal of Social Theory*, 7(4): 463–478.

Houghton, J., Neck, C. and Manz, C. (2003) Selfleadership and Superleadership. In C. Pearce and J. Conger (eds) *Shared Leadership*. Thousand Oaks, CA: Sage.

House, R.J. (1971) A path-goal theory of leader effectiveness. *Administrative Science Quarterly*, 16: 321–339.

House, R.J. and Mitchell, T.R. (1974) Path-goal theory of leadership. *Journal of Contemporary Business*, 3: 81–97.

House, R. and Aditya, R. (1997) The social scientific study of leadership: quo vadis? *Journal of Management*, 23(3): 409–473.

Howell, J.M. and Avolio, B.J. (1992) Charismatic leadership: submission or liberation? *Business Quarterly*, 60(1): 62.

Howell, J.M. and Shamir, B. (2005) The role of followers in the charismatic leadership process: relationships and their consequences. *Academy of Management Review*, 30(1): 96–112.

Huey, J. (1994) The new post-heroic leadership. *Fortune*. February 21: 42–50.

Hughes, J. (2007) *The End of Work: theological critiques of capitalism*. London: Blackwell.

Hunt, J.M. and Weintrub, J.R. (2007) *The Coaching Organization: a strategy for developing leaders*. Thousand Oaks, CA: Sage.

Ibarra, H. and Lineback, K. (2005) What's your story? *Harvard Business Review*, 83: 64–71.

Inns, D. and Jones, P. (1996) Metaphor in organization theory: following in the footsteps of the poet. In D. Grant and C. Oswick (eds) *Metaphor and Organizations*. London: Sage.

lvesson, M. and Sveningsson, S. (2003a) The great disappearing act: difficulties in doing 'leadership'. *Leadership Quarterly*, 14: 359–381.

Jackall, R. (1988) *Moral Mazes: the world of corporate managers*. Oxford: Oxford University Press.

Jackson, B. and Parry, K. (2008) *A Very Short, Fairly Interesting and Reasonably Cheap Book about Studying Leadership*. London: Sage.

Jackson, T. (1998) *Inside Intel: Andy Grove and the rise of the world's most powerful chip company*. New York: Plume.

Janis, I.L. (1972) *Victims of Groupthink – a psychological study of foreign-policy decisions and fiascos*. Boston, MA: Houghton Mifflin Company.

Jones, S. and Gosling, J. (2005) *Nelson's Way: leadership lessons from the great commander*. London: Nicholas Brealey.

Jönsson, S. (ed.) (1996) *Perspectives on Scandinavian Management*. Göteborg: BAS.

Kanter, R.M. (1977) *Men and Women of the Corporation*. New York: Basic Books.

Kanter, M.R. (1983) *The Change Masters: innovations for productivity in the American corporation*. New York: Simon & Schuster.

Kasser, T (2002) *The High Price of Materialism*. Cambridge, MA: MIT Press.

Katz, D. and Kahn, R. (1978) *The Social Psychology of Organizations*. New York: Wiley.

Kelley, R.E. (1992) *The Power of Followership*. New York: Doubleday.

Kelly, S. (2008) Leadership: a categorical mistake? *Human Relations*, 61: 763–782.

Kelly, S., White, M.I., Martin, D. and Rouncefield, M. (2006) Leadership refrains: patterns of leadership. *Leadership*, 2: 181–201.

Kets de Vries, M. (1985) Narcissism and leadership: an object relations perspective. *Human Relations*, 38: 583–601.

—— (1994) The leadership mystique. *Academy of Management Executives*, 8(3): 73–89.

—— (2003) *Leaders, Fools and Imposters: essays on the psychology of leadership*. Lincoln, NE: iUniverse.

Khurana, R. (2002) *Searching for the Corporate Saviour: the irrational quest for charsmatic CEOs*. Princeton, NJ: Princeton University Press.

Klein, N. (2000) *No Logo*. New York: Knopf.

Knights, D. and Willmott, H. (1992) Conceptualizing leadership processes: a study of senior managers in a financial services company, *Journal of Management Studies*, 29: 761–782.

Kodish, S. (2006) The paradoxes of leadership: the contribution of Aristotle. *Leadership*, 2: 451–468.

Kotter, J. (1988) *The Leadership Factor*. New York: Free Press.

—— (1990) *A Force of Change – how leadership differs from management*. New York: The Free Press.

Ladkin, D. (2010) *Rethinking Leadership: a new look at old leadership questions*. Cheltenham: Edward Elgar.

Langfield-Smith, K. (1997) Management control systems and strategy: a critical review. *Accounting, Organizations, and Society*, 22: 207–232.

Lakoff, G. and Johnson, M. (1980) *Metaphors We Live by*. Chicago: University of Chicago Press.

—— (1999) *Philosophy in the Flesh: the embodied mind and its challenge to western thought*. New York: Basic Books.

Laurent, A. (1978) Managerial subordinancy: a neglected aspect of organizational hierarchy. *Academy of Management Review*, 3: 220–230.

Lave, J. and Wenger, E. (1991) *Situated Learning: legitimate peripheral participation*. Cambridge: Cambridge University Press.

Legge, K. (1978) *Power, Innovation and Problem Solving in Personnel Management*. Maidenhead: McGraw Hill.

Lord, R.G. (1985) An information processing approach to social perceptions, leadership and behavioral measurement in organizations. *Research in Organizational Behavior*, 7: 87–128.

Löwendahl, B. (1997) *Strategic Management of Professional Service Firms*. Copenhagen: Copenhagen Business School Press.

Ludeman, K. and Erlandson, E. (2004) Coaching the alpha-male. *Harvard Business Review*, May, 1–10.

—— (2006) *Alpha Male Syndrome*. Boston, MA: Harvard Business School Press.

—— (2007) Channeling alpha male leaders. *Leader to Leader*, Spring, 44: 38–54.

McClelland, D.C. and Burnham, D.H. (1976/2003) Power is the great motivator. *Harvard Business Review*, 81(1): 117–126.

McGee, M. (2005) *Self-help, Inc*. Oxford: Oxford University Press.

McKee, R. (2003) Storytelling that moves people: a conversation with screenwriting coach Robert McKee. *Harvard Business Review*, 81: 51–57.

Mace, M.L. (1950) *The Growth and Development of Executives*. Boston, MA: Harvard Business School Division of Research.

Machiavelli, N. (1515/1997) *The Prince*. London: Penguin.

Macoby, M. (2000) Narcissistic leaders: the incredible pros, the inevitable cons. *Harvard Business Review*, Jan–Feb: 91–102.

Mair, J. (2002) *Schluss mit Lustig*. Frankfurt: Eichborn.

Manz, C.C. (1986) Self-leadership: towards an expanded theory of self-influence processes in organizations. *Academy of Management Review*, 11(3): 585–600.

Manz, C. C. and Sims, H.P. (1990) *SuperLeadership*. Berkeley, CA: Berkeley Publishing Group.

—— (1991) Superleadership: beyond the myth of heroic leadership. *Organizational Dynamics*, 19(4): 18–35.

March, J. and Olsen, J. (1976) *Ambiguity and Choice in Organizations*, Bergen: Universitetsforlaget.

Martin, J. and Meyerson, D. (1988) Organizational cultures and the denial, channeling and acknowledgement of ambiguity. In L.R. Pondy, R.J. Boland and H. Thomas (eds) *Managing Ambiguity and Change*. New York: Wiley.

Maslow, A. (1954) *Motivation and Personality*. New York: Harper & Row.

Maxwell, J.C. (1998) *The 21 Irrefutable Laws of Leadership. Follow them and people will follow you*. Nashville, KY: Thomas Nelson.

—— (1999) *The 21 Indispensible Qualities of a Leader: becoming a persons that people want to follow*. Nashville, TN: Thomas Nelson.

Mayo, E. (1949) *Hawthorne and the Western Electric Company: the social problems of an industrial civilisation*. New York: Routledge.

Meindl, J.R. (1993) Reinventing leadership: a radical, social psychological approach. In J.K. Munighan (ed.) *Social Psychology in Organizations: advances in theory and research*. Englewood Cliffs, NJ: Prentice Hall, 89–118.

—— (1995) The romance of leadership as a follower-centric theory: a social constructionist approach. *Leadership Quarterly*, 6: 329–341.

Meindl, J.R., Ehrlich, S.B. and Dukerich, J.M. (1985) The romance of leadership. *Administrative Science Quarterly*, 30(1): 78–102.

Mintzberg, H. (1998) Covert leadership: notes on managing professionals. *Harvard Business Review*, 76(6): 140–147.

Mintzberg, H. (2009) The best leadership is good management. *Business Week*, August 17.

Mio, J.S., Riggio, R.E., Levin, S. and Resse, R. (2005) Presidential leadership and charisma: the effect of metaphors. *The Leadership Quarterly*, 16(2): 287–294.

Morgan, G. (1980) Paradigms, metaphors, and puzzle solving in organizational analysis. *Administrative Science Quarterly*, 25: 606–622.

—— (1983) More on metaphor: why we cannot control tropes in administrative science. *Administrative Science Quarterly*, 28: 601–608.

—— (1986) *Images of Organization*. Beverly Hills, CA: Sage.

—— (1996) An afterword: is there anything more to be said about metaphors? In D. Grant and C. Oswick (eds) *Metaphor and Organizations*. London: Sage.

—— (1997) *Images of Organization*. 2nd edn. Thousand Oaks, CA: Sage.

Mori, M. (1970) The uncanny valley. *Energy*, 7: 33–35.

Nelson, E.D. and Lambert, R.D. (2001) Stick, stones, and semantics: the ivory tower bully's vocabulary of motives. *Qualitative Sociology*, 24: 83–106.

Nietzsche, F. (1995) *Thus spoke Zarathustra*, New York, Modern Library.

Noon, M. and Delbridge, R. (1993) News from behind my hand: gossip in organizations. *Organization Studies*, 14: 23–36.

Oakes, P.J. and Turner, J.C. (1980) Social categorization and intergroup behaviour: does minimal intergroup discrimination make social identity more positive? *European Journal of Social Psychology*, 10(3): 295–301.

O'Reilly, D. and Reed, M. (forthcoming) Leaderism: an evolution of managerialism in UK public service reform. *Public Administration*.

Oswick, C. and Jones, P. (2006) Beyond correspondence? Metaphor in organization theory. *Academy of Management Review*, 31: 483–485.

Oswick, C., Keenoy, T. and Grant, D. (2002) Metaphor and analogical reasoning in organization theory: Beyond orthodoxy. *Academy of Management Review*, 27: 294–303.

Owen, J. (2005) *How to Lead: what you actually need to do to manage, lead and succeed*. Harlow: Pearson.

Pablo, Z. and Hardy, C. (2009) Merging, masquerading and morphing: metaphors and the world wide web. *Organization Studies*, 30(8): 821–843.

Padilla, A., Hogan, R. and Kaiser, R.B. (2007) The toxic triangle: destructive leaders, susceptible followers, and conductive environments. *The Leadership Quarterly*, 18: 176–194.

Palmer, I. and Dunford, R. (1996) Interrogating reframing: evaluating metaphor-based analysis of organizations. In S. Clegg and G. Palmer (eds) *The Politics of Management Knowledge*. London: Sage.

Parker, M. (1998) Judgement day: cyborganization, humanism and postmodern ethics. *Organization*, 5: 503–518.

—— (1999) Manufacturing bodies: flesh, organisation, cyborgs. In J. Hassard, R. Holliday. and H. Willmott (eds) *Organising the Body*. London: Sage.

—— (2000) *Organizational Culture and Identity*. London: Sage.

Parker, M. and Cooper, R. (1998) Cyborganization: cinema as nervous system. In J. Hassard and R. Holliday (eds) *Organization/Representation*. London: Sage.

Parry, K. and Bryman, A. (2006) Leadership in organizations. In S.R. Clegg, C. Clegg, T. Lawrence and W. Nord (eds) *The Sage Handbook of Organization Studies*. London: Sage.

Parsloe, E. (1999) *The Manager as Coach and Mentor*, 2nd edn. London: CIPD.

Pearce, C. and Conger, J. (eds) (2003a) *Shared Leadership: reforming the hows and whys of leadership*. Thousand Oaks, CA: Sage.

Pearce, C. and Conger, J. (2003b) All those years ago. The historical underpinnings of shared leadership. In C. Pearce and J. Conger (eds) *Shared Leadership*. Thousand Oaks, CA: Sage.

Pedersen, M. (2008) Tune in, break down, and reboot – new machines for coping with the stress of commitment. *Culture and Organization*, 14: 171–185.

Peters, T.J. and Waterman, R.H. (1982) *In Search of Excellence*. New York: Harper & Row.

Peterson, D.B. and Hicks, M.D. (1996) *Leader as Coach: strategies for coaching and developing others*. Minneapolis, MN: Personnel Decisions.

Pfeffer, J. (1977) The ambiguity of leadership. *Academy of Management Review*, 2(1): 104–112.

Pinder, C. and Bourgeois, V. (1982) Controlling tropes in administrative science. *Administrative Science Quarterly*, 27: 641–652

Potter, J. and Wetherell, M. (1987) *Discourse and Social Psychology*. London: Sage.

Pullen, A. and Rhodes, C. (2008) 'It's all about me!': gendered narcissism and leaders' identity work. *Leadership*, 4: 5–25.

Putnam, L.L. and Boys, S. (2006) Revisiting metaphors of organizational communication. In S.R. Clegg, C. Hardy and W. Nord (eds) *The Handbook of Organization Studies*. London: Sage.

Rafaeli, A., Dutton, J., Harguail, C.V. and Mackie-Lewis, S. (1997) Navigating by attire: the use of dress by female administrative employees. *Academy of Management Journal*, 40(1): 9–45.

Readings, B. (1996) *The University in Ruins*. Cambridge, MA: Harvard University Press.

Reed, M. (1990) From paradigms to images: the paradigm warrior turns post-modern guru. *Personnel Review*, 19(3): 35–40.

Rehn, A. and Lindahl, M. (2008) The uncanny organization man: superhero myths and contemporary managemet discourse. In M. Kostera (ed.) *Organizational Olympians: heroes and heroines of organizational myths*. New York: Palgrave Macmillan.

Renesch, J. and DeFoore, B. (eds) (1996) *The New Bottom Line: bringing heart and soul to business*. San Francisco, CA: New Leaders Press.

Rennstam, J. (2007) Engineering work. Ph.D. thesis. Lund: Lund Business Press.

Ricoeur, P. (1978) Metaphor and the main problem of hermeneutics. In *The Philosophy of Paul Ricoeur*. Boston, MA: Beacon Press.

Rost, J.C. (1991) *Leadership for the Twenty-first Century*. New York: Praeger.

Sackmann, S. (1989) The role of metaphor in organizational transformation. *Human Relations*, 42(6): 463–485.

Salam, S. (2000) Foster trust through competence and integrity. In E. Locke (ed.) *Handbook of Principles of Organizational Behaviour*. Oxford: Blackwell.

Sandberg, J. and Targama, A. (2007) *Managing Understanding in Organization*. London: Sage.

Sandjaya, S., Sarros, J.C. and Santora, J.C. (2008) Defining and measuring servant leadership behaviour in organization. *Journal of Management Studies*, 45(2): 402–424.

Schein, E.H. (1985) *Organizational Culture and Leadership*. San Francisco: Jossey-Bass.

Schön, D.A. (1979) Generative metaphor: a perspective on problem setting in social policy. In A. Ortony (ed.) *Metaphor and Thought*. Cambridge: Cambridge University Press.

Scully, J. (1988) *Odyssey: Pepsi to Apple . . . A Journey of Adventure, Ideas and the Future*. New York: Harper and Row.

Selsky, J., Spicer, A. and Teicher, J. (2003) Totally un-Australian! Discursive and institutional interplay in the Melbourne port dispute of 1997–98. *Journal of Management Studies*, 40(7): 1729–1760.

Sennett, R. (1999) *The Corrosion of Character: the personal consequences of work in the new capitalism*. London: Norton & Co.

—— (2008) *The Craftsman*. London: Allen Lane.

Shamir, B. and Eilam, G. (2005) 'What's your story?' A life-stories approach to authentic leadership development. *Leadership Quarterly*, 16: 395–417.

Shapiro, M. (1992) *Reading the Postmodern Polity*. Minneapolis, MN: University of Minnesota Press.

Sinclair, A. (2005) Body possibilities in leadership. *Leadership*, 1: 387–406.

—— (2007) *Leadership for the Disillusioned*. Melbourne: Melbourne University Press.

Sjöstrand, S-E., Sandberg, J. and Tyrstrup, M. (eds) (2001) *Invisible Management: the social construction of leadership*. London: Thomson Learning.

Smircich, L. and Morgan, G. (1982) Leadership: the management of meaning. *Journal of Applied Behavioral Science*, 18: 257–273.

Smith, A. (1776) *An Inquiry into the Nature and Causes of the Wealth of Nations*. London: Dent.

Smith, R.C. and Eisenberg, E. (1987) Conflict at Disneyland: a root metaphor analysis. *Communication Monographs*, 54: 367–380.

Speklé, R. (2001) Explaining management control structure variety: a transaction cost economics perspective. *Accounting, Organizations, and Society*, 26: 419–441.

Spicer, A. (2004) Making a world view: globalization discourse in a public broadcaster. Ph.D. Dissertation, University of Melbourne.

Storey, J. (2004) Changing theories of leadership and leadership development. In J. Storey (ed.) *Leadership in Organizations: current issues and key trends.* London: Routledge.

Sturdy, A. and Fleming, P. (2003) Talk as technique – a critique of the words and deeds distinction in the diffusion of customer service cultures in call centres. *Journal of Management Studies,* 40(4): 753–773.

Sveningsson, S. and Larsson, M. (2006) Fantasies of doing leadership: identity work. *Leadership,* 2(2): 203–224.

Tajfel, H. and Turner, J.C. (1986) The social identity theory of intergroup behaviour. In S. Worchel and W.G. Austin (eds) *Psychology of Inter-Group Relations.* Chicago: Nelson-Hall.

Tebbutt, M. and Marchington, M. (1997) 'Look before you speak': gossip and the insecure workplace. *Work, Employment and Society,* 11: 713–735.

Ten Bos, R. (2007) The new severity: on managerial masochism. *Ephemera,* 7(4): 543–554.

Tepper, B.J. (2000) Consequences of abusive supervision. *Academy of Management Journal,* 43: 178–190.

The Leadership Quarterly (2007) Special issue on 'destructive leadership' 18(3).

Tichy, N.M. (1997) *The Leadership Engine: how winning companies build leaders at every level.* New York: HarperCollins.

Tierney, W.G. (1996) Leadership and postmodernism: on voice and the qualitative method. *Leadership Quarterly,* 7(3): 371–383.

Tinker, T. (1986) Metaphor or reification: are radical humanists really libertarian anarchists? *Journal of Management Studies,* 25: 363–384.

Tourish, D. and Vatcha, N. (2005) Charismatic leadership and corporate cultism at Enron: the elimination of dissent, the promotion of conformity and organizational collapse. *Leadership,* 1: 455–480.

Townley, B. (1997) The institutional logic of performance appraisal, *Organization Studies,* 18(2): 261–285.

—— (2004) Managerial technologies, ethics and managing. *Journal of Management Studies,* 41(3): 425–445.

Tracy, S.J., Lutgen-Sandvik, P. and Alberts, J.K. (2006) Nightmares, demons, and slaves: exploring the painful metaphors of workplace bullying. *Management Communication Quarterly,* 20: 148–185.

Trice, H.M. and Beyer, J.M. (1993) *The Culture of Work Organizations.* Englewood Cliffs, NJ: Prentice-Hall.

Tsoukas, H. (1991) The missing link: a transformative view of metaphors in organization science. *Academy of Management Review,* 16(3): 566–558.

Uhl-Bien, M. (2006) Relational leadership theory: exploring the social process of leadership and organizing. *Leadership Quarterly* 17: 654–676.

Uhl-Bien, M. and Pillai, R. (2006) The romance of leadership and the social construction of followership. In R.P.B. Shamir, M. Bligh, and M. Uhl-Bien (eds) *Follower-centred Perspectives on Leadership: a tribute to James R. Meindl.* Greenwich, CT: Information Age Publishing.

Useem, M. (2001) *Leading Up: how to lead your boss so you both win.* New York: Crown Business.

Van Knippenberg, D. and Hogg, D. (2003) A social identity model of leadership effectiveness in organizations. *Research in Organizational Behavior,* 25: 243–296.

Van Maanen, J. (1991) The smile factory: work at Disneyland. In P.J. Frost *et al.* (eds) *Reframing Organisational Culture.* London: Sage.

—— (1995) *Representation in Ethnography*. London: Sage.

Vega, G. and Comer, D.R. (2005) Sticks and stones may break your bones, but words can break your spirit: bullying in the workplace. *Journal of Business Ethics*, 58: 101–109.

Vroom, V. and Yetton, P. (1973) *Leadership and Decision-making*. Pittsburgh: University of Pittsburgh Press.

Weick, K.E. (1979) *The Social Psychology of Organising*. New York: Random House.

Weick, K. and Sutcliffe, K. (2001) *Managing the Unexpected: assuring high performance in an age of complexity*. San Francisco: Jossey Bass.

Weick, K., Sutcliffe, K.M. and Obstfeld, D. (1999) Organizing for high reliability: processes of collective mindfulness. *Research in Organizational Behavior*, 21: 81–123.

Welch, J. and Welch, S. (2007) Bosses who get it all wrong. *Business Week*, New York: July 23, p. 88.

Wenglén, R. (2005) *Från dum till klok? – en studie av mellanchefers lärande*. Lund: Lund Business Press.

Wenglén, R. and Alvesson, M. (2008) The corrosion of the coach. Working Paper, Lund University.

Western, S. (2008) *Leadership: a critical text*. Thousand Oaks, CA: Sage.

Wetherell, M. (1998) Positioning and interpretative repertoires: conversation analysis and post-structuralism in dialogue. *Discourse and Society*, 9: 387–412.

Williamson, O. (1985) *The Economic Institutions of Capitalism*. New York: Free Press.

Willmott, H. (1994) Business process re-engineering and human resource management. *Personnel Review*, 23(3): 34–46.

Wood, M. (1998) Agency and organization: toward a cyborg-consciousness. *Human Relations*, 51: 1209–1226.

Yukl, G. (1989) Managerial leadership: a review of theory and research. *Journal of Management*, 15: 215–289.

—— (1999) An evaluation of conceptual weaknesses in transformational and charismatic leadership theories. *Leadership Quarterly*, 10: 285–305.

—— (2006) *Leadership in Organizations*. 6th edn. Upper Saddle River, NJ: Prentice Hall.

Zaleznik, A. (1977) Managers and leaders: are they different? *Harvard Business Review*, May–June: 67–68.

INDEX